S0-CCB-548

ROOFS AND SIDING:

A Practical Guide

DON GEARY

RESTON PUBLISHING COMPANY, INC.
A Prentice-Hall Company
Reston, Virginia

Library of Congress Cataloging in Publication Data

Geary, Don
Roofs and siding.

Includes index.
1. Roofs. 2. Siding (Building materials)
3. Dwellings--Maintenance and repair. I. Title.
TH2391.G4 695 78-17946
ISBN 0-87909-752-3

A Prentice-Hall Company
Reston, Virginia 22090

10 9 8 7 6 5 4 3 2 1

Printed in the United States of America

CONTENTS

PREFACE

It seems likely that single-family houses will become obsolete within our lifetime. Prices for land to build on, materials to build with, taxes, utilities, and maintenance costs are all continuing to rise steeply. It would seem that a house can rather quickly become an expensive investment, affordable only by the relatively well-to-do.

Maintenance of a home is expensive, for professional carpenters and contractors are well paid. For repairs or renovations, most homeowners will hire a professional to do the work. Most people just don't feel confident enough with hammer and ruler to attempt more than hanging a picture on a wall. Yet, proficiency at making repairs can come only through practice and experience with the "tools of the trade."

You do not need many tools to do the work covered in this book. With the possible exceptions of aluminum siding and masonry work, you need a simple collection: hammer, ruler, chalk line, utility knife, nail set, shingle bar, ladder, hack saw, and hand-held circular saw. These are all common tools. Lack of information can also deter homeowners from doing their own work. Most of the basic information needed is covered here, although one book cannot cover everything or foresee all problems that can arise when basic guidelines and a careful plan, you should be able to accomplish what you set out to do.

A carefully devised work plan is necessary for any project. All possible tasks must be considered. For example, suppose that while re-covering your roof with asphalt shingles, you discover that the flashing around your chimney needs replacing, or that some of the roof sheathing is rotten and must be replaced. You will have to make the necessary repairs or replacement or the new roof will not be what you expected. Although such further work will usually entail more of an investment in both time and money, you will know that the job has been done correctly and should last many years. Your work plan should be based on information gathered by visual inspection and anticipated results, and you should then follow your plan closely.

Most roof work is dangerous. You should never—for even a second—forget that you are off the ground. To lessen your chances of injury, it is important that you wear the right kind of clothing (proper footwear, for example), use safety equipment if necessary (for example, roof brackets on steep pitched roofs), work with a helper, and be cautious. Don't work if you become overly fatigued. Don't overextend yourself when working on a ladder, and remember that the fastest way to the ground begins with a wrong step.

ACKNOWLEDGMENTS

Few books are solely the work of the writer, and this one is certainly no exception. This book represents years of working with hammer and ruler, as well as research and help from various sources. In particular, I would like to thank the Asphalt Roofing Manufacturers Association, who supplied many of the illustrations and photographs contained within these pages, as well as some of the basic information. The Red Cedar Shingle and Handsplit Shake Bureau also provided invaluable help with the sections covering these materials. Many other companies, both large and small, contributed to the preparation of this book. Photo credits will have to suffice as my thanks. Also of great help were many of the federal government publications offered by the Department of Agriculture, United States Army, and other government agencies.

I would also like to thank my wife, Virginia, for the encouragement she offered in time of need as well as her ability to endure, gracefully, all of those things that make up a writer's life. Other help and encouragement came from a dear friend, Charles Self, another writer who knows well what it's like to look at a blank page.

If you use this book in conjunction with a well-thought-out work plan, a conscientious approach, and determination, you should be able to accomplish what you set out to do. You will, by doing your own maintenance, strengthen your self-confidence and, at the same time, make living in a house affordable.

DON GEARY

1

ASPHALT ROOFING

At least 80 percent of the roofs on American homes are covered with some type of asphalt roofing material, either shingle or rolled roofing. Many good reasons exist for the widespread popularity of asphalt roof coverings: asphalt shingles are relatively inexpensive to buy, easy to apply to a roof deck, and have a life expectancy ranging from fifteen to twenty-five years.

Asphalt shingles are available in a wide range of styles, textures, colors, and application methods. The colors range from white to black, in solid colors or blends, including earthtones. You can choose a roof color that will contrast with siding, window and door trim, and landscape.

Asphalt roofing that is classified by the Underwriter's Laboratories, Inc. (UL) as A, B or C means that it is not easily ignited, will not readily spread flames, and will not contribute to fire hazard by creating flaming brands to endanger adjacent structures. The fire resistance of asphalt roofing is largely because of the mineral granules embedded in the surface of the roofing.

Asphalt roofing products that bear the UL's "wind resistant" label have been tested to withstand winds up to 60 miles-per-hour for two hours, without a single tab lifting. The wind-resistant feature was originally developed for high wind areas, but is included on most asphalt shingle products manufactured today.

PRODUCTION OF ASPHALT PRODUCTS

Asphalt products are made in four steps: dry felt, asphalt, mineral stabilizers, and surfacing (See Figure 1-1).

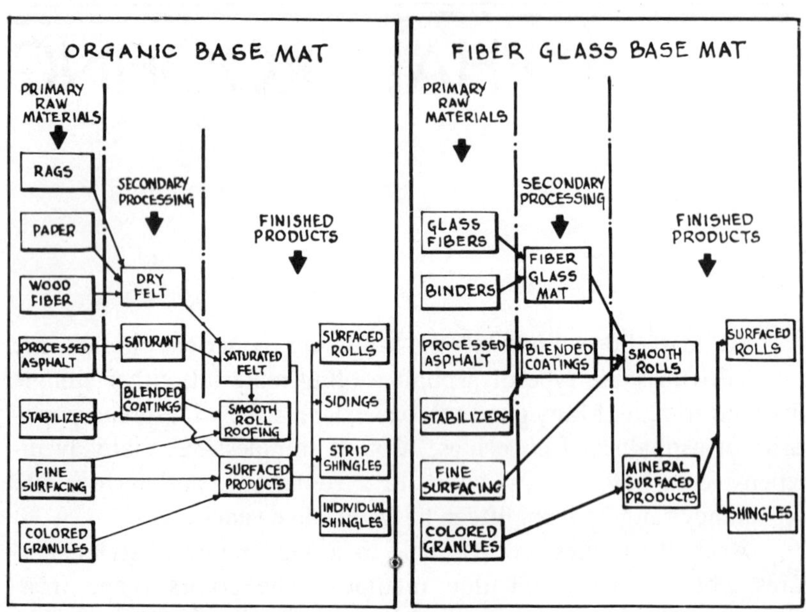

Courtesy of Asphalt Roofing Manufacturers Association

FIG. 1-1. Processing chart for asphalt roofing products; from raw materials to finished roofing.

Dry Felt

Dry felt is made from various combinations of rag, wood, and other cellulose fibers blended in such proportions that the resulting characteristics of strength, absorptive capacity, and flexibility will make an acceptable asphalt roofing product. The manufacture of felt is really an art as well as a science. To know exact proportions of the various ingredients necessary to meet specifications requires long experience on the part of the mill operator. Weight, tensile strength, and flexibility are specified which will enable the felt to withstand any strains which may be placed upon it in the manufacturing processes to which it will later be subjected in the roofing plant, and to enable it to absorb from 1½ to 2 times its weight in asphalt saturants.

Roofing felt is made on a machine very similar to a paper-making machine. The fibers are prepared by various pulping methods, depending on the fiber source. Rag fibers are prepared in beaters after the rags are cut and shredded. Paper fibers are similarly prepared in beaters or other pulping devices, and wood fibers may be prepared by combinations of wood chip cooking devices with attrition mills.

Felt comes off the end of the machine in a continuous wide sheet from which it is cut into specified widths and wound in rolls from 4 to 6 feet in diameter and weighing up to a ton or more each. Felt is specified as to weight in terms of pounds per 480 square feet. This is known as the *felt number* and ranges from 25 to 75.

Asphalt

For 5,000 years asphalt has been used by humans as a preservative, waterproofing, and adhesive agent. The Babylonians used asphalt to waterproof baths and as a pavement. The Egyptians used it to preserve their mummies. Throughout the Middle Ages, asphalt was in common use in Europe. Columbus discovered one of the largest natural deposits on the island of Trinidad in the British West Indies during his third voyage to the new world, around 1498.

Today the petroleum industry provides the material used in the manufacture of asphalt roofing. It is a product of the fractional distillation of crude oil that occurs toward the end of the distilling process, and is known to the trade as *asphalt flux.* Asphalt flux is sometimes refined by the oil refiner and delivered to the roofing product manufacturer in conformance with the manufacturer's specifications. Many manufacturers, however, purchase the flux and do their own refining.

The preservative and waterproofing characteristics of asphalt reside very largely in certain oily constituents. Therefore, in the manufacture of roofing it is necessary to construct the body of the sheet of highly absorbent felt impregnated or saturated to the greatest possible extent with a type of oil-rich asphalt known as *saturant,* and then to seal the saturant in with an application of a harder, more viscous *coating asphalt* which itself can be protected, if desired, by a covering of opaque mineral granules.

The asphalt used for saturants and coatings is prepared by processing the flux in such a way as to modify the temperature at which it will soften. The softening point of saturants varies from 38°C. to 71°C., whereas that of the coating runs as high as 128°C. Asphalt chemists have learned how to regulate this characteristic so that it can be adapted most effectively to resist the temperatures usually found on roofs.

Mineral Stabilizers

It has been found that coating asphalts will resist weathering better and be more shatterproof and shockproof in cold weather if they contain a certain percentage of finely divided minerals called *stabilizers*. Some of the most common materials that have been used as stabilizers include: silica, slate dust, talc, micaceous materials, dolomite, and trap rock. Experience and research have shown that a suitable stabilizer, when used in the proper amount, can materially increase the life of the product in service.

Surfacing

The last step in producing roofing materials is surfacing. Both fine and coarse materials are used in the process. Finely ground minerals are dusted on the surfaces of smooth roll roofings, the back of mineral surfaced roll roofings, and the backs of shingles for the primary purpose of preventing the convolutions of the roll from sticking together after it is wound and to prevent shingles from sticking together in the package. Materials used most for this purpose are talc and mica. These minerals are not a permanent part of the finished product and will gradually disappear from exposed surfaces after the roofing material is applied.

Mineral granules are used on certain roll products and on shingles for the following principal reasons:

1. They protect the underlying asphalt coating from the impact of light rays. Therefore, they should be opaque, dense, and properly graded for maximum coverage.
2. By virtue of their mineral origin, they increase the fire resistance of the product.

3. They provide a wide range of colors and color blends, thereby increasing the adaptability of surfaced asphalt roofings to different types of buildings, and contributing to public acceptance.

The materials most frequently used for mineral surfacing are naturally colored slate, or rock granules either in natural form or colored by a ceramic process. When mineral-surfaced roofing products are being made, granules of specified color or color combinations are added by spreading thickly on the hot coating asphalt and the back coated with talc, mica, or other suitable minerals. The sheet is then run through a series of press and cooling rolls or drums. To ensure proper embedment of the granules, the sheet is subjected to controlled pressure, which forces the granules into the coating to the desired depth.

Some variations in shade of asphalt shingle roofs is unavoidable; slight variations in the texture of the surface of the shingles occur during normal manufacturing operations. The resulting variable absorption and reflection of light causes variations in appearance, but in no way affects the durability of the roofing product.

Shading is especially noticeable on dark colored roofs when viewed from certain angles or under different light conditions. Although shading is less apparent on white or light colored roofs, variation in shade of any kind can usually be made less noticeable through the use of blends of a variety of colors.

When shingles are being made, the sheet material is fed into a shingle-cutting machine. The sheet is cut by a cutting cylinder; pressure is exerted by an anvil roll as the sheet passes between the cylinder and the anvil roll. The cylinder cuts the sheets from the back or smooth side. After the shingles have been cut, they are separated into units that accumulate in stacks of the proper number for packaging. The stacks are moved to manually operated or to automatic packaging equipment where the bundles are prepared for warehousing or shipment.

When roll roofing is being made, the sheet is drawn into a roll-roofing winder. Here it is wound on a mandrel, which measures the length of the material as it turns. When a predetermined amount has accumulated, it is cut off, removed from the mandrel, and passed on for wrapping. After packaging, the rolls are assembled for warehousing or shipment.

From the time the dry felt enters the saturator until the finished products leave the shingle cutters or winding mandrels, the material is rigidly inspected to ensure conformance with specified standards. Some of the important items checked are:

1. Saturation of felt to determine quantity of saturant and efficiency of saturation.
2. Thickness and distribution of coating asphalt.
3. Adhesion and distribution of granules.
4. Weight, count, size, coloration, and other characteristics of finished product before and after it is packaged.

CATEGORIES OF ASPHALT ROOFING

Asphalt roofing and siding products made on a felt base may be classified broadly into three main groups: (1) saturated felts; (2) roll roofing and roll siding; and (3) roofing and siding shingles.

Saturated Felts

Saturated felts, used as underlayment for shingles, for sheathing paper, and for laminations in the construction of built-up roofs, consist of dry felt impregnated with an asphalt or coal tar saturant, but otherwise untreated. Saturated felt paper is commonly referred to as *tar paper*. Saturated felt paper is made in different weights, the most common being no. 15 and no. 30, weighing approximately 15 and 30 pounds per square, respectively. A factory square of roofing equals 108 square feet of material as it comes from the machine. A sales square of roofing is the amount that, when applied, will cover 100 square feet of roof surface.

Roll Roofing

Roll roofing is made by adding a coating of a more viscous, weather-resistant asphalt to a felt that has first been impregnated with a saturant asphalt. Some roll roofings are surfaced with mineral granules to produce a wide range of colors. Some styles are furnished in split rolls designed to give an edge pattern when applied to a roof. (Mineral-surfaced rolls are also embossed to simulate brick or stone for use as sidings on buildings.)

Shingles

All shingles are surfaced with mineral granules. Many weights and patterns of both individual and strip shingles are available, designed for new construction and reroofing. Figure 1-2 shows many of the different types of asphalt roofing products currently produced and used by the roofing industry.

1	2	3			4		5	6
		Per Square			Size			
PRODUCT	Configuration	Approximate Shipping Weight	Shingles	Bundles	Width	Length	Exposure	Underwriters' Listing
Wood Appearance Strip Shingle More Than One Thickness Per Strip Laminated or Job Applied	Various Edge, Surface Texture & Application Treatments	285# to 390#	67 to 90	4 or 5	11-1/2" to 15"	36" or 40"	4" to 6"	A or C - Many Wind Resistant
Wood Appearance Strip Shingle Single Thickness Per Strip	Various Edge, Surface Texture & Application Treatments	Various 250# to 350#	78 to 90	3 or 4	12" or 12-1/4"	36" or 40"	4" to 5-1/8"	A or C - Many Wind Resistant
Self-Sealing Strip Shingle	Conventional 3 Tab	205#-240#	78 or 80	3	12" or 12-1/4"	36"	5" or 5-1/8"	A or C - All Wind Resistant
	2 or 4 Tab	Various 215# to 325#	78 or 80	3 or 4	12" or 12-1/4"	36"	5" or 5-1/8"	
Self-Sealing Strip Shingle No Cut Out	Various Edge and Texture Treatments	Various 215# to 290#	78 to 81	3 or 4	12" or 12-1/4"	36" or 36-1/4"	5"	A or C - All Wind Resistant
Individual Lock Down Basic Design	Several Design Variations	180# to 250#	72 to 120	3 or 4	18" to 22-1/4"	20" to 22-1/2"		C - Many Wind Resistant

Other types available from some manufacturers in certain areas of the Country. Consult your Regional Asphalt Roofing Manufacturers Association manufacturer.

FIG. 1-2a. Typical asphalt shingles.

1	2		3	4		5		6	7
PRODUCT	Approximate Shipping Weight		Sqs. Per Package	Length	Width	Side or End Lap	Top Lap	Exposure	Underwriters' Listing
	Per Roll	Per Sq.							
Mineral Surface Roll	75# to 90#	75# to 90#	One	36' 38'	36" 36"	6"	2" 4"	34" 32"	C
		Available in some areas in 9/10 or 3/4 Square rolls.							
Mineral Surface Roll Double Coverage	55# to 70#	55# to 70#	One Half	36'	36"	6"	19"	17"	C
Coated Roll	50# to 65#	50# to 65#	One	36'	36"	6"	2"	34"	None
Saturated Felt	60# 60# 60#	15# 20# 30#	4 3 2	144' 108' 72'	36" 36" 36"	4" to 6"	2"	34"	None

FIG. 1-2b. Typical asphalt rolls.

Chapter 4 (Reroofing) discusses covering a roof with asphalt shingles. This chapter will examine roll roofing, another type of asphalt roof covering. However, first let us discuss aspects of *pitch*.

Free and effective drainage of rain water from the roof surface is essential if good service from the roof covering material is to be expected. Therefore, it is very important in selecting a finish roof covering to take into consideration the limitations imposed by the "pitch" or slope of the roof deck.

Pitch limitations are indicated in Figure 1-3. Any shingle may be safely used on roofs with slopes of 4-inch rise or more per horizontal foot. However, an exception exists for square-butt strip shingles, which may be used on slopes included within the shaded area in the figure when applied in accordance with low slope specifications (discussed in Chapter 4).

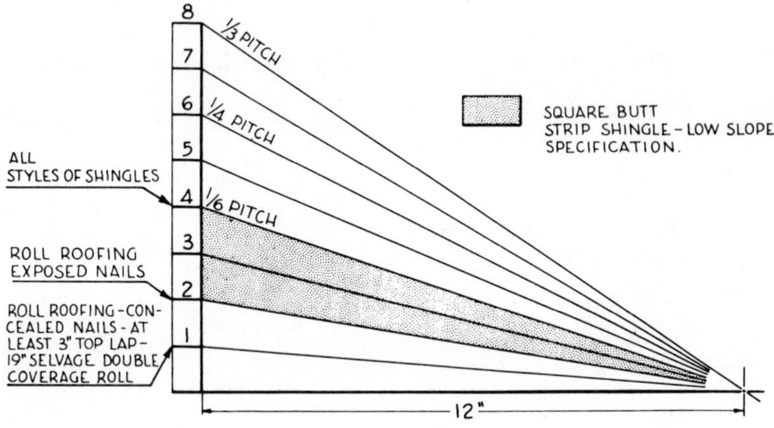

Courtesy of Asphalt Roofing Manufacturers Association

FIG. 1-3. Minimum pitch requirements for different asphalt roofing products.

There are two basic types of roofs: pitched and flat (see Figures 1-4 and 1-5). Pitched roofs are defined as roofs that require both ceiling joists and rafters or trusses. Perhaps the simplest form of pitched roof is the gable roof. Flat roofs (or slightly pitched roofs) are roofs that have the ceiling supported by rafters, upon which the finish roofing is installed.

The slope of a roof is generally expressed as the number of inches of vertical rise in 12 inches of horizontal run. The rise is given first: for example, 4 in 12. This expression indicates a pitched roof that rises 4 inches in height for every 12 inches of slope.

Other than the exception mentioned above for strip shingles, it is best to use roll roofings when the pitch of a roof is less than

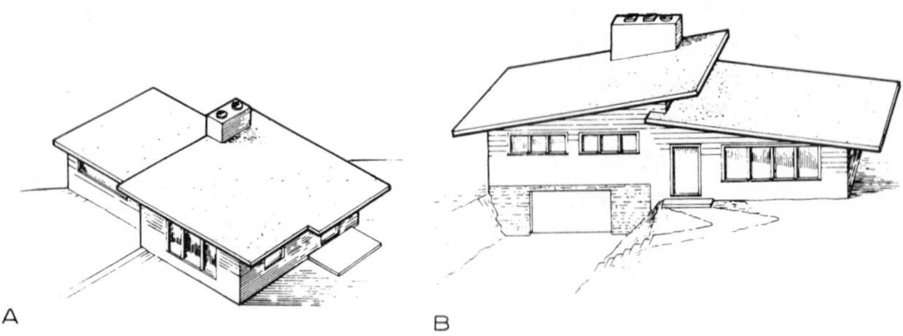

FIG. 1-4. Single roof construction: (A) flat roof; (B) low-pitched roof.

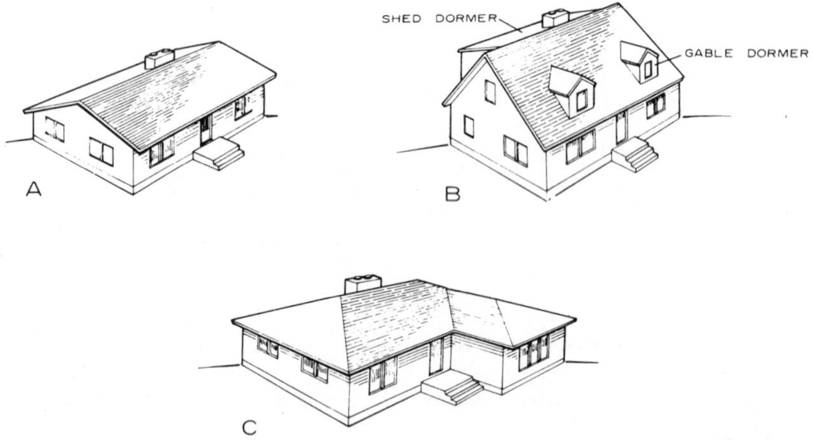

FIG. 1-5. Types of pitched roofs: (A) gable; (B) gable with dormers; (C) hip roof.

4 in 12. In the range from 4 in 12 down to 1 in 12, these two general rules should apply:

1. Roll roofing should be applied using the exposed nail method on roofs with a pitch not less than 2 in 12.
2. Roll roofings should be applied using the concealed nail method with at least a 3-inch top lap, as well as double coverage roofing having a top lap of 19 inches, for roofs having a pitch down to, but not less than, 1 in 12.

The above specifications can be applied to a roof deck having a pitch steeper than the stated minimum.

SAFETY PRECAUTIONS

Before you climb up on your roof, you should keep one thing in mind: it's a long way down. I must assume that, because you are reading this book, you are both willing and able to spend at least one day up on a roof. For the sake of some readers, who may never have been up on a roof, let's mention a few precautions. It is not my intention to alarm the reader unnecessarily, but simply to point out that being up on a roof can be dangerous.

Every year, usually during the warmer months, hundreds of homeowners fall off ladders and roofs while trying to do some type of home repair. In most cases these accidents could have been prevented if only the injured party had not forgotten where he was in the first place.

Several precautions can increase your chances of uninjured success. The first is to wear the proper type of footwear. Some roofing material manufacturers recommend that you wear a pair of sneakers because the tendency of slipping is minimal. But personally, I prefer to wear a pair of military combat boots. The soles of combat boots are thick, a feature you will appreciate after a few trips up a ladder while carrying a bundle of shingles, which weighs around 80 pounds. Combat boots also lace part way up your calf. This means that your ankles will have the necessary support for carrying a load. Also, if you should fall, you have a smaller chance of breaking your ankle than if you had a pair of canvas tennis shoes on.

Also, the soles of combat boots are most commonly made of rubber, which will not slip even on a wet roof surface. Another plus is the toe cap of these boots: you can drop a 20-ounce hammer on your toes and not feel a thing. Try that with any pair of sneakers!

Just because you have on a pair of combat boots, however, don't—even for a second—think you can be like Mercury. For if you should step off a roof, the boots will not keep you afloat, instead, you will drop like a stone.

For all intents and purposes, the only way to get up on your roof will be to climb up a ladder. The following ten ladder safety rules are worth remembering.

1. Carefully and thoroughly inspect any ladder before use, and never use a ladder in need of repair.

2. Make sure that the ladder stands on firm ground before climbing. You should overlap extension ladders a minimum of 3 feet for 36-foot lengths, 4 feet for 48-foot lengths, and at least 5 feet for 60-foot lengths. Also, the top section should be outermost.

3. Ensure that the locks on extension ladders are securely hooked before climbing. Oil moving parts before use. Never attempt to extend a ladder while you are on it.

4. Clean the rungs of the ladder to keep them free of dirt, grease, and oil.

5. Do not stand a ladder in front of door openings unless you are certain no one will open the door and knock the ladder over. One solution is to place an obstacle on the inside of the door, such as a chair or box, or simply lock the door.

6. For safety's sake, extend the ladder at least 3 feet above the roof edge. But never stand on any of the top three rungs of any ladder.

7. Ladder angle against a building is important. A common rule of thumb is: the distance from the base of the ladder to the building should be approximately one-fourth the ladder's height.

8. Try never to place a ladder near electrical lines. But, if you must, be careful not to touch the lines with any part of your body or the ladder.

9. When climbing up or down, always face the ladder and always use at least one hand for support.

10. Store your ladder hung, in a dry, well-ventilated area.

Succeeding courses of roll roofing are installed in the same fashion, finishing the last sheet so that it overlaps the rake by ¼ to ⅜ of an inch.

End laps are treated in the same way as when attaching rolled roofing parallel to the eaves, with a 6-inch-wide overlap and lap cement. The ridge and hips, if present, are also treated in the previously discussed manner.

ROLL ROOFING: CONCEALED NAIL METHOD

Either the concealed nail method or the exposed nail method can be used to attach rolled roofing. There are, however, additional steps when using the concealed nail method (see Figure 1-9).

Begin by attaching a 9-inch-wide strip of roll roofing around the entire perimeter of the roof along the eaves and rake. This strip should overhang the eave and rake by approximately ¼ to ⅜ of an inch and be secured with two rows of roofing nails. Drive the nails 1 inch in from each edge and space them about 4 inches apart.

Next, lay out a full sheet of roll roofing so that it overlaps the edge strips and all edges are flush. Secure the top edge of the full strip by driving nails along that edge, spaced about 4 inches apart. Fold the first strip upward, away from the eave. Then brush a coat of lap cement on top of the edge strip, where the full sheet of rolled roofing will overlap.

ROLL ROOFING: EXPOSED NAIL METHOD

Roll roofing is most commonly applied lengthwise to the roof deck in sheets from 12 to 18 feet long. As an aid to locating the first strip, strike a chalk line at the 36-inch mark, up from the eave. This chalk line will help you to position the top edge of the roll roofing on the roof deck.

Roll out the sheet of roofing so the lower edge and the ends will extend ¼ to ⅜ of an inch over the eave and rake of the roof deck (see Figure 1-6). Drive roofing nails along a line from ½ to ¾ of an inch down from the top edge of the sheet and spaced 18 to 20 inches apart. The top nails are necessary to hold the strip in place (more nails will be used here when the second, overlapping, sheet is applied). Drive roofing nails along the eave and rake on a line approximately 1 inch from the edge of the roofing. Space these nails 2 inches apart and stagger them slightly along the eaves to avoid splitting the roof deck.

Apply the second course of roofing so that it will overlap the first course by approximately 2 inches. Drive nails along the top

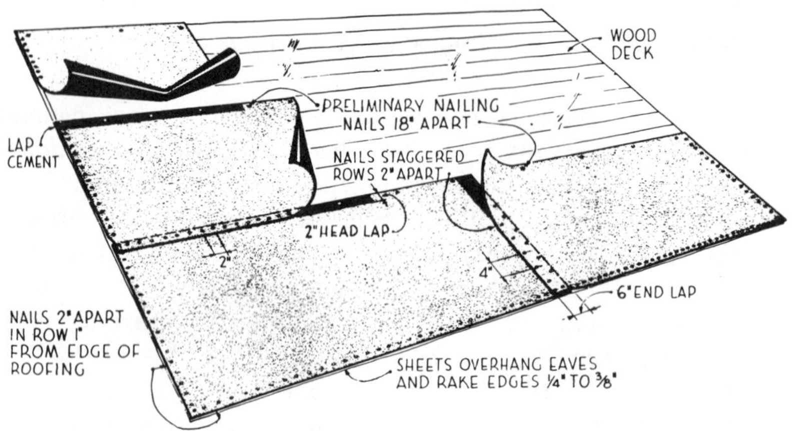

Courtesy of Asphalt Roofing Manufacturers Association

FIG. 1-6. Application of roll roofing by the exposed nail method, parallel to the eaves. Note 6-inch end lap joint.

edge of the sheet approximately 18 inches apart. Positioning the second sheet will be a bit easier if you strike a chalk line 34 inches from the top edge of the first sheet.

After the second sheet has been nailed, only along the top edge, fold back the entire sheet (toward the ridge of the roof). Then apply a coat of lap cement over the top edge of the first sheet where the two sheets overlap. This should be approximately a 2-inch band, along the top of the first sheet. Some roofers also apply a 1-foot-wide band of lap cement along the eaves of the roof deck as added insurance against possible damage by heavy winds.

Next, fold back the second sheet of rolled roofing to its original position so it is embedded in the cement. Nail the overlapping edge of the second sheet in place, spacing the nails approximately 2 inches apart. Stagger the nails slightly to avoid splitting the roof deck, placing them not less than ¾ of an inch up from the exposed edge of the sheet. Nail the edges of the strip 2 inches apart and approximately ¼ to ⅜ of an inch in from the edge.

Apply succeeding courses of rolled roofing in the same manner. The last sheet, however, is trimmed for its entire length so that it ends even with the ridge. Cover the top of the ridge with a cap strip about 12 inches wide and centered over the ridge. Just prior to installing the ridge cap strip, brush a 2-inch band of lap cement on both sides of the ridge for the entire length. Nail the ridge cap strip into place, spacing the nails 2 inches apart and about ¾ of an inch up from the edge. If hips are present on the roof, they are covered with a 12-inch-wide strip in the same fashion as the ridge cap strip (Figure 1-7). Hips should, however, be covered first up to the ridge and then the ridge cap strip can be installed to cover the hip strip ends. It is often very helpful to strike a chalk line approximately 5½ inches on each side of the hip or ridge. This chalk line will help to position the strip.

End lap joints (where the ends of two strips join), should be at least 6-inches wide and cemented the full width of the lap. Stagger the nails in rows, 1 and 5 inches apart, as shown in Figure 1-6. All lap joints should be staggered so that an end lap in one course will never be over or adjacent to an end lap in a preceding course.

Roll roofing can also be attached to a roof deck parallel to the rake. The first step is to strike a chalk line parallel to the rake, approximately 35½ to 35¾ inches from the edge. This line will help to position the roll roofing. The first strip should be placed on the roof so that it overhangs the rake and eave by ¼ to ½ inch. Drive roofing nails 2 inches apart along the eave and rake and

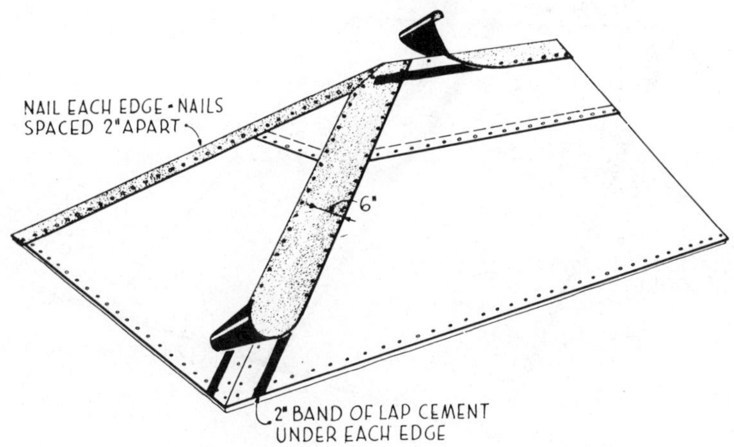

Courtesy of Asphalt Roofing Manufacturers Association

FIG. 1-7. Covering hips and ridges with roll roofing using the exposed nail method.

about 1 inch in from the edges. Nails should also be driven, about 10 to 12 inches apart, along the edge of the roll roofing that will be overlapped by the second sheet. These nails simply help to hold that edge in position.

Lay the second sheet of rolled roofing with a 2-inch overlap on the first sheet (see Figure 1-8). Drive preliminary nails on the far edge of the strip to hold it in position. Then carefully fold back the strip so a 2-inch-wide band of lap cement can be spread on the edge of the first strip. Next, fold back the second strip into position and embed it in the lap cement, overlapping the edges of the first strip by approximately 2 inches. Then drive nails ¾ of an inch in from the lap joint and space them 2 inches apart. Drive roofing nails, spaced the same distance, along the ridge and eave as well.

Then fold back the first full sheet of roofing into place and press into the cement. To ensure firm contact, it is common practice to walk around the edges of the rolled roofing after it has been pressed into the cement. Before you do this, however, you should make certain that you don't have any roofing cement on the soles of your shoes or you will leave tracks all over the roof.

Apply the second and succeeding courses to overlap each preceding course by the predetermined lap (usually 2 inches),

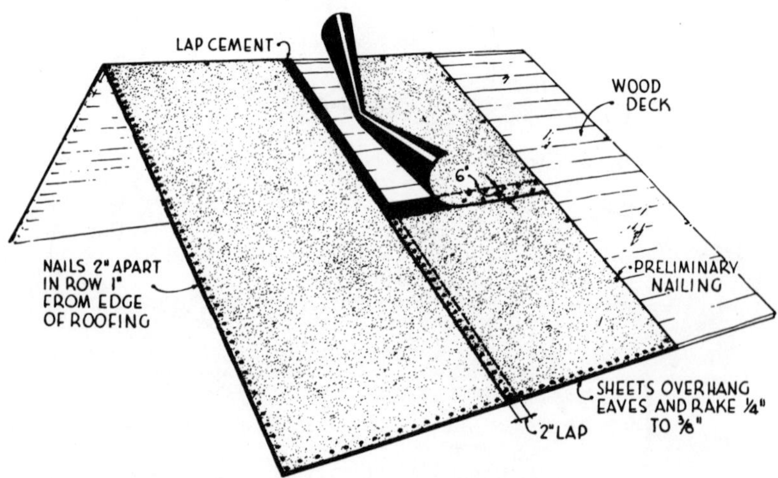

Courtesy of Asphalt Roofing Manufacturers Association

FIG. 1-8. Installing roll roofing parallel to the rake, using the exposed nail method.

securing each course along the upper edge with nails in the same manner as described for the first course. Do not apply nails within 18 inches of the rake edge until the cement has been applied to the edge strip and the overlying sheet has been pressed down into the cement.

Joints should overlap at least 6 inches and be bonded together with lap cement (Figure 1-9). The underlying part of the lap joint should be nailed 1 and 5 inches in from the edge with nails spaced about 4 inches apart. End laps are also staggered so that a lap in one course will never be over or adjacent to a lap in the preceding course.

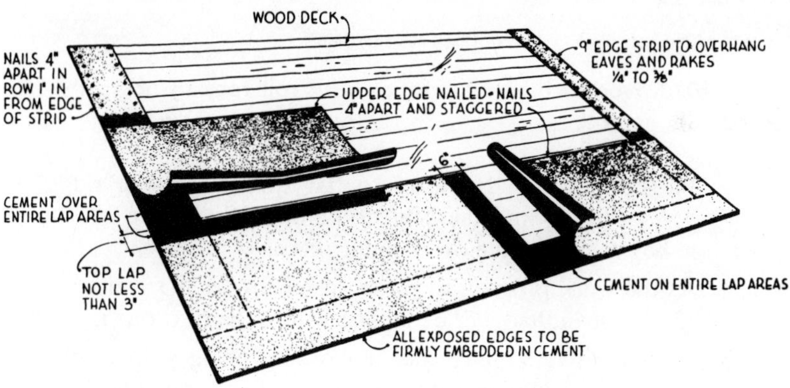

Courtesy of Asphalt Roofing Manufacturers Association

FIG. 1-9. Installing roll roofing parallel to the eaves, using the concealed nail method.

Strips of roll roofing, cut 12 inches × 36 inches are used to cover hips and ridges. These strips are bent lengthwise through their centers so they will lay evenly on the hip or ridge. When applying these strips, start at the lower end of a hip or at either end of a ridge, and "shingle" the pieces in place as shown in Figure 1-10, lapping each piece 6 inches over the preceding one, as follows:

1. Snap a chalk line on each side of the hip or ridge 5½ inches away from the center.
2. Apply the cement from one line over to the line on the other side.

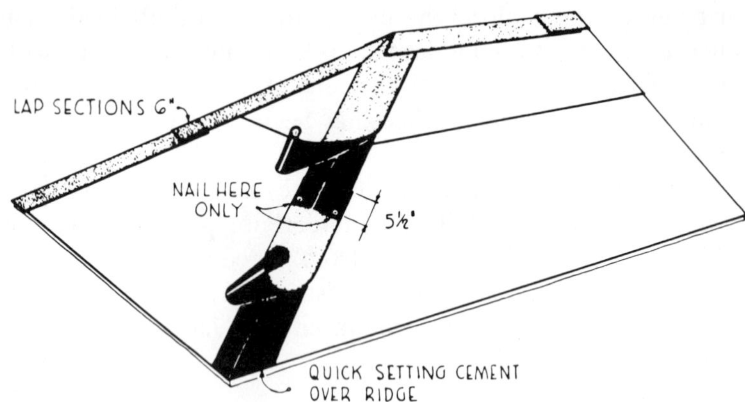

Courtesy of Asphalt Roofing Manufacturers Association

FIG. 1-10. Covering hips and ridges with roll roofing using the concealed nail method.

3. Fit the first folded strip of roofing over the hip or ridge and press it firmly into the cement, nailing only on the end that is to be covered by the overlapping piece.
4. As the work progresses, spread cement over the entire portion of each strip that is to be lapped before the next one is applied.
5. Press the overlapping end of the succeeding strip firmly into the cement and repeat the process to the end of the hip or ridge.

Rolled roofing can also be applied parallel to the rake of a roof. In general, the specifications for horizontal application apply to vertical application except that the sheets are started from the ridge where they are fastened with three or four nails, and unrolled toward the eaves. Sheets should be permitted to hang free, over the eave, until they lie smoothly before they are cemented and nailed to the roof deck.

Application of 19-inch Selvage Double Coverage Roll Roofing

All 19-inch double coverage roll roofing is uniformly produced as a 36-inch-wide sheet, 17 inches of which is intended for exposure and 19 inches for selvage edge. The 19-inch selvage portion is variously finished by different manufacturers. Some saturate the sheet, some saturate and coat the sheet, and others modify in minor respects. Some of these products may be applied with cold asphalt adhesives, some only with hot asphalt, and some with either hot or cold asphalt. It is important to know the type of product being used and to follow the manufacturer's recommendations as to the type of adhesive to use for the best results.

Although the following description illustrates the 36-inch-wide, 19-inch selvage mineral surfaced roofing, any roll roofing may be applied in the same manner, if double coverage of a roof is desired and if the lapped portion of the sheet is 2 inches wider than the exposed portion. This type of roofing is a form of built-up roof.

Nineteen-inch selvage mineral surfaced roofing may be used on roof decks having a rise of 1 inch or more per foot of horizontal run. To ensure adequate pitch, you should make certain that rain water will drain off by gravity, and not stand in puddles and evaporate.

A drip edge, made of noncorrodible, nonstaining material, is used along the eaves and rakes, applied directly to the edges of the roof deck. Metal drip edge is designed to allow water runoff to drip free of underlying construction. The drip extends back from the edge of the deck not more than 3 inches and is secured with appropriate roofing nails spaced 8 to 10 inches apart along its inner edge as shown in Figure 1-11.

Begin installing this type of roofing by first cutting the 19-inch selvage portion from a strip of roofing. Apply this sheet parallel to the eave so that it projects ¼ to ⅜ of an inch beyond the edge of the drip edge, along the eave and at the rake ends. Secure this selvage portion to the deck with three rows of roofing nails. The top

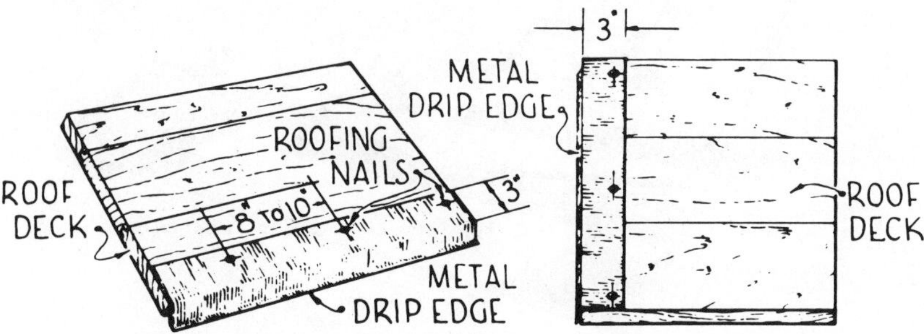

Courtesy of Asphalt Roofing Manufacturers Association

FIG. 1-11. Metal drip edge is applied to the edges of the roof deck prior to installing double coverage roll roofing.

row is 4½ inches down from the top edge of this strip, while the lower row is about 1 inch from the bottom edge of the sheet. The center row of nails is driven halfway between the upper and lower rows of nails. All nails are spaced approximately 12 inches apart in slightly staggered rows.

Apply the first row of roofing with the end and lower edge flush with the rake and eave edge and edge of the starter strip. Then secure it with two rows of roofing nails through the selvage portion. The first row of nails should be 4¾ inches below the upper edge and the second row 8½ inches below the first. All roofing nails should be spaced approximately 12 inches apart, in staggered rows.

Next, fold back this first strip over the nail rows and apply a coat of the recommended roofing cement to the entire starter strip. Then, fold back the first course into position and press it into the cement.

Attach succeeding courses of this type of roofing material to the roof deck in a similar fashion. Each course overlaps the succeeding course the full 19-inch width of the selvage edge and is nailed along the top edge in the same manner as the first strip.

After each course is nailed along the top edge, lift away the mineral-surfaced exposed part of the sheet, exposing the selvage portion of the underlying sheet. Then apply a coat of cement to this area at a rate recommended by the manufacturer of the roofing material (see Figure 1-12). Apply cement to within ¼ of an inch

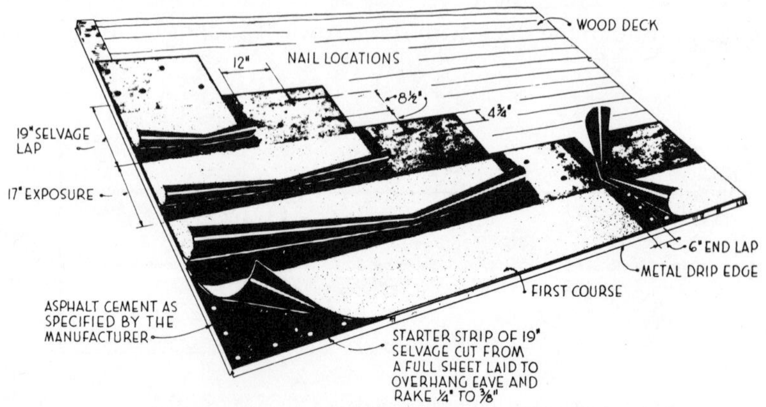

Courtesy of Asphalt Roofing Manufacturers Association

FIG. 1-12. Installing 19-inch double coverage roll roofing parallel to the eaves.

of the edge of the exposed portion of the underlying sheet. Then fold back the overlying sheet into position and press it firmly into the cement. Apply enough pressure over the entire cemented area, using a broom or light roller to ensure complete adhesion between the sheets at all points.

It is important that the cementing agent be spread so that when pressure is applied to the overlying sheet, the cement is brought all the way to the edge of the surfaced section.

As with all types of rolled roofing, all end laps are 6 inches wide. The underlying mineral-surfaced portion of the lap is first secured to the deck surface with a row of roofing nails located 1 inch back from the end of the normally exposed part of the roofing. Nails are commonly spaced in a row 4 inches apart. Asphalt cement is then spread evenly over 5½ inches of the 6 inch lapped area and the overlying sheet is then folded back down into position and pressed firmly into the cement. (See Figure 1-13.)

Secure the overlying sheet to the deck surface with a row of roofing nails located 1 inch back from the end of the selvage portion of the sheet on 4-inch centers. Stagger all end laps so that an end lap is never adjacent to an end lap in a preceding course.

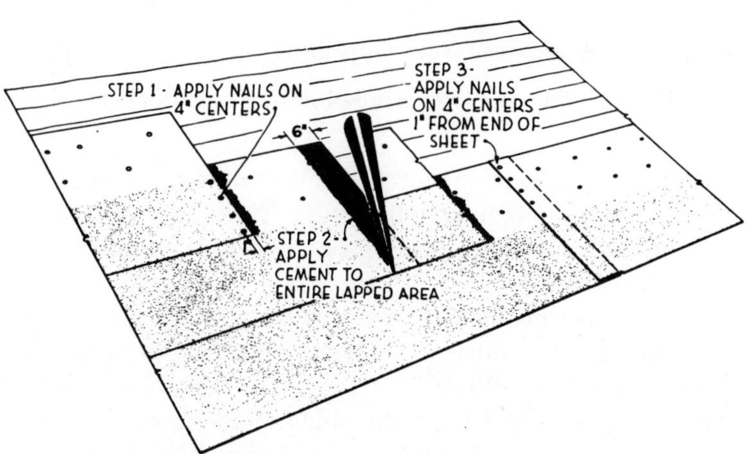

Courtesy of Asphalt Roofing Manufacturers Association

FIG. 1-13. End lap joints are accomplished in three steps when installing double coverage roll roofing. (1) Apply nails on 4-inch centers; (2) apply cement to entire area to be lapped; and (3) nail top sheet only in area to be covered by succeeding course.

Nineteen-inch selvage double coverage roll roofing can, of course, be applied parallel to the rake of the roof deck. In general, the specification for horizontal application applies to vertical application, except that the first sheet is located so that it overhangs the rake instead of the eave. In addition, all end laps are constructed so that the up roof sheet overlies the lower one, as shown in Figure 1-14.

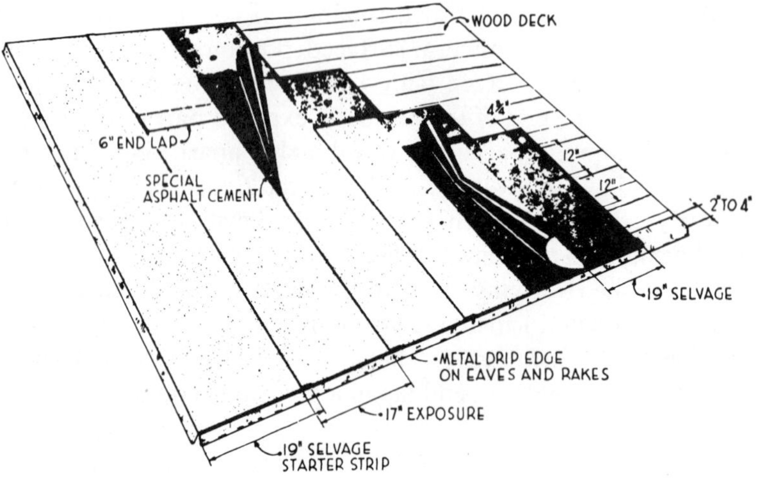

Courtesy of Asphalt Roofing Manufacturers Association

FIG. 1-14. Attaching double coverage roll roofing parallel to rake.

Hip and ridge treatment is similar to the concealed nail method of installing regular roll roofing. The sheets of roofing are butted and nailed as they come up on either side of a hip or ridge (see Figure 1-15).

Begin by cutting strips of roofing 12 × 36 inches across the sheet for use as hip and ridge covering. Bend the pieces lengthwise through their centers. When applying, start at the lower end of a hip or at either end of a ridge and shingle the pieces to the hip or ridge, lapping each one over the preceding one by a distance equal to the length of the selvage portion. It may be helpful, when installing hip and ridge caps, if you proceed as follows:

1. Snap a chalk line on each side of the hip or ridge 5½ inches away from the peak.

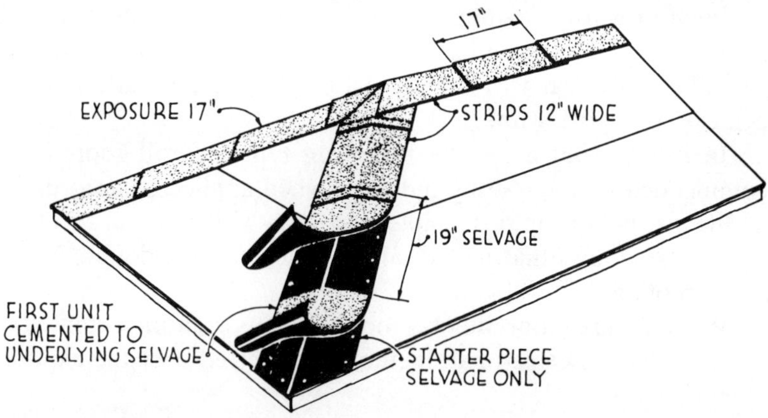

Courtesy of Asphalt Roofing Manufacturers Association

FIG. 1-15. Hip and ridge treatment when installing double coverage roll roofing.

2. Cut a selvage portion from one strip and apply it as a starter, using nails 1 inch above each edge on 4-inch centers to secure it in place. Apply asphalt cement over its entire length.
3. Fit the next folded strip of roofing over the hip or ridge and press it firmly into the cement, nailing only on the end that is to be covered by the overlapping piece.
4. As the work progresses, spread asphalt adhesive over the selvage portion of each strip that is to be lapped before the next one is applied.
5. Press the overlapping end of the succeeding strip into the cement and repeat the process to the end of the hip or ridge.

GENERAL COMMENTS ON ROLL ROOFING

All types of rolled roofing are installed in a similar manner. Because of these similarities, a few general comments about this type of roof covering follow.

First, it is not a good practice to apply rolled roofing when the outside temperatures are at or below 7°C. All rolled roof coverings become very brittle at these temperatures and have a tendency to crack when unrolled. If you must work at lower temperatures, you can increase your chances of success by storing the roofing in a warm place for at least 24 hours prior to unrolling.

Even in warm weather, it is good practice to unroll the roofing carefully and let it lie in the sun before attaching it to the roof deck. The sun's heat will slightly soften the material and make it much easier to work with.

In heavy wind areas the following types of roll roofing are recommended by the roofing industry, when applied in accordance with the instructions in this chapter: 18-inch-wide mineral surfaced, 65-pound smooth, blind nailed, and 19-inch selvage double coverage roll roofing.

When a maximum life of a roof covering is an important consideration, the concealed nail method is preferred over the exposed nail method.

Use only the lap cement or quick setting cement recommended by the manufacturer of the roofing product. Cements should be stored in a warm place until ready for use. If necessary, cement may be warmed by placing the container in hot water. However, never attempt to heat asphalt cement directly over a flame, for it is flammable.

Nails are an important consideration for application of roll roofing directly to a wooden roof deck. Use 11 or 12 gauge, hot-dipped galvanized roofing nails. These nails are commonly ⅜ of an inch in diameter with large heads and shanks ⅞ of an inch to 1 inch in length. When installing roll roofing over an existing covering, you must use roofing nails that are long enough to penetrate at least ¾ of an inch into the roof sheathing.

Assuming that the roof deck supporting structure (rafters) are rigid enough to prevent standing puddles of water after a rain, the following minimum roof pitches are safe for the type of application indicated:

Specification	Acceptable Minimum Pitch
Exposed nail method—2-inch top lap	2 inches per foot
Concealed nail method—3-inch top lap	1 inch per foot
Concealed nail method—double coverage 19 inch	1 inch per foot

Installed properly, a roof covered with roll roofing will give at least 15 years of service, with a life of 25 years not uncommon. Roll roofing, while not the most attractive roof covering, is probably the most utilitarian asphalt roof covering, and the easiest to install. Chapter 4, "Reroofing," covers asphalt shingles, the most common form of asphalt roof covering.

2

CEDAR SHINGLES AND HANDSPLIT SHAKES

The Red Cedar of the Pacific Northwest is truly a remarkable tree. Hundreds of years ago, the Indians along the northern Pacific coast used tall, majestic cedars as a center of their culture. They built shelters and tribal longhouses from boards that were cut from cedar. They built dugout canoes from sections of cedar trees. They wove the stringy bark into blankets and clothing and even used the pleasantly aromatic boughs from the cedar tree for bedding. They also buried their dead in coffins made from cedar. But probably the most spectacular use of cedar was for the elaborately carved tribal totem poles. Because the Red Cedar of the Pacific Northwest was such an important part of their lives, the Indians referred to it as "the tree of life." (See Figure 2-1.)

The Western Red Cedar (*Thuja Plicata*) has also played an important role in the building of America during the past century, particularly in the form of shingles and shakes. They have graced the exteriors of countless thousands of homes from modest cottage to stately mansion. Cedar shingles and shakes are the products of a distinctive natural material. The giant Western Red Cedar tree, which grows in Washington, Oregon, Idaho, and British Columbia, produces a uniquely beautiful clear run of pure "heart-wood" texture and grain.

A handy rule-of-thumb in choosing between red cedar shingles and shakes for roofing is that the heavy, handsplit-and-resawn shake tends to create strong dominating roof architecture while the

Courtesy of Red Cedar Shingle and Handsplit Shake Bureau

FIG. 2-1. The Indians of the Pacific Northwest used Western Red Cedar for many building projects, including totem poles.

shingle, being more uniform in its lines, is more gentle in character. (See Figure 2-2.)

Handsplit cedar shakes are produced from clear, straight-grained wood. No two shakes are exactly the same, although shake artisans maintain enough similarity in their products to allow proper application.

TYPES OF SHAKES

To increase adaptability, and to tailor their product for sidewalls as well as for roofs, manufacturers of "Certi-Split" shakes produce three distinctive types, based on texture and method of manufacture: handsplit-and-resawn, tapersplit, and straight-split. All "Certi-Split" shakes can be used effectively on roofs. The handsplit-and-resawn type is designed to give the most rugged texture and heaviest butt-lines. Tapersplit and straight-split shakes impart a more uniform texture to roofs, when rugged effects are not desired.

Courtesy of Red Cedar Shingle and Handsplit Shake Bureau

FIG. 2-2. Examples of cedar shakes and shingles.

Although all three types may be used on sidewalls, tapersplit and straight-split varieties are usually preferred, with the shorter lengths favored. For a more detailed discussion of cedar shingle and shakes for sidewall application, see Chapter 10, "Shingle Siding."

Handsplit cedar shakes are, as their name implies, made by hand. The process of making handsplit shakes begins with selected cedar logs that have been cut to specified lengths. The resulting blocks or *bolts,* as they are called, are then trimmed to remove the bark and sapwood. In the case of tapersplit or straight-split types, individual shakes are then rived from the block with a heavy steel blade called a *froe.* To obtain a tapered thickness for tapersplit shakes, the blocks are turned—end on end—after each shake is split off the block.

The froe has a long and interesting history in America. In the past the froe was always used instead of a saw to make shingles and even boards from straight-grained wood. A froe consists of a wedge-shaped blade, at least 13 inches long, with a short, wooden handle attached at one end at a 90 degree angle to the blade. The froe is struck with a *froe club,* which is a wooden or sometimes steel mallet. (See Figure 2-3.)

Courtesy of Red Cedar Shingle and Handsplit Shake Bureau

FIG. 2-3. A froe and froe club being used to make handsplit cedar shakes.

A froe is first placed, with the handle in a vertical position, on top of a block of cedar. The end of the blade is then struck with the froe club, forcing the blade of the froe down into the block, going with the grain. As the blade of the froe is driven down into the block, the handle is pulled or pushed toward or away from the user. This action will often split off a shingle because of the natural straightness of the grain.

In colonial times a saw was rarely used for cutting with the grain; splitting with a froe and froe club was much easier. An experienced user could split 1-inch wide shingles from a large block of wood in a fraction of the time needed to saw the same size pieces. To this day the makers of handsplit cedar shakes still use the froe and froe club to rive shakes from blocks of cedar.

To produce the handsplit-and-resawn shakes, blocks of cedar are split into thicker than normal boards and then passed through a thin band saw to form two shakes, each with a handsplit face and a flat-sawn back. Expert sawyers guide the boards diagonally through the saw to produce shakes with thin tips and thick butts. After the shakes are hand-split (and resawn if necessary) they are packaged. Experienced shake packers bundle the finished shakes in a standard size frame, compressing the bundles slightly and binding them with wooden bandsticks and steel strapping.

"Certi-Split" Shakes

"Certi-Split" shakes are produced in two lengths: 18-inch and 24-inch. The shakes vary considerably in width and, to a small degree, thickness. Some have more texture than others, and there may be variations in color. These variations are the pleasing result of craftsmanship applied to a natural material. It is this handsplit appearance that has brought shakes to the attention of architects, builders, and homeowners who desire character and warmth in the designs of their homes, rather than mechanical monotony.

It is wise always to specify "Certi-Split" when ordering handsplit shakes. To ensure high standards, "Certi-Split" shakes are inspected at frequent unannounced intervals. The experienced inspectors, employed by and responsible only to the Red Cedar Shingle & Handsplit Shake Bureau, police the quality of shakes. Shake bundles that have undergone the Bureau's scrutiny carry an identifying "Certi-Split" label under the bandstick. This constant supervision raises the value of the "Certi-Split" name from that of a trademark to a guarantee of consistent and reliable manufacture. Since shake-making is a craft that involves individual skill, great variances in product are possible; the "Certi-Split" label is assurance that your shakes are the finest.

INSTALLING CEDAR SHINGLES AND SHAKES

Roofing with cedar shingles and shakes is only slightly different from shingling with asphalt shingles. Basically, exposure is different for the various types of shakes and shingles. For example, a 10-inch exposure may be used with 24-inch-long shakes. When this exposure is strictly adhered to, a square of 24-inch-long shakes will cover 100 square feet of roof area. Standard exposure can, of course, be reduced but then proportionately more material and labor will be required. Standard exposure should not be increased when shingling a roof but can be increased when covering a sidewall of a house. Standard exposure for the most common types of cedar shingles and shakes are listed below:

24-inch shakes	10-inch exposure
24-inch shingles	7½-inch exposure
18-inch shingles	5½-inch exposure
16-inch shingles	5-inch exposure

To determine the required number of shingle or shake bundles you will need to cover your roof, you must find the area of the roof. Divide the area of the roof by 100 (one square of shingles) to arrive at the number of squares of shingles or shakes you will need to cover the roof at standard exposures. Don't forget to allow for double coursing at the eaves: with shingles, one square will provide about 240 lineal feet of starter course; with shakes, one square will cover about 120 lineal feet. Also allow about one extra square of shingles for every 100 lineal feet of valleys, and about two squares extra for shakes.

Nails

Nails are extremely important. Be sure to use rust-resistant nails. Zinc-coated or aluminum nails are both excellent. Don't skimp on nail quality: why spend time fastening red cedar shingles with short-lived nails? (See Figure 2-4.)

For new construction, or when covering a roof deck that has had the old roof covering removed, it takes about two pounds of 6*d* nails per square of 24-inch shakes, two pounds of 3*d* nails for 16-inch or 18-inch shingles, and two pounds of 4*d* nails for 2-inch shingles, provided that all shakes or shingles are spaced according to the standard exposure table above.

The roof deck itself, on which you will be attaching cedar shingles, may be either spaced or solid depending on your location. In snow-free areas, spaced sheathing is practical, using 1 × 6's spaced on centers equal to the weather exposure at which the shakes will be laid, but not over 10 inches. In areas in which wind-driven snow is common, solid sheathing is recommended. (See Figure 2-5.)

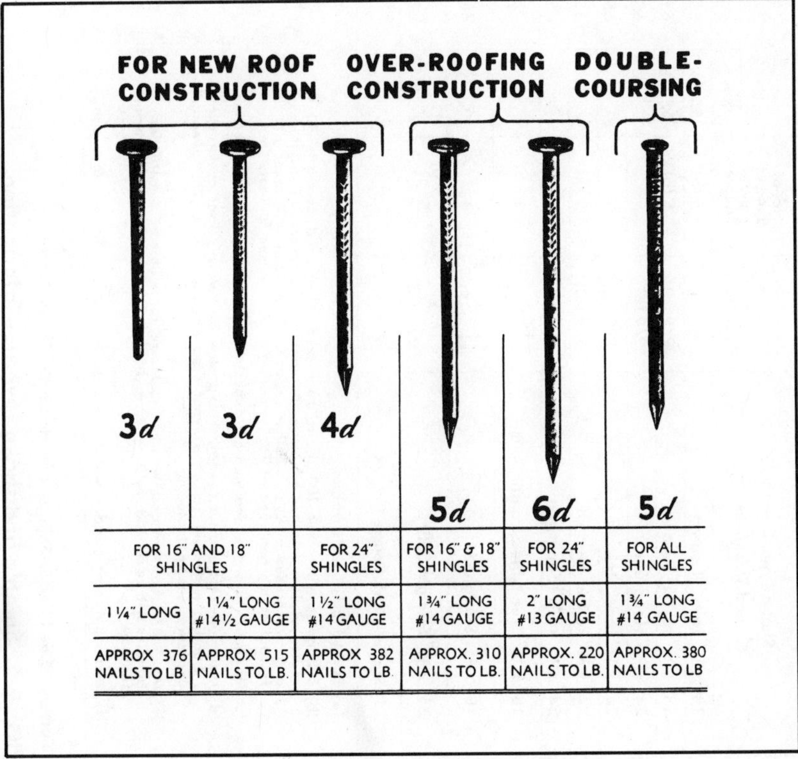

FOR NEW ROOF CONSTRUCTION
OVER-ROOFING CONSTRUCTION
DOUBLE-COURSING
3d
3d
4d
5d
6d
5d
FOR 16" AND 18" SHINGLES
FOR 24" SHINGLES
FOR 16" & 18" SHINGLES
FOR 24" SHINGLES
FOR ALL SHINGLES
1 1/4" LONG
1 1/4" LONG #14 1/2 GAUGE
1 1/2" LONG #14 GAUGE
1 3/4" LONG #14 GAUGE
2" LONG #13 GAUGE
1 3/4" LONG #14 GAUGE
APPROX 376 NAILS TO LB
APPROX 515 NAILS TO LB.
APPROX 382 NAILS TO LB
APPROX. 310 NAILS TO LB.
APPROX. 220 NAILS TO LB.
APPROX. 380 NAILS TO LB

FIG. 2-4. The various types of nails used to attach cedar shingles.

Shake Type, Length and Thickness	No. of Courses per Bundle	No. of Bundles per Square	Approximate coverage (in sq. ft.) of one square, when shakes are applied with 1/2″ spacing, at following weather exposures (in inches):								
			5½	6½	7	7½	8½	10	11½	14	16
18″ x ½″ to ¾″ Resawn	9/9 (a)	5 (b)	55 (c)	65	70	75 (d)	85 (e)	100 (f)			
18″ x ¾″ to 1¼″ Resawn	9/9 (a)	5 (b)	55 (c)	65	70	75 (d)	85 (e)	100 (f)			
24″ x ⅜″ Handsplit	9/9 (a)	5		65	70	75 (g)	85	100 (h)	115 (i)		
24″ x ½″ to ¾″ Resawn	9/9 (a)	5		65	70	75 (c)	85	100 (j)	115 (i)		
24″ x ⅜″ to 1¼″ Resawn	9/9 (a)	5		65	70	75 (c)	85	100 (j)	115 (i)		
24″ x ½″ to ⅝″ Tapersplit	9/9 (a)	5		65	70	75 (c)	85	100 (j)	115 (i)		
18″ x ⅜″ True-Edge Straight-Split	14 (k) Straight	4								100	112 (l)
18″ x ⅜″ Straight-Split	19 (k) Straight	5	65 (c)	75	80	90 (j)	100 (i)				
24″ x ⅜″ Straight-Split	16 (k) Straight	5		65	70	75 (c)	85	100 (j)	115(i)		
15″ Starter-Finish Course	9/9 (a)	5	Use supplementary with shakes applied not over 10″ weather exposure.								

(a) Packed in 18″-wide frames.

(b) 5 bundles will cover 100 sq. ft. roof area when used as starter-finish course at 10″ weather exposure; 6 bundles will cover 100 sq. ft. wall area when used at 8½″ weather exposure; 7 bundles will cover 100 sq. ft. roof area when used at 7½″ weather exposure; see footnote (m).

(c) Maximum recommended weather exposure for three-ply roof construction.

(d) Maximum recommended weather exposure for two-ply roof construction; 7 bundles will cover 100 sq. ft. roof area when applied at 7½″ weather exposure; see footnote (m).

(e) Maximum recommended weather exposure for sidewall construction; 6 bundles will cover 100 sq. ft. when applied at 8½″ weather exposure; see footnote (m).

(f) Maximum recommended weather exposure for starter-finish course application; 5 bundles will cover 100 sq. ft. when applied at 10″ weather exposure; see footnote (m).

(g) Maximum recommended weather exposure for application on roof pitches between 4-in-12 and 8-in-12.

(h) Maximum recommended weather exposure for application on roof pitches of 8-in-12 and steeper.

(i) Maximum recommended weather exposure for single-coursed wall construction.

(j) Maximum recommended weather exposure for two-ply roof construction.

(k) Packed in 20″ wide frames.

(l) Maximum recommended weather exposure for double-coursed wall construction.

(m) All coverage based on ½″ spacing between shakes.

Courtesy of Red Cedar Shingle and Handsplit Shake Bureau

FIG. 2-5. Shingle and shake coverage information.

Reroofing with Cedar Shingles

Cedar shingles and shakes can, of course, be attached to a roof deck with an existing roof covering of asphalt shingles provided the existing deck and covering is in sound condition. A rule of thumb, often used by professional roofers, is that a roof can be re-covered up to a maximum of three times. If, as time moves on, a fourth roof covering is needed, it is installed as if it were in new construction after all the old roofing has been removed. If it is determined that the existing roof covering must be removed, refer to Chapter 4, Reroofing, for complete information.

When overroofing you must remove a 6-inch strip of the old roofing along the eaves and gables, and install 1-inch-thick boards in their place. These boards provide a strong base at the perimeter of the new roof, concealing the old roof from view. The boards will also raise the edges of the gable ends of the roof, causing water to run down the roof rather than run off the ends of the house. In addition, the old ridge covering or ridge cap must be removed and replaced with cedar bevel siding. The butt (thicker) edges are overlapped at the peak and the new shingles are attached over the bevel strips.

Valley Installation

Valley flashing should be installed before you begin attaching the shingles. Because they are one of the most vulnerable areas in sloped-roof construction, valleys must be built with extreme care and with materials of maximum durability to avoid leaks. On handsplit cedar shake roofs, valleys may be either of the "open" type (covered with roofing felt and sheet metal) or of the "closed" type (covered with hand-fitted shakes). The open valley is used more often by professional roofers because it is less time consuming to construct. The open valley is also the easiest of the two types for the relatively inexperienced homeowner to install.

For maximum life, open valleys should be painted on both surfaces with a good grade metal paint and underlaid with 15-pound saturated roofing felt. Lay this strip of roofing felt down the center of the valley before installing the flashing material. The metal valley sheets should be at least 20 inches wide and with a 4- to 6-inch headlap. Valley metal should be galvanized iron not less than 26 gauge, preferable heavier, and ideally center and edge crimped. As the roof shakes are laid, those that adjoin valleys are trimmed parallel to the valleys to form a 6-inch wide gutter. (See Figure 2-6.)

To construct closed valleys, should you want to use them, first nail a 1 × 6-inch wood strip into the center of the valley and cover it with roofing felt as in open valleys. Next, shakes in each course are edge-trimmed to fit into the valley, then laid across the valley with an undercourse of 18 to 24 gauge, prepainted galvanized iron, which has a 2-inch headlap, and which extends at least 10 inches under the shakes on each side of the valley.

Any structural members, pipes, or vents that protrude through the roof deck should be flashed and counterflashed on all edges to prevent leakage. Flashing should extend at least 6 inches under the shakes and should be covered by counterflashing.

Courtesy of Red Cedar Shingle and Handsplit Shake Bureau

FIG. 2-6. Metal valley, at least 26 gauge galvanized iron, painted for antirust protection, center and edge crimped, is nailed into place along the edges.

On new construction, chimney flashing should be built in by the mason. If the masonry work has been completed, however, flashing strips should be inserted between bricks to a depth of ¾ of an inch by removing the mortar, then filling over the flashing with bituminous mastic. Against wooden walls, such as dormers, flashing can be inserted under the butts of the shakes or siding.

Before you install flashing, paint it on both sides after first cleaning with mineral spirits or gasoline. Flashing strips that must be bent to sharp angles should be painted after bending to the required angle. Flashing that is crimped to form a water stop in the centers of valleys should be given a double coat of paint over the crimped area.

When painting metal flashing material it is always best to give it a first coat of a special metal primer. After this initial coat has sufficiently dried you can then give the flashing a second (and possibly third) coat of finish color. Use a heavy-bodied lead and oil paint (if available) or bituminous paint on all roof metal, allowing it to dry thoroughly before installing. As an alternative, you might consider using flashing with a baked-on enamel coating; although this type is slightly more expensive, it eliminates the necessity of painting. Baked-on enamel flashing material is readily available in most parts of the country.

One other time-saver in metal flashing are metal vent pipe flashing collars, available in standard waste and vent pipe sizes. These collars slip snugly over pipes and extend out over the roof deck, forming a watertight seal over the pipe.

Attaching the Shakes

Before beginning the installation of cedar shakes to a roof, a 36-inch-wide strip of 15-pound roofing felt is attached along the eave line and over the roof sheathing. The beginning or starter course at the eave line should be doubled; as a design measure, the bottom course can be tripled. In addition, after each course of shakes is attached, an 18-inch-wide strip of 15-pound roofing felt is attached over the top portion of the shakes, extending onto the sheathing above, with the bottom edge of the felt positioned at a distance above the butt equal to twice the weather exposure. For example, if 24-inch shakes are being installed with the standard 10-inch exposure, the bottom edge of the felt should be applied 20 inches above the shake butts; the strip will then cover the top 4 inches of the shakes and extend 14 inches onto the sheathing. (See Figure 2-7.)

The first double (or possibly tripled) course of shakes should extend 2 inches over the eave boards. This 2-inch projection over the edge of the eave is necessary to prevent water from working its way back under the roofing.

As you attach the shakes to the roof deck keep in mind that individual shakes should be spaced apart approximately ½-inch, to allow for possible expansion. These joints or "spaces-between-shakes" should be broken or offset at least 1½-inches in adjacent courses. Also, the joints in alternate courses should not be in direct alignment in three-ply roof construction.

When applying straight-split shakes, which are of equal thickness throughout, the froe-end of the shake (the end from which they have been split, and which is smoother than the other end) should be laid uppermost. This will ensure a tighter and more weather-resistant roof. Furthermore, the use of roofing felt underlay between courses is not necessary when straight-split or tapersplit shakes are applied in snow-free areas at weather exposures less than one-third the total shake length. This applies to three-ply roof construction.

Courtesy of Red Cedar Shingle and Handsplit Shake Bureau

FIG. 2-7. The first course of shakes is applied over the starter course.

Nails are driven into the shakes until the head just meets the surface but not further (nails have less holding power when the heads are driven into the shake surface). Use two nails for each shake, driving them about 1 inch in from each edge, and from 1 to 2 inches above the butt-line of the following course. Never use more than two nails, even for wide shakes, because often a nail driven into the center of the shake will split the shingle right down the center.

Be sure that the nails you use are long enough to penetrate at least ½ inch into the sheathing. The 6*d* size, which is 2 inches long, normally is adequate, but longer nails should be used, if necessary, because of shake thickness and/or weather exposure. On handsplit cedar shakes laid over other roofing materials, longer nails must be used to reach the roof sheathing below. (See Figure 2-8.)

Courtesy of Red Cedar Shingle and Handsplit Shake Bureau

FIG. 2-8. Be sure to use nails long enough to penetrate at least ½ inch into the sheathing on the roof deck. Nails used in overroofing are longer than those used in new construction.

The rules for sitting and working on a roof are: (1) work in front of you; (2) keep materials above your position; (3) be able to reach your working area; and (4) move to the right if you are right-handed, or to the left if you are left-handed. Following these rules, carry and apply as many courses at a time as you can comfortably reach without moving. It may be from five to eight courses. Be guided by the length of your arm and don't try to overreach; this could result in a mishap.

When you reach the midway point between the eave and ridge you should check your course spacing. Measure up from the lower edge of the last course to the ridge line and divide for the adjusted exposure, so that the tips of the shakes in the next-to-the-last course just come to the ridge. An economical 15-inch starter finish shake can then be applied. This saves time of trimming shakes at the ridge. Then, cap the roof with factory-manufactured hip and ridge units. These units should be doubled at each end of the ridge, and should be nailed on each side with two 8*d* nails. Work from each end of the ridge, and apply a saddle in the center. (See Figure 2-9.)

If valleys are present, carry eight to ten courses of shingles into the valley and then check to make sure that they are straight. If necessary, make adjustments for those courses that are out of line, so one course doesn't disappear. To obtain straight valleys, it is always best to strike chalk lines along both sides of the valley, along the point at which you want to end each course. For quality valleys, in addition to using chalk line guides, be sure that the grain of the shingles is the same as it is in the main body of the roof. As insurance against leaks you should keep nails as far from the center of the valley as possible. (See Figure 2-10.)

Ridge Caps and Hip Caps

When the entire roof deck has been covered with shingles or shakes you can install the ridge cap and, if present, the hip caps. For this final course at the ridge line, as well as for the hips, uniform shakes should be selected. A strip of 15-pound saturated roofing felt, at least 8 inches wide, should be attached first over the crown of all hips and ridges. Hips and ridges should always be covered with shakes or shingles—rather than metal caps, for example—to achieve a harmonious appearance. As mentioned earlier, you can use prefabricated hip and ridge units, if available, or you can cover ridge and hips with individual shakes on the spot.

Courtesy of Red Cedar Shingle and Handsplit Shake Bureau

FIG. 2-9. An example of a finished ridge or hip cap. Note how edges are beveled.

Courtesy of Red Cedar Shingle and Handsplit Shake Bureau

FIG. 2-10. Shakes are cut parallel to valleys as courses are applied over the metal valley. Keep nails as far from the center of the valley as possible.

If you are constructing the ridge and hip caps on the house, select shakes that are approximately 6 inches wide. Then, as a guide, tack two wooden straight edges (1 × 4's) on the roof, 5 inches from the center line of the hip and ridge, one on each side. Double the starting course of shakes. Nail the first shake on the hip in place with one edge of the shake resting on the guide strip. Then, cut back the edge of the shake that projects over the hip on a bevel. Cut back the shake on the opposite side of the hip to fit over the first shake. Apply shakes of the following courses alternately in reverse order. (See Figure 2-11.)

Ridges are similarly constructed. Weather exposure should be the same as that given the shakes on the body of the roof. It is

Courtesy of Red Cedar Shingle and Handsplit Shake Bureau

FIG. 2-11. Factory assembled "hip-and-ridge" units "finish" the hips and ridges. Hip-and-ridge units should be applied at the same exposure as field of roof, and longer nails should be used to ensure adequate penetration.

obviously important that shakes on hips and ridges be attached with nails of sufficient length to reach through all underlying shakes, bevel siding (if used), and the roof deck sheathing below. (See Figure 2-12.)

In laying a cap along an unbroken ridge that terminates in a gable at each end, start laying the cap at each end so that it meets in the middle of the ridge. At that point nail a small saddle of shake butts to splice the two lines. Always double the first course of capping at each end of the ridge.

Courtesy of Red Cedar Shingle and Handsplit Shake Bureau

FIG. 2-12. An example of a finished ridge.

VARIATIONS WITH CEDAR SHAKES

Among the many roof variations that may be achieved with handsplit shakes is that produced by reducing the exposure of each course from the eaves to the ridge. This requires shakes of several lengths, however.

A very serviceable graduated exposure roof may be built by starting at the eaves with 24-inch-long shakes, laid with 10 inches of shingle exposed to the weather. Lay one-half of each roof area with shakes of this length, reducing the exposure gradually to about 8½ inches. Finish off the job with 18-inch shakes, starting with 8-inch exposures and reducing this to 5-inch exposures by the last course. The resulting appearance exaggerates the actual distance from the eaves to the ridge.

Although split-shake roofs are less likely to drip rainfall or snow from the gables than are roofs of smoother materials, gable-drip and icicles can be eliminated by inserting a single strip of cedar bevel siding the full length of each gable end with the thick edge flush with the sheathing edge. The resulting inward pitch of the roof surface keeps moisture away from the gable edge. In addition to concealing the old roofing materials (in reroofing), the gable edge will be more visually pleasing.

For a truly unique-looking roof, consider using a mixture of fairly smooth and very rough handsplit shakes. This will produce a roof with a rugged appearance and will be much more interesting to look at than a roof composed entirely of rough shakes.

PRECAUTIONS

Properly applied roofs of handsplit red cedar shakes should not leak, even under the most severe weather conditions. Such roofs, however, should not be subjected to unusual exterior strains. If it is necessary to walk over a roof for any reason, boards should be used for a walkway. Workmen should wear soft-soled shoes when applying a shake roof; under no circumstances should they wear hob-nailed or cleated-soled footwear, which will damage the shingles or shakes.

As handsplit shakes are thicker than ordinary roofing materials, the butt lines at the eaves tend to spread rain water over a slightly wider zone, especially on handsplit-and-resawn shake roofs. Wider guttering than is normally used will avoid splashing or runoff over the outer lip. Handsplit shakes with a thickness of ¾ inch or less require 5-inch gutter widths. For thicker shakes, 6-inch widths are better. Treated or painted wood gutter is the most pleasing, aesthetically.

Most cedar roofs are not treated, although under special circumstances when a preservative is desirable (conditions of heat or humidity, for instance) treatment of the shingles with a fungicidal chemical will inhibit bacterial growth such as moss, fungus, and mildew. Heavy-bodied paints or oils, which form roof surface coatings, should not be used on shake or shingle roofs.

Extreme care should be taken in applying some chemicals, such as pentachlorophenol solutions, because of their toxic nature. Manufacturer's directions should be followed to the letter. Shake roofs should be cleaned periodically, normally on an annual basis, of any accumulation of debris such as leaves, because such foreign matter can adversely affect roof service and life. (See Figure 2-13.)

Courtesy of Red Cedar Shingle and Handsplit Shake Bureau

FIG. 2-13a. Photo of a home before over-roofing with red cedar shakes.

Courtesy of Red Cedar Shingle and Handsplit Shake Bureau

FIG. 2-13b. After shot of same house.

3

SLATE ROOFS

HISTORICAL USES OF SLATE

Slate has been used as a roof covering for hundreds of years. Slate roofs have been in use in France, England, and Wales for centuries. One of the earliest references to the use of slate for roofs is in the construction of the roof of the Saxon Chapel at Stratford-on-Avon, Wiltshire, England, built during the eighth century. After almost 1200 years of constant exposure to all kinds of climatic changes, the slate roof is still in sound condition although covered with moss.

Slates were used to cover old castles at Carnarvon and Conway in North Wales during the twelfth century. These slates were thick and rough, as the workers of that time had little skill at splitting and trimming the slate. Today, modern architecture requires slate craftsmen to reproduce the handiwork of these early workers on special treatment, rough, and thick slate roofs.

The first reference in literature to authentic slate quarrying is the mention of the Penrhyn quarries by a Welsh bard in 1570. In 1580, Sion Tudor addressed some verses to the Dean of Bangor, Rowland Jones, requesting a shipload of slate. It is fitting that the introduction of the world to so vast an industry should have come through the agency of people of such importance as the Dean of the Church and a poet of distinction.

During the next two hundred years little is known of the growth of the industry. But gradually, from the local market around Penrhyn, it had grown to considerable importance by the end of the eighteenth century. Quarry methods were crude and transportation difficult until 1850 when the Welsh slate industry began to grow rapidly for several reasons: the extensions of railways and the resulting widening of the market; the growth of new towns; improvements in rural dwellings; removal of restrictive tariffs; and increased foreign demand.

In France the rapid development of the slate industry also dates from about 1850 and for nearly the same reasons. The quarrying of slate on the continent had begun long before this, however, and at Angers, France—a famous modern slate-mining center—a slate-roofed castle built in the twelfth century is still standing.

In North America probably the oldest slate quarry is in the Peach Bottom district at the Pennsylvania-Maryland border, opened in about 1734. In Virginia, the first quarry was opened about 1787 to provide slate for the roof of the state capitol. Slate was first quarried in Georgia in 1850. From such beginnings, slate quarrying grew and spread until it became an established industry. From the very first, Welsh slate workers played an important part in the development of slate quarrying in America. It is a matter of record that about 1877, 150 skilled slate workers left the Bethesda district in North Wales to work in American quarries. Many years before that, however, as the industry was beginning, towns with Welsh names, such as Pen Argyl and Bangor, arose in Pennsylvania, as Welsh slate workers settled there.

CHARACTERISTICS OF SLATE

The major difference between slate and other stone is the natural slaty cleavage of the former, which permits it to be more easily split. A second direction of fracture or "scallop," usually at right angles to the slaty cleavage, is called the *grain*. Roofing slates are commonly split so that the length of the slate runs with the grain. The nature of the surface after splitting depends on the character of the rock from which it is quarried. Many slates split to a smooth, practically even and uniform surface, while others are somewhat rough and uneven. As a result, a wide range of surface effects are available for the finished roof.

Slate quarried for roofing stock is of dense, sound rock, exceedingly tough and durable. Slate, like any other stone, becomes harder and tougher after exposure to the elements. It is practically nonabsorptive; tests on Pennsylvania slate showed a porosity of 0.15 to 0.4 percent.

Color

Slate from certain localities contains narrow bands of rock differing to various degrees in chemical composition and color from the main body of the stone. These bands are called *ribbons*. Ribbons containing no injurious constituents and of a desirable color are acceptable in slate for roofs. Slates of this type, when trimmed so that the ribbons are eliminated, are known as *clear slate*. Slates that contain sound ribbons are sold as *ribbon stock*. The color of slate is, of course, determined by its chemical and mineralogical composition. Since these factors differ in various localities, it is possible to obtain roofing slates in a variety of colors and shades.

It is truly remarkable to find a natural product possessing, in addition to the other qualities mentioned above, such unlimited possibilities in color effect. The use of slate for roofing makes it possible to obtain a surface of uniform or contrasting colors in cold or warm values. Moreover, if the design of the building requires a roof of one general color, various shades of the same color may be used to provide an interesting variation up and down, or across the roof or interspersed throughout. A low-eaved, prominent roof surface may require a quiet or contrasted blending of the autumnal colors of nature to allow the structure to blend in with its intimate surroundings. Slate not only permits a roof of permanent color, but by the selection of "weathering" slate, one may take advantage of the mellowing effect of both age and weather.

Weathering

Upon exposure to the weather, all slate is changed slightly in color. The extent of this color change varies with different slate beds, being barely perceptible in certain slates. Those slates in which the color changes only slightly are classed as "permanent" or "unfading" slate. Those in which the final result is more marked

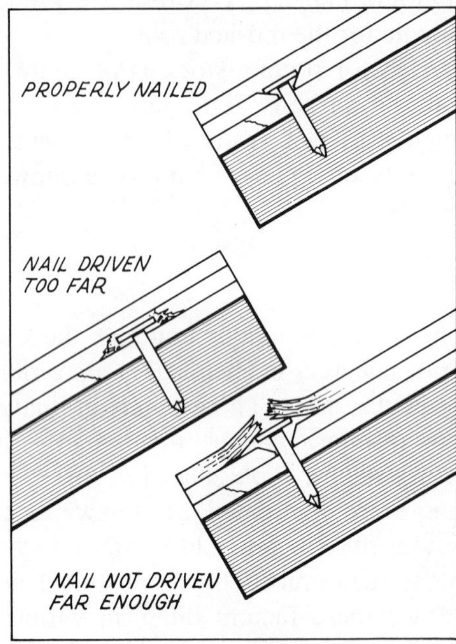

FIG. 3-1. Examples of nailed slate.

and varied are known as "weathering" slates. Weathering is the natural result of exposure to the weather of the coloring minerals in the slate. When color is an essential consideration, this characteristic should be considered. Slate cutters and quarry operators know from experience the probable nature and extent of the changes in the original color, although different quarries in the same state, and often in the same locality, may produce a wide range of colors in both permanent and weathering slates.

To take the fullest advantage of the various possible effects, the source of the slate, as well as its ultimate color effect, should be taken into consideration when planning a roof of slate.

There are eight basic slate colors: black, blue-black, grey, blue-grey, purple, mottled purple-green, green, and red. These color designations should be preceded by the word "unfading" or "weathering," according to the ultimate color effect desired.

Location of Slate Quarries

Active roofing slate quarrying in the United States is confined to the states of Maine, Maryland, New York, Pennsylvania, Vermont, and Virginia. The chief production of Pennsylvania slate is from the Lehigh district, including parts of Northhampton and Lehigh counties. The Peach Bottom district extends from York and Lancaster counties, Pennsylvania, across the line into Harford County, Maryland. The active Vermont district lies in Bennington and Rutland counties, and extends into Washington county, New York. The Maine slate deposits occur in Piscataquis county, located in the center of the state. Virginia operations are now conducted on the Arvonia belt of Buckingham and Fluvanna counties and near Esmont.

SELECTING MATERIAL

In the United States, roofing slates are sold by the "square," the same measurement as for other roof coverings. A square of roofing slate, however, means a sufficient number of slate shingles of any size to cover 100 square feet of a pitched roofing surface, when laid with the approved or customary standard lap of 3 inches. Slates for surfacing flat roofs are usually laid tile fashion, without overlapping, in which case a square of roofing slate would cover an area greater than 100 square feet.

The quantity of roofing slate per square varies from 686 pieces for the 10 × 6 inch size to 98 pieces for the 24 × 14 inch size, which includes the allowance for a 3-inch head lap. (See Table 3-1.)

It should be noted that for roofs of comparatively little slope, when a 4-inch lap is required, an additional quantity of roofing slate must be purchased. For steep roofs or siding, when a lap of 2 inches is sufficient, fewer slates will be required. Slate, however, is always sold on the basis of quantity required for a lap of 3 inches even for flat roofs.

The commercial standard thickness of roofing slate is 3⁄16 of an inch. "Commercial standard" is the quarry run of production, and allows tolerable variations above or below the 3⁄16-inch standard.

A square of roofing slate will vary in weight from 650 to 8,000 pounds for thicknesses from the commercial standard 3⁄16-inch to 2 inches. The commercial standard thickness will weigh from 650 to 750 pounds per square. For estimating the dead load on the roof construction, it may be taken at a maximum of 800 pounds per

TABLE 3-1
Dimensions of Slate Shingles for Roof Application

Face Dimensions in Inches	Minimum Number to Square (3-inch lap)	Face Dimensions in Inches	Minimum Number to Square (3-inch lap)
10 × 6	686	16 × 10	221
10 × 7	588	16 × 12	185
10 × 8	515	18 × 9	213
12 × 6	533	18 × 10	192
12 × 7	457	18 × 11	175
12 × 8	400	18 × 12	160
12 × 9	355	20 × 10	169
12 × 10	320	20 × 11	154
14 × 7	374	20 × 12	141
14 × 8	327	20 × 14	121
14 × 9	290	22 × 11	138
14 × 10	261	22 × 12	126
14 × 12	218	22 × 14	109
16 × 8	277	24 × 12	115
16 × 9	246	24 × 14	98

square or 8 pounds per square foot, including saturated felt and nails as well as the slate itself.

No piece of roofing slate should have fewer than 2 nail holes. The standard practice is to machine punch 2 holes in every roof slate at the quarry where the slate has been cut.

LAYING A SLATE ROOF

In the laying of any roofing material, workmanship is as essential as the selection of the proper roofing materials. The more enduring the material, the more important the workmanship becomes. Slate, the most long lasting roofing material known, should be laid by roofers of experience and training. It is a mistake to assume that those without some type of qualifications can properly lay slate. For instance, the nailing of cedar shingles and the nailing of slate are entirely different processes. The heads of slating nails should just touch the slate and should not be driven home to draw the slate, but left with the heads just clearing the slate so that the slate hangs on the nail. The opposite is true of cedar or asphalt shingles, when nails are driven flush with the surface of the shingle. If nails are driven into roofing slate in the same fashion, the slate can shatter around the nail hole or the head can be crushed and eventually the slate could ride up over the nailhead and be blown off in a heavy wind. Problems with slate roofs are often attributed to the slate itself when actually the root of the problem lies in improper nailing. All nails should penetrate the sheathing and not the joints between the roofing boards (or sheathing). This is especially important near the ridge of the roof.

There should be no through joints from the roof surface to the felt below. The joints of each course should be well broken with those below. If this simple precaution is neglected, it is possible that water may find its way through the joints and eventually cause the felt to deteriorate and result in leaks.

When random-width roofing slate is used, the slate should be jointed as near the center of the under slate as possible and not less than 3 inches from any under joint. (See Figure 3-2.) When all slates are of one width, this is automatically done by starting every other course with a half slate or, when available, a slate one and one-half times the width of the others.

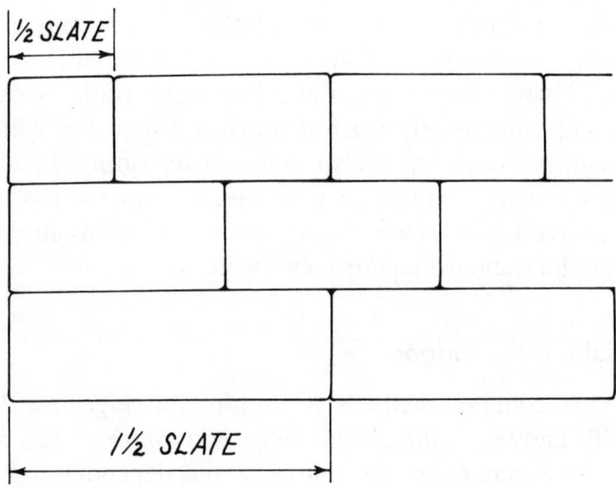

FIG. 3-2. Joints between the courses of slate must always be broken.

The exposure of a slate is the portion not covered by the next course of slate above and is thus the part of the slate that is exposed to the weather. The standard lap of the alternate courses used on sloping roofs is 3 inches and is the basis upon which all roofing slate is sold and quantity computed. The proper exposure to use is then obtained by deducting 3 inches from the length of the slate used and dividing by two. For example, the exposure for a 24-inch slate is: 24″ − 3″ = 21″ ÷ 2 = 10½″ exposure. Table 3-2 will be helpful in determining proper exposure for sloping roofs.

TABLE 3-2
Exposure in Inches for Sloping Roofs

Length of Slate in Inches	Slope 8 inches to 20 inches per foot, 3-inch lap
24	10½
22	9½
20	8½
18	7½
16	6½
14	5½
12	4½
10	3½

Sloping roofs that have a rise of between 8 and 20 inches per foot of horizontal run should be laid with a 3-inch lap. Buildings in southern or southwestern parts of the country may be safely roofed with a lap of only 2 inches, provided that quality workmanship is used while laying the slate. For steep roofs, such as the mansard and other nearly vertical roofs, a 2-inch lap will usually be sufficient. A 2-inch lap is also sufficient for siding. In some sections of the country—northern areas, for example—it is common practice to overlap 4 inches. Check other slate roofs in your area to see what the standard lap for your locale is.

Finishing the Ridges

The two common methods of finishing the ridge of a slate roof are usually known as the *saddle ridge* and *comb ridge,* but each may have other names and certain variations depending on the part of the country. With a saddle ridge, the regular roofing slates are extended to the ridge so that the pieces of slate on the opposite sides of the roof butt flush. On top of the last regular course of roofing slate at the ridge is laid another course of roofing slate, called the *combing slate,* and the pieces on the opposite side of the roof are butted flush. The combing slate is usually laid with the grain horizontal and should be wide enough (almost to the edge of the underlying course) so that the roof ridge is uniform with the rest of the roof. Or, the saddle ridge slate can be half the width of the regular size slate used on the roof. For example, if 20 inch × 12 inch slates are used on the roof with an 8½ inch exposure, 12″ × 8″ slates, laid horizontal, could be used for the ridge.

You will notice, in Figure 3-3, that the combing slates overlap and break joints with the underneath slate. In this way, all of the nails in the combing slate are covered by succeeding slates except for the nails in the last or finishing slate on the ridge, and these nails must be covered with roofing cement. Nails for the saddle ridge slates are driven between the joints in the slates below.

The comb ridge is laid in the same manner as the saddle ridge except that the combing slate of the north or east side extends beyond the ridge line as shown in the detail in Figure 3-3. This extension should not be more than 1 inch. The comb ridge may be laid with the combing having a vertical or horizontal grain. In either case, the edge of the slate should be set in roofing cement, as shown, and the nailheads covered with roofing cement. If the top or combing course is projected 1⁄16 of an inch to ⅛ of an inch above the under top courses, it will make a much better finish and will be more easily filled with roofing cement.

A variation of the standard comb ridge is known as the *cox-comb ridge* in which the combing slate alternately projects on either side of the ridge.

A variation of the saddle ridge is known as the *strip saddle ridge,* also shown in Figure 3-3. This type of ridge is laid in a similar manner to the saddle ridge except that the combing slates do not overlap but butt flush; also, each combing slate has four nails. The combing slate may be the same width as the regular roofing slate or narrower. All exposed nailheads must be covered with roofing cement, as should the edges of the combing slates on both ends of the ridge.

As Figure 3-3 illustrates, the top courses of the regular roofing slate have the edges set in roofing cement. This is done to prevent wind damage and actually does little to help waterproof the roof.

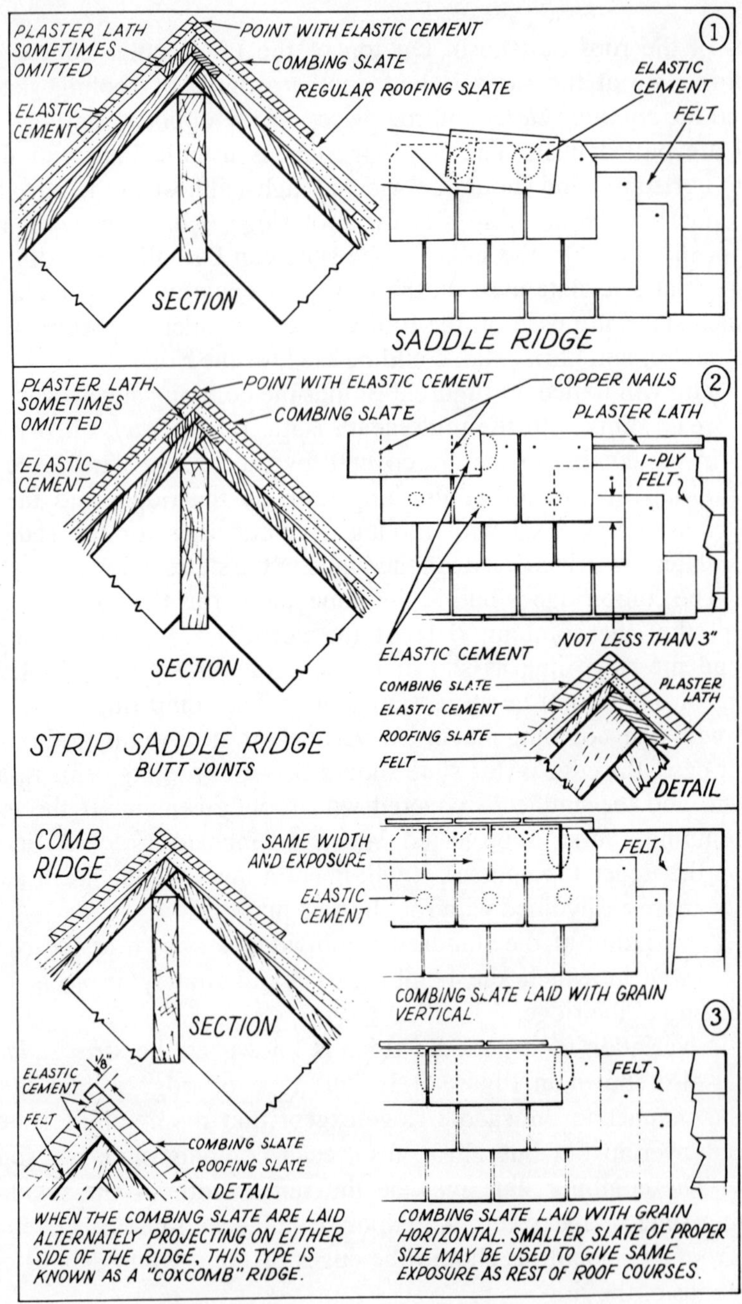

FIG. 3-3. Standard details for slate ridges.

SLATE HIPS

There are several methods of forming hips on slate roofs; Figure 3-4 illustrates the most common types of slate roof hips in this country.

The *saddle hip* may be formed by placing on the sheathing forming the hip one or two cant strips and running the roofing slate up to these strips. On top of the cant strip and the slate are laid the hip slates which are usually the same width as the exposure of the slates on the rest of the roof. As Figure 3-4 (1) demonstrates, four nails are used to fasten the hip slate to the roof. The nails are driven into the cant strip and do not go between the joints of the slate (as do the nails for the saddle ridge). The heads of the nails are, of course, covered with roofing cement. The next slate to be laid covers the preceding nailheads and the cement. Roofing cement is also placed on the joint between the roofing slate and the saddle hip slate before the saddle hip slate is nailed into place. A variation of the saddle hip is known as the *strip saddle hip* and is often used on less expensive work. A strip saddle hip may be formed of narrower slates laid with butt joints, which do not necessarily line up with the course of the slate on the roof.

Another type of hip is known as the *mitered hip,* in which the slates forming the roof courses and the hip are all in one plane (see Figure 3-4 [2]). The hip slates should be cut accurately to form tight joints, and these joints should be filled with roofing cement. Nails are driven so they will be covered by succeeding mitered hip slates.

One variation of the mitered hip is commonly known as the *fantail hip* (see Figure 3-4 [4]). A fantail hip is laid the same as the mitered hip except that the bottom edge of each piece of hip slate is cut at an angle to form a fantail.

Another very popular type of hip is the *Boston hip,* in which slates are woven in with the regular courses of roofing slates, as shown in Figure 3-4 (3). The nailheads are covered with roofing cement and the lower part of succeeding slate rests in this cement. In addition to the roofing cement, metal flashing is sometimes woven in with each course of mitered hips. That metal flashing is not necessary is evidenced by older roofs, in which master slate craftsmen covered hips only with slate.

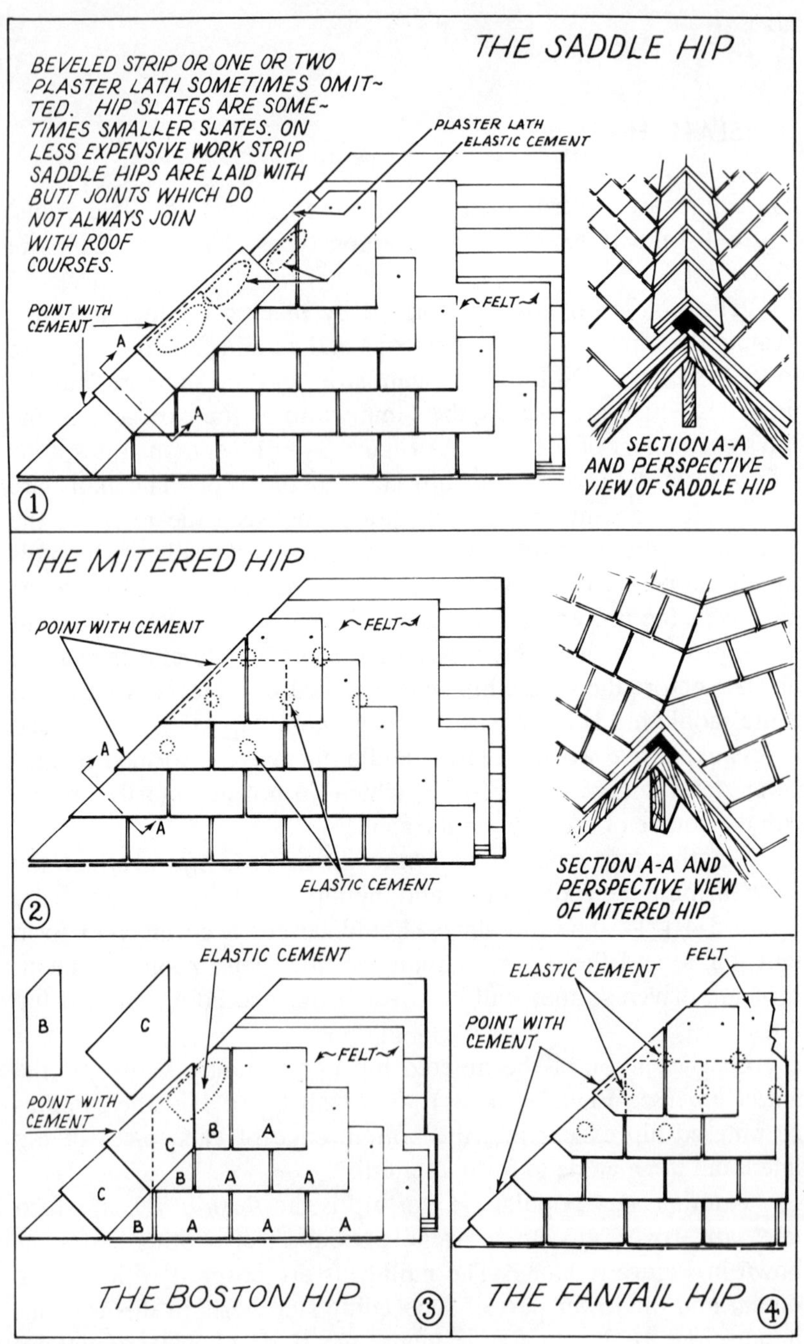

FIG. 3-4. Standard details for slate hips.

VALLEYS

There are two methods of forming valleys: open and closed. The open valley is, without a doubt, the most popular method, not only with slate roofs but with all kinds of finish roof coverings. Although many people consider the closed valley to be more pleasing in appearance, its use seems to be limited only to very high quality work. Variations of the closed valley, frequently used in connection with the graduated or textural roofs, are the round valley and the canoe valley.

Open Valleys

The open valley (Figure 3-5) is formed by laying strips of metal flashing in the valley angle and lapping the slate over it on

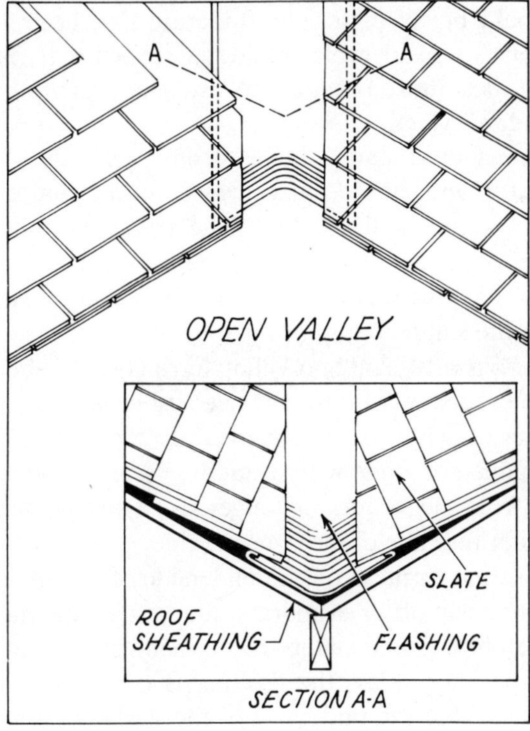

FIG. 3-5. Detail of open valley.

either side, leaving a space between the slate edges to act as a channel for water running down the valley angle. The width of the valley, or the amount of space between the slate edges, should increase uniformly toward the bottom of the valley. The amount of this increase, or taper, is usually 1 inch for every 8 feet. For example, in a valley 16 feet long, the distance between slates will be 2 inches greater at the bottom than at the top, as the width increases at the rate of ½ inch in 8 feet on each side of the valley. This permits a uniform width of about two-thirds the width of the slate under the slate adjacent to the valley. The difference in width or taper allows the slate to be laid closer to the valley at the upper end than at the lower end and takes care of the increase in water received. This tapering of the valley also has the very practical effect of allowing any ice that forms to free itself and slide down as it melts.

You must allow for this increase in width in the valley when placing the flashing strips. Valley flashings are generally laid in pieces up to 8 feet long. The best theoretical manner of handling the taper would be, of course, by tapering the sheets of flashing. As this involves considerable additional expense in labor, time, and material, it is more practical to use sheets of flashing shorter than the standard 8 feet.

The slate should start 2 inches from each side of the valley center at the top and should taper away from the center at the rate of ½ inch for every 8 lineal feet. The metal flashing should be wide enough to extend up under the slate, not less than 4 inches (preferably 6 to 8 inches), and as far as is possible without being punctured by the slating nails.

When two roofs forming a valley have considerable difference in slope or the roofs are of different size and cause a large variation in the volumes of water to be delivered into the valley, the flashing should be crimped or made with a standing seam to break the force of the water from the steeper or longer slope and prevent its being driven up under the slate of the opposite side.

Condensation forming on the underside of the valley flashing, when not free to run off or evaporate, may attack the metal or roof sheeting. Therefore, some slaters recommend not using felt paper under metal flashing unless the flashing is copper. If felt is used, they recommend that the underside of the flashing be painted with a quality oil-base paint.

Closed Valleys

A closed valley is formed with the slate worked tight to the valley line and pieces of metal placed under the slate, as shown in Figure 3-6. The size of the sheet to be used is determined by the length of the slate and the slope of the adjoining roofs. Each sheet should extend 2 inches above the top of the slate on which it rests so that it may be nailed along the upper edge of the roof sheeting without the nails penetrating the slate. Each sheet should be long

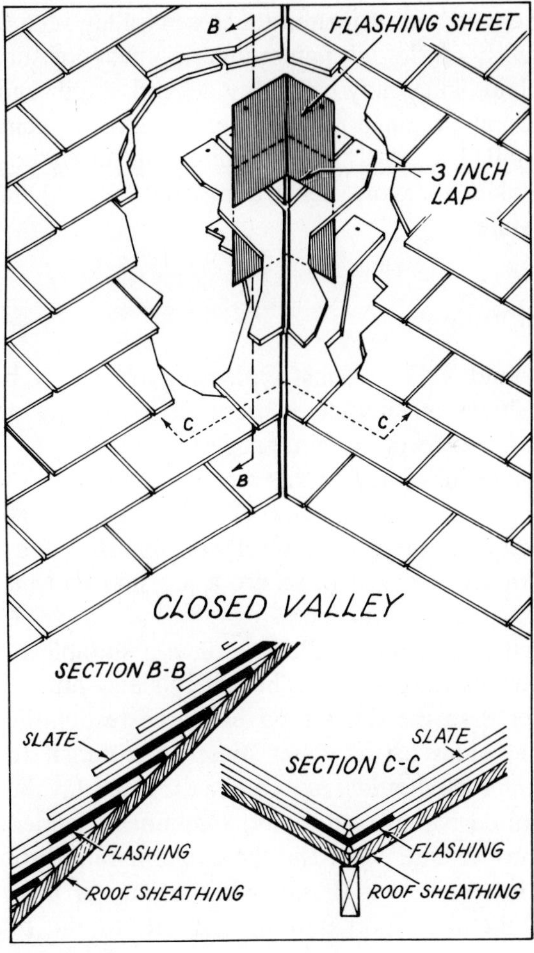

FIG. 3-6. Detail of closed valley.

enough to lap the sheet below by at least 3 inches and should always be set back of the butt of the slate above so that it will not be visible. These sheets are separated by a course of slate. Each sheet must be wide enough so that the vertical distance from the center of the valley to a line connecting the upper edges of the sheet will be at least 4 inches. This dimension depends on the nailing of the slate, which should not penetrate the sheets.

Some roofers form the sheets with a center crimp, thus stiffening them and forming a straight line on which to set the slates. This also prevents water from one slope forcing its way above the sheet on the other slope.

Another method of forming a closed valley is to lay sheets of flashing directly on the felt paper covering the roof sheeting before the slate is laid. They may be of any desired length and should lap in the direction of the flow of water at least 4 inches. Flashing should be nailed every 18 inches along the outer edge and care should be taken to avoid penetrating the sheet of flashing when nailing the slate.

Round Valleys

The round valley forms a pleasing transition between two interesting slopes when used in connection with a graduated or textural roof. However, if not properly laid out, it will mar an otherwise beautiful roof. For this reason, laying out a round valley should only be attempted by a worker with a thorough knowledge of slate. It requires the most careful workmanship and experienced knowledge of the problem to secure a job that will be both pleasing in appearance and watertight.

Primarily, the round valley requires a suitable foundation to establish the general contour. The valley slates must be at least 4 inches longer than the slates used in the corresponding courses of the roof. The sides of the slates must be trimmed to the proper radius and the tops shouldered to make the slates lay flat.

The round valley slates are sometimes bedded in roofing cement. If proper care is used in the trimming and fitting, no flashing should be necessary. If the workmanship is not dependable, flashings of metal or prepared roofing cut to the proper radius should be used as a precautionary measure. Flashings should always be used, however, wherever ice may form.

The radius of the round valley starts as a maximum at the eaves and gradually diminishes to practically zero at the ridge. For appearance, as well as to facilitate laying the valley slates, the distance across the eaves should not be less than 24 inches. If the roof condition will not permit this, the canoe valley should be used.

Canoe Valleys

The canoe valley is a variation of the round valley; it is laid in the same manner except that the radius at the eaves and ridge is practically zero. The radius is gradually increased until it is at a maximum halfway between the eaves and the ridge.

FLASHING

In addition to ridges, hips, and valleys, flashing should be used at all other intersections of vertical or projecting surfaces through the roof or against which the roof abuts, such as walls, parapets, dormers, sides of chimneys, and so on. Flashings used over or under the roof covering and turned up on the vertical surfaces are known as *base flashings*. Metal built into the vertical surface and bent down over the base flashing is termed a *cap* or *counterflashing*.

Base flashings should be extended under the uppermost row the full depth of the slate or at least 4 inches over the slate immediately below the metal. The vertical leg must be turned up not less than 4 inches and preferably 8 inches on the abutting surface. Where a vertical surface butts against the roof slope, it is necessary to build in the base flashing with each course of slate laid. Turn out 4 inches on the slate and at least 8 inches above the roof. If the roof stops against a stuccoed wall, a wood strip 4 inches wide having a beveled top edge should be secured to the wall. The base flashing is then turned over the slate at least 4 inches and bent up vertically at least 3 inches on the board. Except in unusual cases, it will be found satisfactory to turn the base flashing out 4 inches on the roof surface and up on the vertical surface from 6 to 8 inches for either sloping or flat roofs. Posts, flagpoles, scuttles, and so forth, where projecting through the roof, should have base flashings. Vent pipes should have base flashings in the form of special sleeves or ready-made roof flashing units.

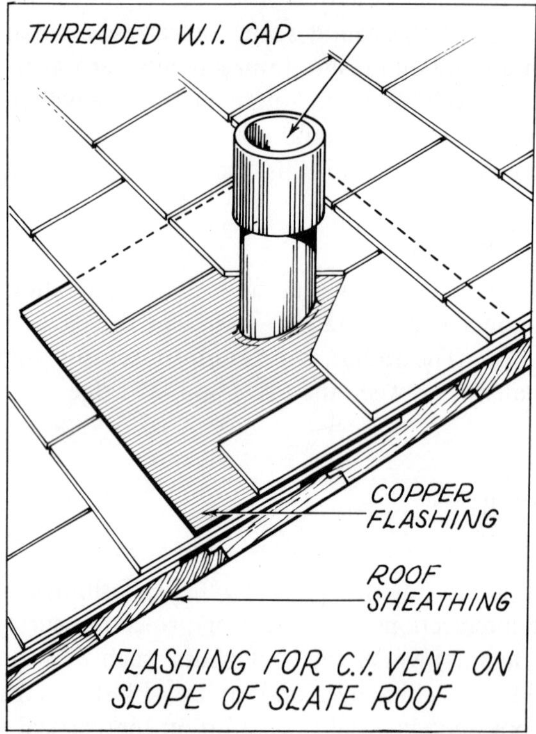

FIG. 3-7. An example of flashing around a waste pipe on sloped slate roof.

Where the base flashing is not covered by vertical slate, siding, or the like, a cap flashing must be used. This member should be built into the masonry joints not less than 2 inches, extended down over the base flashing 4 inches, and the edge bent back and up ½ inch. Reglets in stone or concrete are usually about 1 inch wide and 1 inch deep. The flashing should be formed and laid in the bottom of the cut and thoroughly caulked with a suitable caulking compound. After caulking, the reglet is filled to the surface with roofing cement. For a uniform looking finished job, it is common practice to paint over the roofing cement a color that closely resembles the masonry (see Figure 3-8).

You will notice in the drawing that all exposed and unfastened flashings have the edge of the strip turned under ½ inch. This is done to give the strip stiffness against wind. This rigidity helps to hold the flashing in place and also helps to prevent snow from packing up underneath.

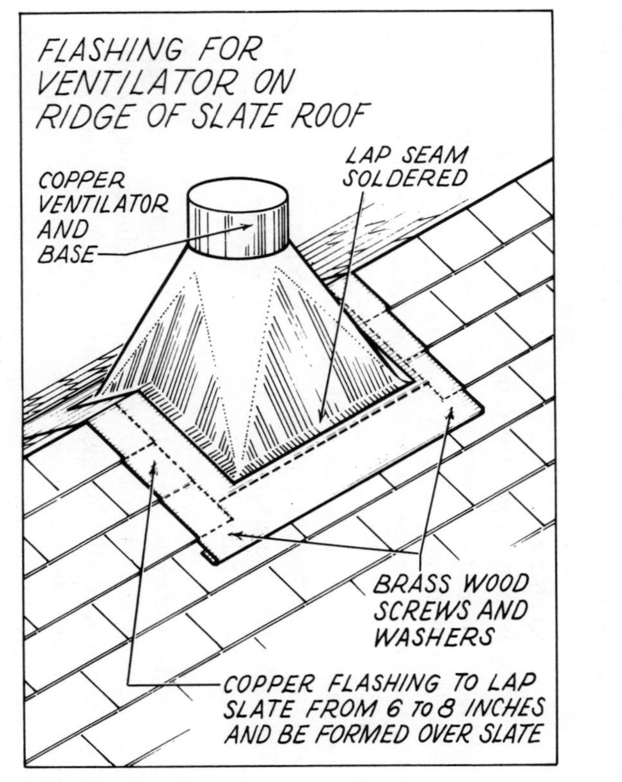

FIG. 3-8. Detail of flashing for ridge projection.

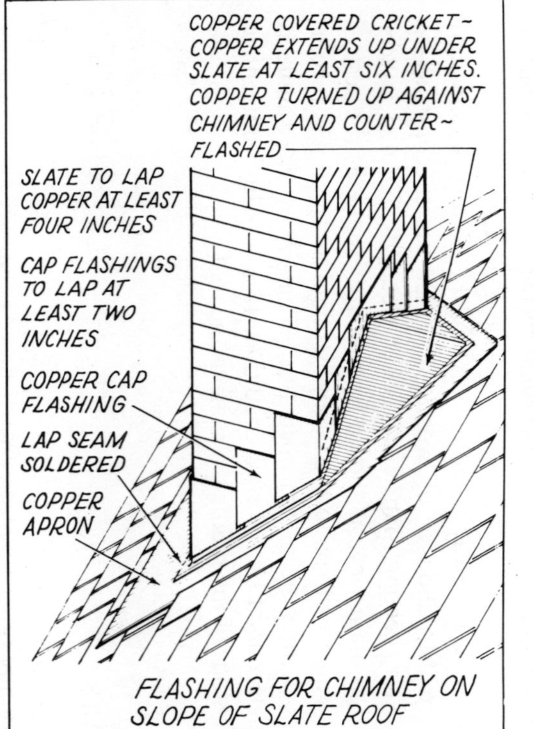

FIG. 3-9. Flashing for chimney on slope of slate roof, commonly called a cricket.

Where a chimney or other vertical surface breaks through the roof at a right angle to the slope, a saddle or cricket must be built to throw the water away from the back of the vertical member. If the roof construction is of wood, use light rafter construction covered with sheeting, paper, and sheet metal. If the area is very large and in plain view, it should be slated the same as the rest of the roof. Valleys will be formed with the main roof and it is recommended that they be of the open type. The size of the saddle is largely determined by the roof condition. It is usually sufficient to make the slope of the saddle the same as the roof.

NAILS

Like any other type of construction, a slate roof can only be as strong and enduring as its weakest part, and the majority of slate roof failures over a period of years may be attributed to the punching of the nail holes, the nailing of the slate, and the nails themselves.

Before nails came into extensive use, the slate on roofs were held in place by wooden pegs driven through the slate and into the roof lath. Later, it was common practice to hang the slate to the laths or battens by means of heavy wire hooked through the slate and over the laths. The wiring method is sometimes used today when the slate is laid directly on steel construction.

Nailing is the most widely used method of securing slate to a roof, and careful attention should be given to the choice of nails used. The important considerations involved are size, shape, and material used to make the nails.

For all practical purposes, the ordinary diamond point and smooth shaft are sufficient for slating nails. The shaft, since it supports a greater weight and must resist a small shearing stress, should be larger than that of the shingle nail. To prevent the slate from being lifted up over the nail after being laid, the diameter of the head should be greater than that of common shingle nails.

The temptation to use shingle nails instead of slating nails should be discouraged, for the slight saving in cost on the entire roof cannot approach the cost of repairs which may develop as a result of poor nail choice.

Plain or ordinary galvanized nails should not be used for laying slate. Nails having a copper content, such as "yellow metal," or cut zinc nails are sometimes used. It is important that the nails used are the type that will resist atmospheric corrosion. Copper or copperweld nails have been used in the past with lasting success.

Under ordinary conditions, it will be found satisfactory to use 3*d* nails for commercial standard slates up to 18 inches in length. Use 4*d* nails for the longer slates and 6*d* nails on hips and ridges. Thicker slates require longer and heavier gauge nails. The proper size may be determined by adding 1 inch to twice the thickness of the slate being laid.

Nails suitable for slate roofing purposes are made in three forms, each of which has its advantages (see Figure 3-10). The copper wire nail is used generally for nailing flashing, sheeting, and sometimes for shingling. It is not the best choice for slate work, because it is too light and has a small head. The slating nail, as Figure 3-10 shows, is especially adapted for slating, as it is of heavy gauge and has a wide, flat head. These features make it much more desirable than the common wire nail. The regular cut nail is not recommended. While the shaft is of proper thickness, its head is too small.

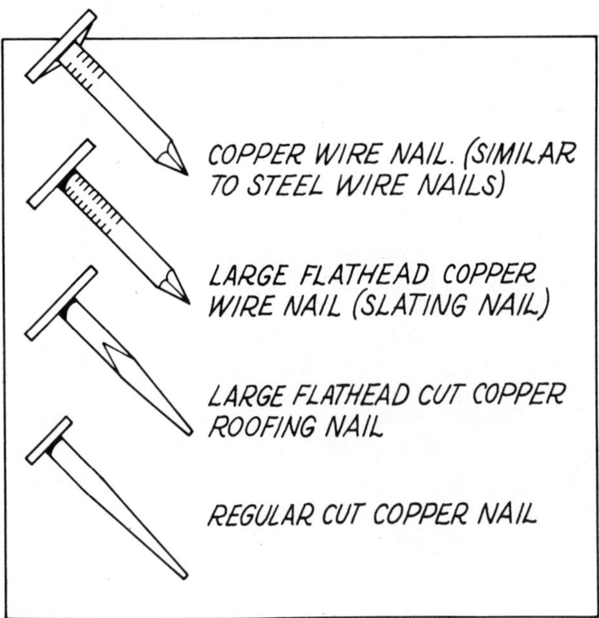

FIG. 3-10. The common types of nails used to attach slate to roofs.

The cut nail is made from sheets and is of a different shape than any of those made from wire. The enlargement of the shaft gives it more stiffness than the wire nail.

A slate roof will last longer than the installer. However, even though slate possesses long-lasting qualities, such as its ability to withstand water, climatic changes, and gaseous fumes in the air, as well as being fireproof, a permanent roof cannot be expected to last unless it is properly laid and its fastenings selected for the same enduring qualities.

4

REROOFING

Eventually, all roofs need replacement of the existing covering; the only possible exceptions are slate and ceramic tile roofs, which seem to last forever. Asphalt shingles have a life expectancy of from ten to twenty-five years depending, of course, on climate, relative air quality, construction, installation, and expected life of the existing shingles.

The biggest enemy of roofing is the sun, which causes roofing to become dried-out, brittle, and faded. Wind, rain, hail, snow, and temperature change all play a part in the demise of a roof covering. Signs of a weathered roof are: excessive mineral granules, and cracked, blistered, curled, or missing shingles (see Figure 4-1). Check the base of downspouts for signs of excessive granule loss. Inspect the attic with a flashlight for signs of leaks (and mildew, which is a sign of inadequate ventilation).

If your roof is relatively new and has suffered limited damage from a storm or from falling objects, or has developed a small leak, chances are that it can be repaired easily. Damaged shingles or shingles that have been blown away in a high wind can be replaced. But if your roof is at least fifteen years old and some of the above problems seem to be recurring, it is likely that you need a new roof. The best and only way to determine if it is time to replace your roof is to climb up on the roof and inspect the shingles (see Figure 4-2).

Courtesy of Asphalt Roofing Manufacturers Association

FIG. 4-1. Worn shingles often curl up at the edges.

Courtesy of Asphalt Roofing Manufacturers Association

FIG. 4-2. When shingles become brittie, they should be replaced.

PRELIMINARY STEPS

Once you have determined that you need a new roof, you will have to figure out how much material you will need to complete the job. This is most easily accomplished by actually measuring one side of your roof, assuming that both sides of your roof are the same. If they are not, you will have to make adjustments to your calculations. Measure the length of the eaves and rake. A 100-foot steel tape measure will prove helpful. Multiply the length of the eaves by the length of the rake to arrive at the square footage for one side of your roof. Double this figure and you will have a square foot total for your entire roof. To this figure must be added the square footage of dormers, garage roofs, capolas, and anything else that is to be reroofed. For example: the eaves of a house measure 40 feet and the rake measures 16 feet; 40 feet × 16 feet = 640 square feet for one side of the roof. Multiplied by two, the total square footage of the roof is 1,280 square feet. A square of roofing shingles will cover 100 square feet; so, to cover this particular roof, you will need thirteen squares of roofing shingles, plus an extra bundle to cover mistakes and to cover the ridge.

If you have a hip roof, it will take a bit more calculating to determine the required number of roofing shingles. Essentially, you must determine the square footage of two triangles and two parallelograms. The formula for the area of a triangle is Area = ½ base × height. The formula for a parallelogram is Area = height × ½ length of ridge plus length of eaves. To illustrate with an example, see Figure 4-3.

You will also have to renew the flashing when reroofing a house. Roofs are, more often than not, complicated by the intersection of other roofs, adjoining walls, or other projections through the deck, such as chimneys and soil stacks, all of which create opportunities for leakage. Therefore, special provisions must be made for turning the weather at these points. Such construction is commonly called *flashing*. Careful attention to flashing is essential to good roof performance, regardless of the type of construction or cost. All flashing is installed before the finish roof covering is attached. A full discussion of flashing techniques will be covered later in this chapter.

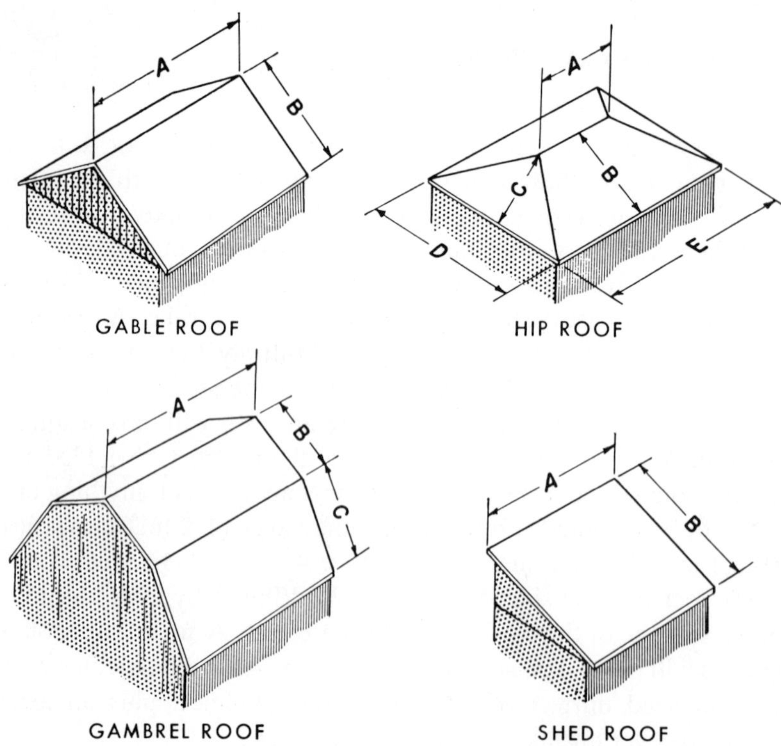

Gable Roof.—Multiply roof length (*A*) by rafter length (*B*). Multiply by 2.
Hip Roof.—Step 1: Add roof length (*A*) and eaves length (*E*). Divide by 2. Multiply by rafter length (*B*). Multiply by 2. Step 2: Multiply longest rafter length (C) by eaves length (*D*). Step 3: Add figures obtained in steps 1 and 2 for total roof area.
Gambrel Roof.—Add rafter lengths (*B* and C). Multiply by roof length (*A*). Multiply by 2.
Shed Roof.—Multiply roof length (*A*) by rafter length (*B*).

FIG. 4-3. Methods of determining area of roof.

Generally speaking, new asphalt shingles can be installed over an existing roof covering. Exceptions are, of course, slate and tile roofs, which do not permit nails to be driven through them. Cedar shakes on a roof are often removed before a new roof covering of asphalt shingles is attached (Figure 4-4). Cedar shakes, because of their rugged texture, do not provide a smooth, flat deck which is necessary for reroofing. In some cases, professional roofers will not remove cedar shake roofs, but will, instead, attach "feathering strips" between the courses of shakes to provide a smooth roof deck.

Courtesy of Asphalt Roofing Manufacturers Association

FIG. 4-4. In many cases, old, worn shingles will have to be removed.

As you can see in Figure 4-5, the rake and eaves also require special treatment.

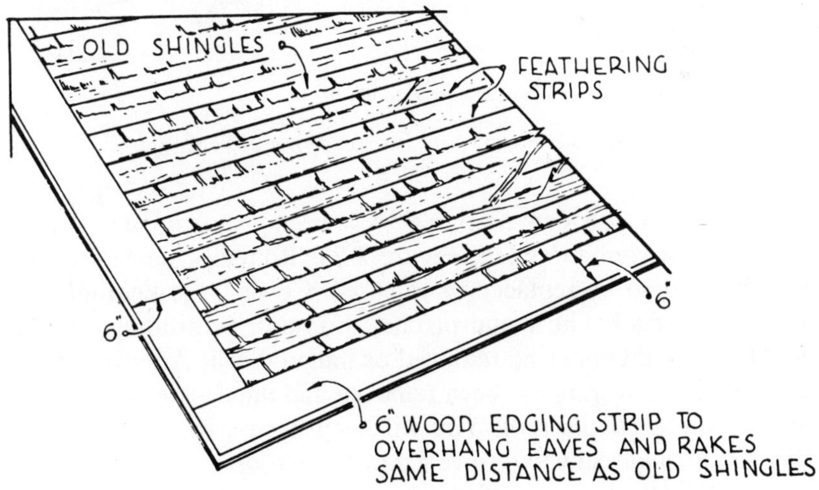

FIG. 4-5. Feathering strips can be used to make an old shingle roof level.

Professional roofers will remove an existing asphalt shingled roof after it has been reroofed three times. This is called a *tear off* and amounts to taking off all of the existing roof covering down to the bare wood roof deck. A common procedure is to remove the existing roof covering with large shovels. Both asphalt and wooden shingles can be removed this way (Figure 4-6). It is easier to work from the top of the roof down to the eaves. Everything is removed from the roof deck: old shingles, nails, existing flashing, vent caps, and old felt paper.

Courtesy of Asphalt Roofing Manufacturers Association

FIG. 4-6. A shovel is a handy tool for removing old shingles.

Once the wooden roof deck has been exposed, you should inspect it for soundness (see Figure 4-7). Rotted or damaged roof sheeting should be replaced or repaired. Cover large knotholes in the existing deck with metal patches. Loose or protruding nails in the deck should either be removed or nailed down. After all of the existing roof covering has been removed and the deck repaired, you should sweep off the roof. You will then have a roof deck that is flat, sound, and ready to receive a new finish roof.

The first step in reroofing a bare wooden roof deck is to cover it with no. 15 saturated felt paper, as in new construction (Figure 4-8). The felt paper is rolled out, parallel to the eaves and stapled

Courtesy of Asphalt Roofing Manufacturers Association

FIG. 4-7. Inspect the roof deck for soundness. Rotted or damaged sheeting must be replaced or repaired.

Courtesy of Asphalt Roofing Manufacturers Association

FIG. 4-8. Number 15 asphalt saturated felt paper must be applied to a roof deck after a tear-off or in new construction.

or nailed to the deck. Start at the bottom of the deck and roll the paper across the roof until you have covered the roof with rows from the eaves to the ridge. Rows of saturated felt paper should overlap at least 2 inches, and where ends join, lap them 4 inches. Lap the felt 6 inches from both sides over all hips and ridges. The felt underlayment on a wooden roof deck performs three vital functions:

1. It ensures that shingles will be applied over a dry roof deck, thus avoiding the buckling and distortion of shingles that may be caused by their application over wet, moisture-laden roof boards. When the roof deck is of plywood, delamination of the plywood resulting from moisture absorption is prevented.
2. If shingles are either lifted up or, in extreme cases, damaged or torn by abnormally high winds, the felt underlayment prevents the entrance of wind-driven rain onto the roof deck or into the interior of the house.
3. The underlayment serves to prevent any direct contact between the shingles and resinous areas in the wood roof deck which, because of chemical incompatibility, would be damaging to the shingles.

In many cases it will not be necessary to remove existing roof coverings provided that the strength of the roof deck is adequate to support the weight of new additional roofing, as well as the usual snow and wind loads. Also, the existing roof deck must be sound and able to provide good nail-holding capabilities.

If the existing roof covering is to remain on the roof, some surface preparation is still required. You must remove all loose or protruding nails and realign old shingles. You should also replace any missing shingles with new ones. The main idea is to provide a smooth deck to receive the new asphalt shingles. Saturated felt paper is not necessary when you are attaching new asphalt shingles on a roof with an existing roof covering.

After the roof deck has been worked on so it is ready to receive a new covering, your next step is to install metal drip edge along the rakes and eaves. (See Figure 4-9.) Then you will have to install flashing wherever there is a break in the roof: valleys, chimneys, dormers, vertical walls, soil stacks, and anything else that breaks the roof surface.

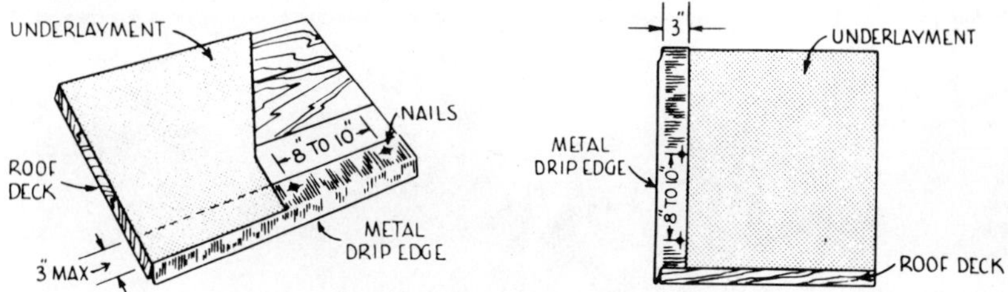

Courtesy of Asphalt Roofing Manufacturers Association

FIG. 4-9. Apply metal drip edge to the eaves (left) and rake (right).

INSTALLING FLASHING

Although there are several ways of installing flashing on a roof, our discussion will be limited to open valleys; they work well and are the easiest for the do-it-yourself homeowner to install.

Before any valley flashing is installed, a 36-inch-wide strip of 15-pound saturated felt paper is centered and run down the length of the valley. Secure this paper with only enough nails to hold it in place. Then lay metal flashing material into the valley and nail into place at least 6 inches from the center of the valley. Next, spread a band of asphalt adhesive along the edges of the flashing to provide a watertight seal, as shown in Figure 4-10. Finally, strike two chalk lines along both sides of the valley to indicate where the shingles are to end.

A valley should be wider at the bottom than at the top. A valley should be 6 inches wide at the top and diverge at the rate of ⅛-inch for every foot as the valley approaches the eave. As an example, a valley 8-feet long will be 6 inches wide at the top and 7 inches wide where it meets the eave. As shingles are laid into position, along the chalk line marks at the valley, place a daub of cement under each shingle to prevent water from penetrating between the courses. Valley flashing is needed wherever two sloping roofs join at an angle, causing runoff along the joint.

Special treatment is recommended where an open valley occurs at a joint between a dormer roof and the main roof through which it projects. Here, after the underlay is applied, apply the main roof shingles to a point just above the lower end of the valley. The course last applied is fitted close to and flashed against the wall of the dormer under the projecting edge, as in Figure 4-11. Apply

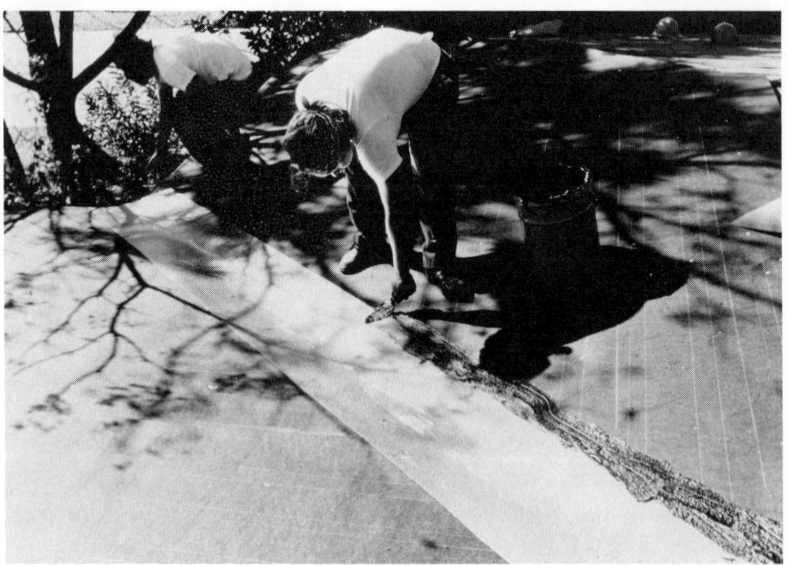

Courtesy of Asphalt Roofing Manufacturers Association

FIG. 4-10. After valley flashing is attached a band of roofing cement is spread along the edges.

Courtesy of Asphalt Roofing Manufacturers Association

FIG. 4-11. Shingles are laid on main roof up to lower end of valley.

the first strip of valley lining and the bottom end, cut so that it extends ¼ inch below the edge of the dormer deck, with the lower edge of the section that lies on the main deck projecting at least 2 inches below the point where two roofs join.

Then cut the second or upper strip of flashing on the dormer side to match the lower end of the underlying strip. Cut the side that lies on the main deck to overlap the nearest course of shingles. This overlap is the same as the normal lap of one shingle over another, depending on the type of shingle being used. In the case of the 12-inch-wide, 3-tab square butt strip shingles, it extends to the top of the cutouts.

Apply the following courses of shingles over the valley lining, the end shingles in each course being cut to conform to the guidelines (chalk lines), and bedded in a 3-inch-wide strip of plastic asphalt cement. The valley construction is completed in the usual manner as indicated in Figure 4-12.

Figure 4-13 shows how the joint between a vertical wall and the rake of an abutting roof is treated when new asphalt shingles are being applied over an old roof. After leveling the old shingles, replacing any broken or worn shingles, and otherwise setting the old roof joint into first-class order, apply a strip of smooth roll roofing 6 or 8 inches wide over the shingles abutting the wall sur-

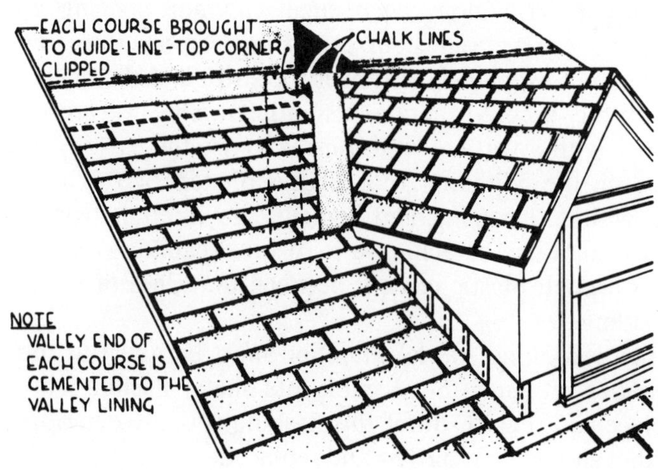

Courtesy of Asphalt Roofing Manufacturers Association

FIG. 4-12. Dormer flashing and valley completed

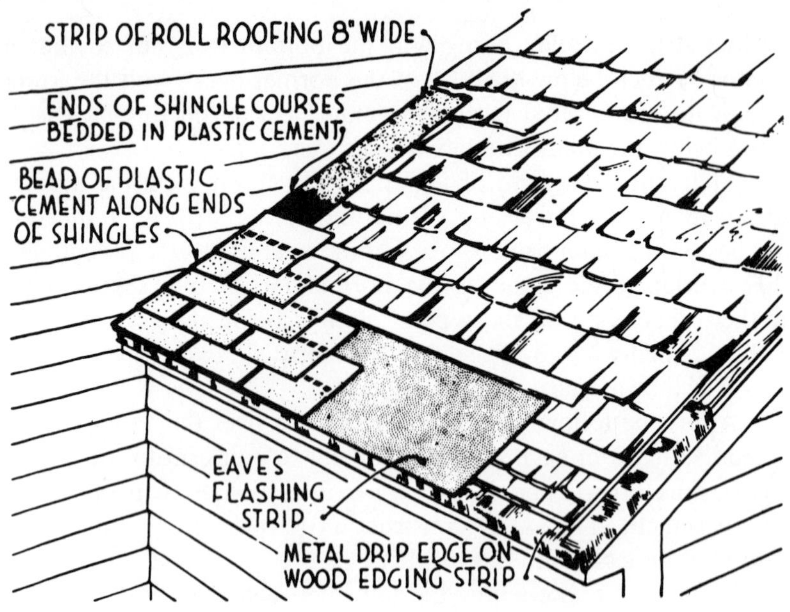

Courtesy of Asphalt Roofing Manufacturers Association

FIG. 4-13. Flashing against a vertical wall when reroofing over old shingles.

face. Nail this strip along each edge with nail spacing approximately 4 inches. As each course of shingles comes to this joint, brush a band of asphalt cement over the strip, and the new shingles are then firmly secured therein. Essentially, what we are trying to accomplish with a vertical wall joint is to use the existing flashing. The area on the adjoining roof that is on top of this flashing is built up with roll roofing and cement. An improved appearance and a tight joint can be achieved by using a caulking gun to apply a bead of asphalt plastic cement between the edges of the shingles and the siding.

When reroofing, special attention must be given to the flashing around a chimney. Serviceable old metal flashing should be left in place and reused. But if this flashing is badly deteriorated or damaged, it should be removed and replaced.

Side and base flashing are first applied to the chimney. Apply a strip of rolled roofing approximately 8-inches wide on the reconditioned roof surface at the front and sides of the chimney (Figure 4-14). It should be laid so that it abuts the chimney on

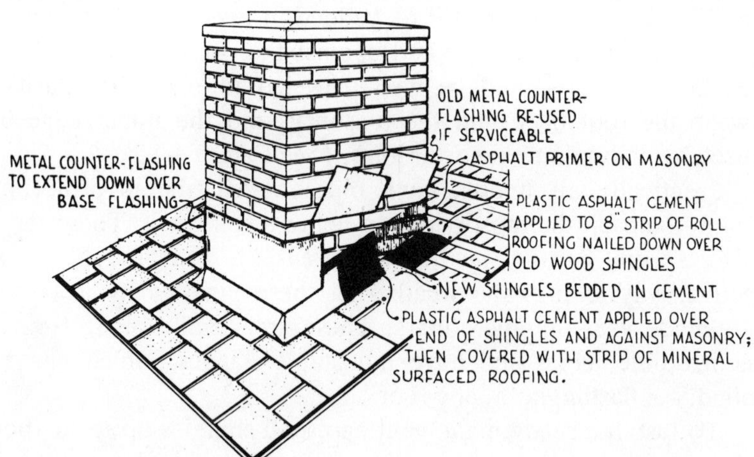

Courtesy of Asphalt Roofing Manufacturers Association

FIG. 4-14. Chimney flashing details using old cap and counter flashing.

all sides and should be secured to the old roof with a row of nails along each edge. At the junction where it meets the chimney, a heavy coat of plastic asphalt cement should be applied, and the strip itself coated with a plastic asphalt cement. The end shingle of each new course is applied along the chimney edge and should be cut so that it will be about ¼-inch from the brickwork when finally embedded in the cement, which should then be squeezed through the joint at the point where the shingle abuts the chimney.

The masonry should then be cleaned with a wire brush for a distance of 6 to 8 inches above the roof deck, and a suitable asphalt primer applied to the masonry. After applying the primer, trowel plastic asphalt cement over the shingles for a distance of approximately 2 inches up the chimney, against the masonry surface, for 4 to 6 inches. Then, press a strip of mineral-surfaced roll roofing wide enough to cover the cement into the cement, as shown in Figure 4-14, the side pieces being returned around and over the ends of the front piece, and around the back of the chimney for a distance of about 6 inches.

If the original construction did not provide a cricket behind the chimney, the base flashing at this point should consist of a 36-inch-wide strip of mineral-surfaced roll roofing, applied to lie 24 inches up the roof over the old roofing and 12 inches up the rear face of the chimney. It should be bedded in plastic asphalt cement applied over the old roofing and against the primed masonry surface. The cement should be well troweled into all irregularities between the roof deck and the masonry, and the upper edge be secured by nailing into a mortar joint. (See Figure 4-15.)

Practically all houses have pipes or ventilators projecting through the roof, the most common being a soil stack. These pipes call for special flashing methods. The easiest, and probably most effective, way to turn the weather at these pipes is by installing ready-made vent or pipe collars. These are usually made from a noncorrodible metal and have adjustable flanges, which can be applied as a flashing to fit any roof.

To install a ready-made vent cap, nail shingles up to the bottom edge of the pipe, and continue attaching shingles until half the pipe is covered by the edges of shingles. Then the cap is slid down over the pipe and succeeding courses of shingles are attached over it. It is important, for waterproofness, that the cap be nailed only along the top edges. As shingles are nailed over, do not drive any nails into the flat part of the vent cover. Some roofers will add a coat of roofing cement on the up-roof side of the vent as added insurance against water gaining access to the roof below.

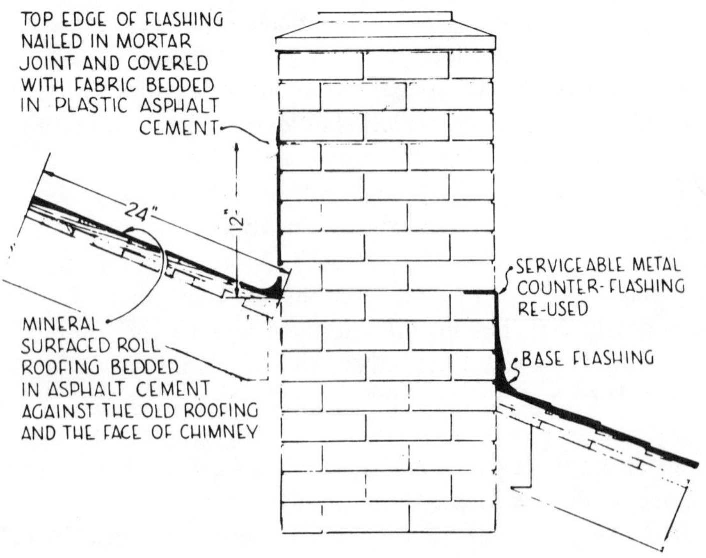

Courtesy of Asphalt Roofing Manufacturers Association

FIG. 4-15. Detail of top of base flashing over chimney.

After all of the metal flashing and drip edge have been attached to the roof deck, you can begin the task of shingling the roof. If the old roof has been taken off, you will proceed as if in new construction. (See Chapter 1.) Reroofing over an existing asphalt shingle roof will be covered later in this chapter.

SHINGLING THE ROOF

Before applying the first course of shingles, apply a starter strip (see Figure 4-16). This can be either a row of shingles, with the top edge of the shingle against the eave, or a 9-inch-wide or wider starter strip of mineral-surfaced roll roofing. In either case, attach the starter strip parallel to the eaves and about ¼ to ⅜ of an inch over the edge. Nail the starter strip on a line 4 or 5 inches up from the edge of the eave and with nails spaced so they will not be exposed at the cutouts or spaces between the shingle tabs in the first course of shingles.

The first course of shingles is started with a full shingle while succeeding courses are started with full or cut strips depending on the style of shingles being applied and the desired pattern. There are three major spacing variations for square butt strip shingles: *breaking thirds, breaking halves,* and *the quick method.*

Courtesy of Asphalt Roofing Manufacturers Association

FIG. 4-16. A starter strip can be easily cut from a shingle.

Courtesy of Asphalt Roofing Manufacturers Association

FIG. 4-17. The starter strip is nailed in place before the first course of shingles is applied. Starter strips overhang ¼ to ⅜ of an inch.

When it is desired that cutouts break joints on thirds, start the second course with a strip from which 4 inches has been cut, the third course with a shingle from which 8 inches has been cut, and the fourth course with a shingle from which the entire first tab has been cut off. This will cause the cutouts to break joints on thirds with the course below. Courses five, six, and seven may repeat the process, or may continue by removing 1⅓ tabs and 2 tabs respectively from each first strip before applying it at the rake. Thus, shingles are placed so that the lower edges of the butts are aligned with the top of the cutouts of the underlying course.

When it is desired that the cutouts break joints on halves, the second course is started with a strip from which 6 inches has been cut from the first tab, the third course with a strip from which the entire first tab has been removed, the fourth course with one-half a strip, and so forth, thus causing the cutouts to be centered on the tabs of the course below.

Some authorities recommend—and some applicators prefer—to start each succeeding course after the first, up to and including the sixth, with a strip from which an additional half of a tab has been removed, the seventh course being started with a full strip

Courtesy of Asphalt Roofing Manufacturers Association

FIG. 4-18. A full-width shingle is used for the first course and a shingle with 4 inches removed is used for the second course.

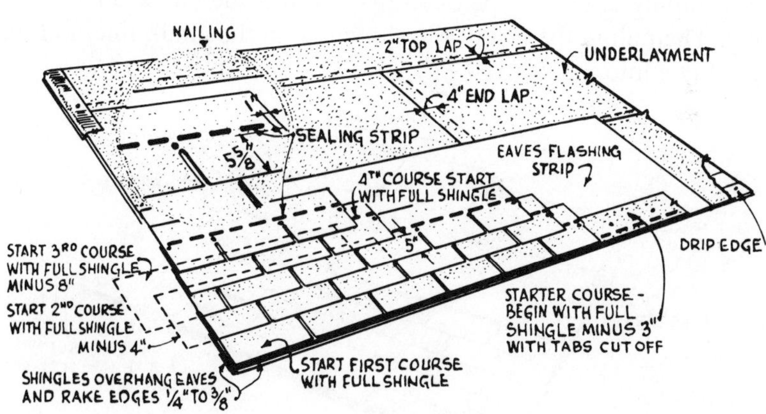

Courtesy of Asphalt Roofing Manufacturers Association

FIG. 4-19. Three-tab square butt strip shingles, with cutout joints broken on thirds.

(see Figure 4-20). This is to conserve the applicator's time if very much scaffolding is needed for the job: it is referred to as the *quick method* of spacing.

Random spacing can be achieved by removing different amounts from the rake tab of succeeding courses in accordance with the following general principles:

1. The width of any rake tab should be at least 3 inches.
2. Cutout centerlines of any course should be located at least 3 inches laterally from the cutout centerlines in both the course above and the course below.
3. The rake tab widths should not repeat closely enough to cause the eye to follow a cutout alignment.

Starting the first course with a full-length strip indicates the length of the starting tab of each succeeding course to produce satisfactory random spacing (Figure 4-21). It will be helpful to strike a chalk line, parallel to the eaves, as a guide for the first row of shingles. This is especially helpful when the old roof covering has been torn off. Strike the chalk line 12 inches up the roof (from the edge of the eaves) across the entire length of the roof. Twelve inches is the standard width of a 3-tab, square butt shingle. If you are installing another type of shingle, adjust the chalk line accordingly. Then align the top of the shingle with the chalk line and nail the shingle into place.

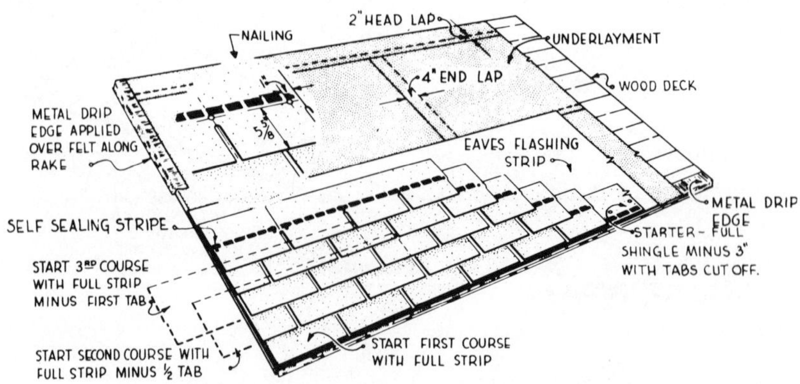

Courtesy of Asphalt Roofing Manufacturers Association

FIG. 4-20. Three-tab square butt strip shingles with cutouts centered over the tabs in the course below.

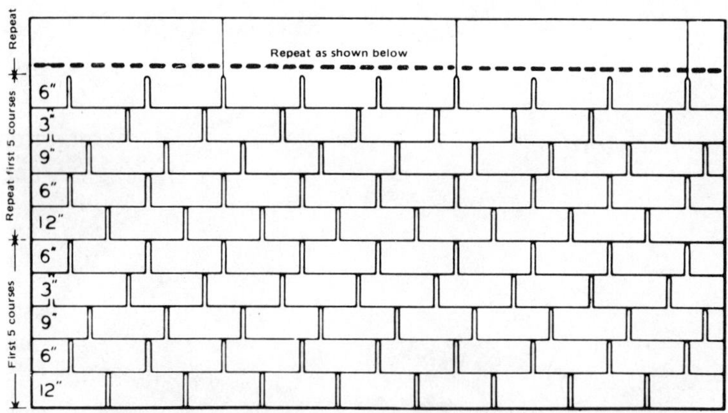

Courtesy of Asphalt Roofing Manufacturers Association

FIG. 4-21. Random spacing of three-tab square butt strip shingles.

If you are installing new shingles on a roof on which the existing asphalt shingles have not been removed, you will find it advantageous to use the edges of the old shingles as a guide for aligning the new shingles. First remove approximately 3 inches along the top edge of the first row of shingles, so that the new shingles do not bridge the butts of the old shingles in the course above. Apply the first course, starting at a rake with a full-length shingle. Locate roofing nails ⅝ of an inch above the cutouts, and 1 inch and 12 inches in from the edges. Use four nails for each shingle. Do not place nails in or above the factory-applied adhesive strips.

Use full-width shingles for the second and succeeding courses, aligning the top edges with the butt edges of the old shingles in the next course (Figure 4-22). This will reduce the exposure of the first course to 3 inches, which is usually concealed when gutters are installed, and will provide an automatic 5-inch exposure for each succeeding course. Roofers who use this method say it gives them a smoother, more uniform, and faster application, with a new horizontal nailing pattern 2 inches below the old.

Since nails should be long enough to penetrate through the roofing material and at least ¾ of an inch into wooden decks, or through a plywood deck, nails used for reroofing are longer than nails used in new construction or in reroofing where the existing roofing material has been removed (Figure 4-23). For reroofing over old wooden shingles, use 1¾-inch-long nails. For reroofing

Courtesy of Asphalt Roofing Manufacturers Association

FIG. 4-22. Apply shingles across and up the roof, using the bottom edges of the old shingles as a guide.

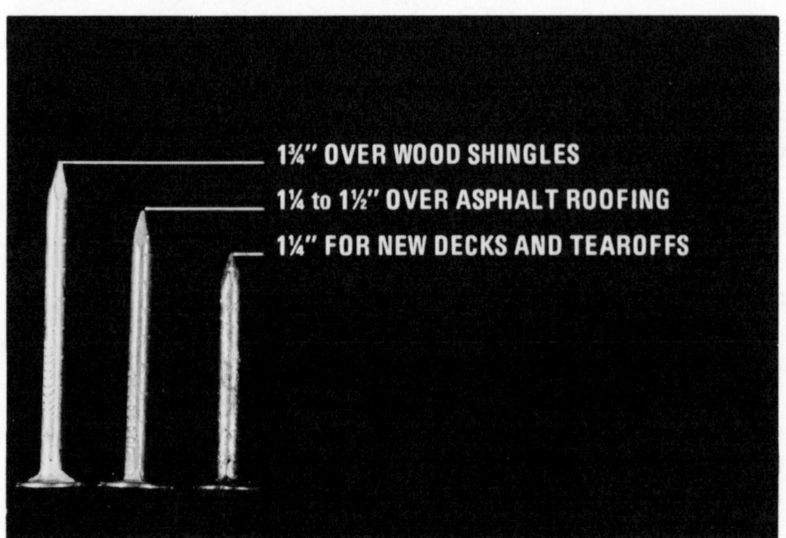

Courtesy of Asphalt Roofing Manufacturers Association

FIG. 4-23. It is important to use the right size roofing nails for the type of roofing you are doing.

over old asphalt roofing, use nails 1¼ to 1½ inches in length. For tearoffs, nails 1¼ inches in length are recommended, which is the same as for new construction.

Shingles are applied across and up the roof. This approach tends to minimize color shading problems because it blends together shingles from different bundles. When nailing a shingle, start from the end nearest to the shingle last applied and proceed across. This will prevent buckling. Nails should be driven straight so that the edge of the nailhead will not cut into the shingle. Nailheads should be driven flush and not countersunk into the surface of the shingle. Make sure that no cutout on an end joint is less than 2 inches from any nail in an underlying course. If you make any nailing mistakes, correct them as they happen.

Proceed up and across the roof in this manner. When you come to a soil stack, trim a shingle to fit and check alignment, both horizontally and vertically (Figure 4-24). Then apply asphalt cement under shingles around the vent stack. Set shingles into the cement and apply additional cement around the base of the stack.

Courtesy of Asphalt Roofing Manufacturers Association

FIG. 4-24. Shingles are cut to fit around soil stacks and vent pipes.

When you come to a vertical wall—that is, the front of a dormer—apply full shingles up to the edge. Next, apply a coat of cement at the base of the wall. Then snap a chalk line to indicate where the finish course of shingles will be applied. Apply additional cement in a wavy pattern where the finish course will be set, as indicated by the chalk lines. Then, embed cut shingles into this cement as a finish course. No nails are used for this finish course; the shingles are simply pressed into the cement (Figure 4-25). This procedure is completed by applying additional cement where the finish course of shingles meets the sidewall.

Eventually, as you nail down courses of shingles, you will come to the ridge of the roof and, if you are working on a hip roof, the hip. Continue laying the course of shingles until finally the last course extends over the ridge, or the edge of the shingle extends over the hip.

When the entire roof has been covered with courses of asphalt shingles, you can cover the hips and ridge. Hips are covered first. Begin by trimming the new shingles where they intersect at the hip. Then measure and snap a chalk line on both sides of the hip.

Courtesy of Asphalt Roofing Manufacturers Association

FIG. 4-25. Cut shingles are embedded in cement to finish off vertical wall joints: no nails are used.

Cut the ridge shingles where they pass over the ridge, and strike chalk lines on both sides of the ridge as well (Figure 4-26).

Shingles for hip and ridges can be cut quickly and easily from the tabs of matching shingles. For example, a 3-tab shingle will yield exactly three pieces of hip or ridge cap when cut at the tab slot. The tops of the shingles, when cut to a taper, will permit a neater application (Figure 4-27). The shingles are then lined up with the chalk lines and nailed into place with the recommended 5-inch exposure. Secure the shingles with a nail on each side of the hip or ridge, located 5½ inches from the exposed end and 1 inch up from the edge.

Both hip and ridge shingles should be bent lengthwise along their centerlines to have an equal amount of exposure on each side of the hip or ridge. In cold weather, warm the shingles before bending. For ridges, always apply the laps away from the direction of the prevailing winds. If you are uncertain of the direction of the prevailing winds, look at other houses in the area to see which way their ridge caps face or remember which direction the ridge cap faced on the house you are working on. Where hips intersect with

Courtesy of Asphalt Roofing Manufacturers Association

FIG. 4-26. Strike chalk lines on either side of the ridge and hips. These lines will help to keep ridge and hip caps straight.

Courtesy of Asphalt Roofing Manufacturers Association

FIG. 4-27. Tapered ends on cap shingle tabs look neater.

the ridge, apply cement to provide a watertight seal. Do not use metal hip or ridge material because corrosion might discolor the roof.

The last shingle for the ridge is face nailed with one nail on each side of the ridge. These nailheads must be covered with a daub of cement to ensure protection against water damage.

COMPLETION OF REROOFING

After the hip and ridge cap have been installed, the job of reroofing your house is almost complete. You should then go back over the work and check for damaged shingles, which may have been caused by dropping a tool on the roof or walking too many times in one spot. Remove any damaged shingles by drawing the nails from the damaged shingle and also from the shingle immediately above. Then replace with a new shingle and renail. Damaged shingles can cause leaks, and they also hurt the overall appearance of the new roof.

Next, go back and apply a daub of cement under the edges of all shingles that end in valleys (Figure 4-28). This gives added protection against water seepage. While you still have the cement and trowel handy, you should go back to any vent or soil stacks and carefully place a daub of roofing cement on the up-roof side of these breaks in the roof (Figure 4-29). Don't forget to apply additional cement around chimneys, vertical wall junctions, and anyplace else that breaks up the roof line (Figure 4-30).

Courtesy of Asphalt Roofing Manufacturers Association

FIG. 4-28. A spot of cement is put under each shingle where it meets a valley.

Courtesy of Asphalt Roofing Manufacturers Association

FIG. 4-29. Cement is placed on the up-roof side of soil stacks and vent pipes.

Courtesy of Asphalt Roofing Manufacturers Association

FIG. 4-30. A bead of caulking should be run around chimneys after the finish roofing has been installed.

Finally, before you climb off the roof, sweep it off (Figure 4-31). This will be a good opportunity for you to inspect your work. Check over the entire roof and pay extra attention to any area that breaks the normal roof lines. Check that cement has been applied to all necessary areas, as outlined above. When you are satisfied that the job is complete, you can climb down off the roof, knowing that it should not give you any trouble for fifteen to twenty-five years.

Courtesy of Asphalt Roofing Manufacturers Association

FIG. 4-31. Sweep off the roof and inspect the work. Correct any errors before they cause problems.

GENERAL COMMENTS

As with any remodeling job, there are a few tricks of the trade or helpful tips that can make the work go smoother and help you to obtain professional looking and performing results. The following helpful hints might prove useful.

Eave flashing is required wherever the January daily temperature averages −4°C. or less, or wherever there is a possibility of ice forming along the eaves and causing a backup of water. Two methods of flashing against leakage from this cause are used, depending on the slope of the roof and the possibility of unusually severe icing conditions. A course of 90-pound mineral-surfaced roll roofing or a course of smooth roll roofing not less than 50 pounds is installed to overhang the underlay and metal drip edge from ¼ to ⅜ of an inch. It should extend up the roof far enough to cover a point at least 12 inches inside the interior wall line of the building (Figure 4-32). When the overhang of the eaves requires the flashing to be wider than 36 inches, the necessary horizontal lap joint is cemented and located on that portion of the roof deck, extending beyond the exterior wall line of the building.

When you have the new shingles delivered to the job site, make sure they are stored properly. Asphalt shingles should be

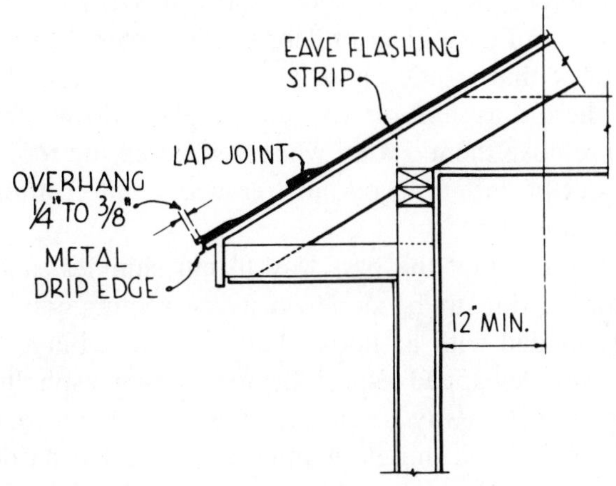

Courtesy of Asphalt Roofing Manufacturers Association

FIG. 4-32. Eave flashing strip for normal pitched roof.

stored off the ground, stacked no higher than 4-feet high and covered with a tarp. Do not use a plastic cover unless it has been ventilated to prevent the formation of moisture underneath the cover. Do not store shingles overnight on the roof.

A bundle of asphalt shingles weighs approximately 80 pounds and, depending on shingle type, there are three to four bundles of shingles to a roofing square. Obviously, the shingles will have to be carried up onto the roof before they can be installed. Eighty pounds is a great deal of weight for a person to carry, especially if one is not in good physical shape. Consider this point before you decide to do your own roofing. I have found that the best way to carry shingles is to throw a bundle up onto my shoulder, center and balance the load, approach the ladder and climb up onto the roof. I climb up the ladder, holding on with one hand and leaning forward slightly. When my head passes above the eave, I very carefully step off the ladder and onto the roof deck. Carrying shingles up onto a roof is a balancing act that takes a bit of practice and is probably the most dangerous part of reroofing because of the extra load and different balance. You should probably carry half bundles of shingles until you feel more secure.

One other point about carrying shingles: never throw or drop a bundle of shingles down on the roof deck. The weight of a falling bundle could break through the deck and do all kinds of damage to the roof, the rooms below, and you. Work carefully.

Keep the roof deck clear of debris at all times. Nothing should be on the deck that would cause you to trip and fall. If you are tearing off the old asphalt or wooden shingles, throw them off the roof as you remove them. Later, when you sweep the roof off, clean any debris out of gutters to permit free water runoff after the new roof has been installed.

I have found that the best way to cut shingles, and there is always some cutting to be done on every roofing job, is with a utility knife loaded with a "hook blade." A hook blade is a razor blade that was developed especially for cutting asphalt shingles. By the way, the best way to cut shingles is from the back of the shingle. The front of a shingle is mineralized, much harder to cut, and will tend to dull a hook blade quickly. For long cuts on a shingle—as with a starter strip, for example—I use the straight edge of another shingle as a cutting guide.

For protection against high winds, it is best to use shingles manufactured to conform to the Underwriter's Laboratories' standard for Wind-Resistant Shingles. Wind-resistant shingles, often called "self-sealing shingles," have a factory-applied adhesive across the middle of each shingle. After these shingles are applied to a roof deck, the sun's rays heat up this adhesive and help to bond it to the shingles below. Although self-sealing shingles were originally developed for high wind areas, they are now standard in most parts of the country.

For extra protection against wind damage, some roofers apply a spot of quick-setting roofing cement, about the size of a fifty-cent piece, under each shingle tab. The top of the shingle is then pressed against the adhesive to ensure a good bond. This additional adhesive may be worth considering along eave and rake edges in high wind areas.

5

REPAIRING AND PREVENTING LEAKS

One of the basic, underlying principles of a home is to seal you and your family off from the elements. The exterior surfaces of a house will do the job of protecting you from these forces of nature year after year with almost no attention from you. In fact, about the only time a homeowner thinks about his roof is when it leaks. At that point, of course, there is no time to prevent the leak, only to make the necessary repairs before related interior damages can occur.

Interestingly enough, about 95 percent of all roof (and sidewall) leaks can be prevented by periodic checking of the roof system and correction of any potential problem areas before they become a reality. The latter part of this chapter will cover preventative maintenance; first, we'll describe what to do when you discover that water has somehow gained entrance into the interior of your home.

When water falls on a roof surface it will run off toward the earth, seeking the fastest and most direct route. If a roof surface is in sound condition—no holes, for example—water will run to the edges of the roof and then fall to the ground, or into a rain gutter where it will be carried to the ground. If, however, there are breaks in the roof surface, water will run into these as it seeks a faster way to the ground. The ideal roof covering is denser than water and, therefore, will not absorb water. All modern roofing materials fall into this denser-than-water category but many underlying subroofing materials (sheathing, for example) are not as dense as water and therefore will absorb to the saturation point. The fact that subroofing materials will absorb water, and cause leaks, is of little importance unless there is some type of break in the finish roofing material, and this is where most leaks start.

LOCATING THE LEAK

Roof leaks are almost always discovered during a rainstorm, although some are common during winter thaws when ice dams build up at the eaves. Usually, water seeking a quicker way to the ground runs into crevices, cracks, or holes under lower courses of shingles, under felt paper, between sheathing, along rafters, and into the attic. Once in the attic the rain water flows between ceiling joists for the room below and then drips down from a light fixture or down an interior wall. All of these possibilities can make finding a leak somewhat of a mystery, but one place to begin looking for the source of the leak is in the attic space.

Attic

Using a flashlight, try to find where the rain water is entering the attic space. If you find water dripping down into the attic, put a suitable container under the drip to prevent further damage. If you cannot find any areas that seem to be leaking enough to cause all of the water you are getting down below, you will have to try a different approach. While still in the attic space look for dark colored areas in the sheathing, as these are usually an indication that water is present in that area. You can also turn off all lighting in the attic space and look for daylight showing through any holes in the roof deck. Other areas to check for leaks are around waste pipes and the chimney (either for the furnace or fireplace). Check the area around where pipes or chimney pass through the roof deck or where the chimney runs up the sidewall of the house. The small space between the stonework and the sidewall is always caulked but in time some of this caulking will crack and shrink, leaving a space where wind-blown water can gain entrance into the house. You can usually see daylight through these cracks, when they are present. If you do, stick the end of a wire coat-hanger through the hole to mark the area for patching from the outside.

Other areas to check are around attic ventilators and windows. Here again look for daylight shining through around the edges or seams and dampness or darker colored wood around the area.

If insulation is present, as it should be, on the attic floor or between the roof rafters, finding the source of the leak will, in most cases, be a bit more difficult than if insulation were not present. Chances are good that you will have to remove a lot of the insulation just to find the source. Once it has been found and repaired you will have to reinstall the insulation. Fiberglass batting or rolled sheets can be placed outside in the sun to dry and then reused, but loose insulating fill often cannot be reused. If you were to reinstall the damp or wet insulation you would be setting up an ideal mold and mildew breeding ground. Keep in mind that you would also be reducing the effectiveness of the insulation by installing it wet.

Checking Outside

If you cannot find the leak inside the attic, then you should continue your search outside. First, you should not climb up on the roof when it is still raining, unless it is absolutely necessary. Wet shingles are very slippery and they will be difficult to walk on, especially on steeper pitched roofs. Begin by first looking at your roof from the ground; it may be helpful to use a pair of binoculars for close inspection from the ground. You will have a general idea of the location of the leak (front or back roof, left or right side, for example), and while this does not necessarily rule out other areas, your best bet is to start looking for the source of the leak in this general area.

One area that is a common source of leaks are the valleys where two roofs join. Often leaves, twigs, branches, and other debris will fall on a roof and build up in valleys, usually where the valley drains into a gutter. The debris builds up in the gutter, preventing water runoff, and on the roof itself. When heavy rains fall, the water is prevented from running freely off the roof and, in fact, builds up and actually soaks in between the layers of shingles.

Obviously, the easiest and best remedy for this type of problem is to remove all of the debris. The water can then run off the roof freely. This should solve the problem unless, of course, there was extensive damage to the roof deck. To prevent such possible damage, you should periodically check all of the valleys, gutters, and downspouts, and remove any obstructions before they have a chance to build up and prevent the free runoff of rain water.

Sometimes the valley flashing gets damaged or possibly the valley was damaged when the shingles were installed. As chapter 4 on reroofing explained, shingle nails should not be driven any closer than 6 inches from the center of the valley. Sometimes, especially during a heavy rain, even this 6-inch minimum is not enough and the rain water overflows the valley as it runs down the roof. If it is determined that the valley nailing is at fault, the best solution is to apply roofing cement to all of the nailheads that hold the edges of the shingles to the valley. Work carefully to avoid damaging the valley flashing.

If you discover that some of the valley flashing has been damaged, a patching material is available that can be used instead of installing new flashing. Called Flashband, it is made by the Evode Company and is simple to use. Flashband is a pliable, self-stick aluminum sealing tape, possessing excellent weather resistance and light reflectivity. It will adhere firmly to all surfaces (porous surfaces, such as brick or cement, may require painting first, however, to ensure a solid bond). Flashband is applied with hand pressure and provides an instant, sure, watertight bond that grows stronger with time, giving lasting protection against wind, driving rain, and even snow. (See Figure 5-1.)

To use Flashband, simply cut off a length long enough to cover the area being patched, peel off the backing paper, press down over the area, and smooth into position. It will readily conform to contours. The patch strip should be large enough to overlap the surrounding surfaces by at least 1 inch all around. The patch is finished off by smoothing down with a cloth pad, roller, or squared sectioned piece of wood. Flashband will last indefinitely, both in the package or in service as a patch. Every do-it-yourself homeowner should have a roll of this patching material handy for on-the-spot patching jobs. (See Figure 5-2.)

Another area that is frequently a source of leaks is the flashing around chimneys and waste pipes that run through the roof deck. As with valleys, wind-blown debris builds up on the up-side of the roof over these breaks in the roof deck and prevents the free flow of water off the roof. Chances are good that you will be unable to

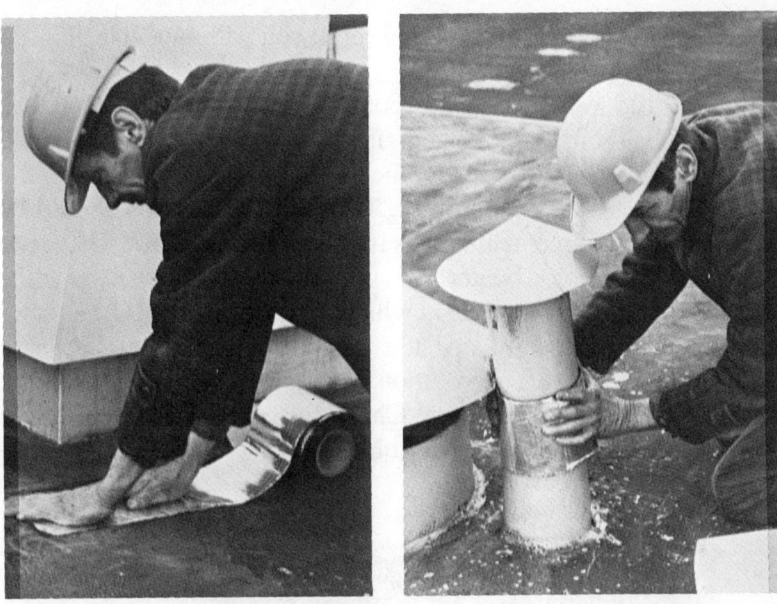

FIG. 5-1. Flashband is attached with hand pressure for a quick patch.

FIG. 5-2. Flashband is handy for all types of exterior repairs.

see these problem areas from the ground; you will have to climb up on the roof for your inspection.

Check the area on the up-roof side of these protrusions, not only for debris but for cracked, loose, or missing caulking and roofing cement. Another area is where the flashing is attached to the chimney or pipe (see Figure 5-3). This joint or junction should be sealed with roofing cement to ensure keeping water out. Often, as the old caulking dries, water can get into the space between the chimney and flashing where it will either freeze, causing greater expansion of the opening, or the water will run down into the interior of the house. The solution here is to apply new caulking or roofing cement over the area. Check this area annually to make sure that the caulking is doing its job of keeping the water out.

FIG. 5-3. Flashband is handy for repairs to joints around waste pipes.

REPAIRING SHINGLES

Loose, curled, broken, or missing shingles can also allow water to seep into the house. In high wind areas, special shingles are used which have daubs of roofing cement on the face of each shingle. As the sun beats down on the roof surface, some of this cement melts slightly, creating a tight bond between shingles. On older houses, these wind-resistant shingles may not have been used and therefore, when rain is accompanied by high winds, water is blown under the edges of these shingles.

To fasten down loose shingles, place a few daubs of roofing cement under each tab of these shingles. Use either a caulking gun filled with roofing cement or a small putty knife and a can of the same type of roofing cement. Simply lift the edges of the shingle, place the cement, and press the shingle down into the adhesive. (See Figure 5-4.) The same treatment should be used for shingles with curled up edges: lift up, apply the cement, then press the shingle down into the cement. You will find that the shingles are

FIG. 5-4. Seal down shingle edges with the aid of a caulking gun filled with roofing cement or caulking.

much easier to work with when you do this type of repair work on a sunny day. The sun's rays will heat up the shingle and make it easier to lift. If you have to work on a cold or overcast day, be careful as shingles tend to be a bit brittle and can break easily.

If shingles are torn, but still in place, they can be repaired with roofing cement. Place a few daubs of the cement under both sides of the tear, press the shingle back into place, and then apply a coat of the cement over the tear. If shingles are missing or torn off they should be replaced. Before you can replace a damaged asphalt shingle you must first remove the nails that hold it in place. You will also have to remove the nails in the shingles above the damaged shingle. Begin by lifting the tabs on the shingle above and inserting the edge of a pry or shingle bar under the shingle, and under the nails that hold it in place. Press down on the pry bar and the nails should come out. Work carefully so you won't damage the shingle not in need of repair. Next, remove the nails in the damaged shingle in the same manner. Common roofing practice is to drive four nails into each shingle. When all of the nails have been removed, slide the damaged shingle out of place.

Slide the new shingle into place and align the bottom edge with the other shingles in that course. Now you must nail the new shingle into place. Since exposed nailheads are potential leak spots, you should nail the shingle under the tabs of the shingles above. Use the nail holes in the shingle above (the one that was not replaced, but had its nail removed). Place new nails into these holes and then, using the pry bar and hammer, drive the nails into the roof deck. The reason for using the pry bar and hammer, rather than nailing directly, is that you will not be able to lift the old, undamaged shingle high enough to hit the nail directly, unless it is very warm and the shingle becomes pliable. The nails in the shingle above will hold the top edge of the new shingle; four other nails must be driven into the new shingle directly on its surface, but concealed. Use the pry bar and hammer to drive these nails in the same fashion. Drive one nail about 1 inch in from each edge and two more about ⅝ to 1 inch above the tab cutouts. Again, work carefully to avoid damaging the existing or new shingles, and keep all nailheads concealed. If you find that you must face nail (drive the nail so that its head is exposed) cover the exposed heads with roofing cement. (See Figures 5-5, 5-6, 5-7, and 5-8.)

FIG. 5-5. Torn shingles should be repaired.

FIG. 5-6. Pry out the nails holding the damaged shingle with the aid of a shingle bar.

FIG. 5-7. Slip a new shingle into place and align with other shingles in the row.

FIG. 5-8. Carefully nail the new shingle into place.

Flat roofs or roofs with only a slight pitch are almost always covered with roll or selvage edge rolled roofing (see Chapter 1). Problems often occur when water does not run off this type of roof but, instead, lays in puddles. This usually is the result of low spots in the roof. Other problems will occur when blisters are present on a rolled roof. In either case these problems should be repaired, using a similar approach. The blister or low spot must be opened up, dried, and re-covered with a suitable patch.

Repairing Blisters

Begin patching a blister by first cutting across its face with a sharp utility knife. If you dip the blade in turpentine, it will cut smoother. Once the blister has been opened, check the inside to make sure that there is no water present; if there is, then the area must be dried, either by leaving the blister open and letting the sun dry the area or by using a portable hair dryer. Using a hair dryer is often necessary in cold weather or when you can't depend on the sun. When the area is completely dry, use a small putty knife to force roofing cement under both sides of the cut. Next, press the cut edges of the blister down into the roofing cement until they lie flat. Then apply a good coat of roofing cement over the top of the cut. Before this dries, cut a patch (from rolled roofing material) large enough to extend 2 inches beyond the original cut. Press this patch down into the roofing cement and nail it in place, spacing the nails about 2 inches apart. The last step is to cover all of the exposed nailheads with a coat of roofing cement. Some professional roofers will also give the edges of the patch an additional coat of the cement.

Repairing Low Spots

Low spots, which are potential leakers, are repaired in a similar manner except that instead of installing one layer of patch, several layers are attached one on top of another until the area has been built up to a height equal to the rest of the roof. Sometimes, however, the real cause of the low spot is sagging rafters. The only sure way to correct this problem is to jack the rafter just slightly higher than the surrounding rafters, then nail an additional rafter (2 × 6 or 2 × 8) directly to the sagging member. When the jack is removed the sag should have been corrected by the addition of an extra rafter.

Of course, some leaks are the direct result of storm damage; a tree branch falling on the roof, for example. Such leaks require immediate attention if you hope to protect the contents of your house from serious damage. Usually there is structural damage that will require extensive repairs. The idea is to stop rain water from running into your home, and to stop it as soon as possible. The only immediate solution is to cover the hole or damaged area as soon as possible to prevent more water from coming into the house.

As soon as possible after the damage occurs, turn off all power at the fuse box, then get your hands on a large tarp or strong piece of plastic, and cover the hole or damaged area with the tarp. For best results, one edge of the tarp should be over the ridge of the roof and tied down (either to a stake in the ground or around a chimney or waste pipe). The other edge of the tarp should be below the damaged area, and secured so it won't move. Needless to say, installing a tarp over a damaged roof can be dangerous, but it remains as the only quick remedy for unexpected damage. Chances are that you will not be able to stop all of the water from coming into the house but by covering the damaged area you will stop most of the water. I do not recommend that you try to cover a damaged roof with a tarp unless you are concerned about related damages from water. Obviously, climbing up on a roof during a storm is very dangerous, but if you want to lessen the damages, the tarp method is the only quick solution.

SEASONAL CHECKS FOR LEAK PREVENTION

As mentioned earlier, almost all leaks can be prevented by simply being aware of the conditions up on your roof and keeping potential problem areas in sound condition. An effective leak prevention program can be accomplished with two periodic checks: spring and fall.

Spring Checks

In the spring you should inspect your roof for damages that may have begun during the colder winter months. Gutters and downspouts may have been forced out of alignment by the weight of ice and snow. Ice may, in fact, have caused some of the joints between part of the gutter downspout system to open up, thereby reducing the effectiveness of the system. Check the gutters and downspouts by spraying a stream of water up onto the roof and watching for any leaks in the system. Repairs or realignment should be done if necessary. Scrape and repaint any sections of gutter or downspout to prevent rust damage.

Check for curled, torn, or missing shingles. Repair as outlined in this chapter. Check for blisters or low spots on flat roofs that may be a result of heavy snow loads. Also, check all flashing in valleys and around chimneys or waste pipes. Apply a coat of roofing cement or caulking where necessary.

Look closely at the shingles along the eaves of the house, as this area often suffers damage from melting snow and ice dams. Repair or replace shingles as necessary. Spring is also a good time to determine if you need a new roof shingling job. You therefore have several months either to plan to do the job yourself or to shop around for the best price from a competent contractor.

Fall Checks

In the fall you should make sure that your roof is in sound condition and able to withstand the punishment of the coming winter months. Your fall check should include all of the items that were checked in the spring. Based on the information you gathered from the spring check, you will know where your emphasis should be: ice and snow problems, for example.

In addition, your fall check should include a thorough cleaning of gutters and downspouts to ensure that melting snow and rain water will be carried quickly off the roof. To be effective a fall check should be done after most of the leaves have fallen off the trees. By doing the maintenance at this time you can reasonably expect the gutters and downspouts to remain clear of debris throughout the winter months.

Barring any unforeseen catastrophes, your roof should give you from ten to twenty-five years of good service, provided that you are aware of the conditions and forces that attack the roof surface. A conscientious program of periodic checks and maintenance, when necessary, will help your roof do its job. You will also be saving hundreds of dollars over the life of your roof by finding and correcting problems before they get out of hand.

6

GUTTERS AND DOWNSPOUTS

The best protection against water damage from the outside is to create efficient ways for rain and snow runoff water to be directed away from the house. Water that is allowed to collect around the foundation of a house will, more often than not, find its way into the interior of the house (usually the basement) and cause many problems. The most common method of catching and directing water from a roof surface is, of course, rain gutters and downspouts.

The most common type of gutter is one that is hung from the edge of the roof or fastened to the edge of the facia. Gutters are made from wood, galvanized metal, copper, aluminum, and even vinyl. Some are bare or galvanized metal; others have a factory-applied enamel finish. Shapes are either half-round or formed, and widths range, for residential installation, from 4 inches to 6 inches.

The size gutter used depends on the size of the roof area serviced by the gutter. For roofs with an area of up to 750 square feet, a 4-inch gutter should suffice. For roofs with a roof area of between 750 to 1500 square feet, a 5-inch gutter is commonly used. For roofs with a square footage of over 1500 feet a 6-inch gutter is most effective.

Lengths of gutters range from 10 feet to 30 feet long. The easiest (and most readily available) gutter length for the homeowner to work with are 10-foot lengths. Joints between the sections of gutters are made with a slip joint connector for inside and outside corners. Ends are easily covered with end caps, available in both right and left ends. (See Figure 6-1.)

Gutters must, of course, be sloped toward a downspout. Standard sloping calls for a drop of about 1 inch for every 20 feet of gutter run. It is also common practice to use one downspout for a 35-foot gutter length. For greater lengths, two downspouts are used, one at each end of the gutter.

Downspouts must be large enough to carry off quickly the water collected by the gutters. The number and size of downspouts to be used will be determined by the total area of the roof and the

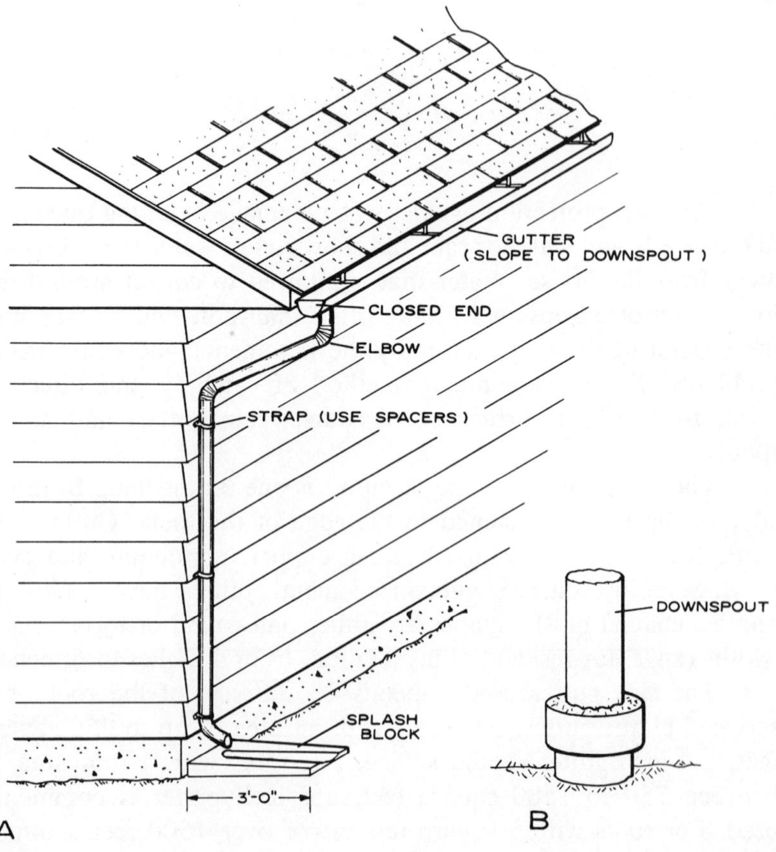

FIG. 6-1. Typical gutter and downspout installation showing (A) elbows, end caps, downspout straps, and (B) top of drain into dry well.

total length of the gutters. Additional downspouts may be used to connect one roof with another—where two roofs join, for example. Generally speaking, one 3-inch-wide downspout is used for every 1000 square feet of roof area serviced by gutters.

Downspouts are connected to the gutter with elbows. Downspouts are fastened to the side of the house with straps, which hold the downspout securely to the sidewall. The end of the downspout should almost always end with an elbow to direct further the flow of water away from the foundation. If just an elbow is used to finish off the downspout, then a splash block should be used to divert further the flow of water from the foundation and prevent erosion at this point.

In many cases, where the ground around the foundation is level, for example, a splash block will not be enough to divert the flow of water. Here, it is most common to install a dry well. In densely populated areas, town ordinances often prohibit the discharge of rain water into the street or street sewer so a dry well must be constructed in these cases. Dry wells range from simple rock-filled holes to giant concrete caverns (which should be built by a qualified contractor). Building a simple, functional dry well will be covered later in this chapter.

INSTALLATION

Although one person can install gutters and downspouts, the work will be much easier to accomplish if two workers are involved.

Gutters

Begin by measuring the length of all facia boards on the sides of the house where the gutters will be installed. Determine how the gutters will run around the house and make a note of how many inside corners, outside corners, slip joint connectors, and end caps will be needed. You will also need sections of gutter that have a downspout outlet. The gutter is attached to the facia boards with either gutter spikes and ferrules or strap hangers (spaced approximately 2½ feet apart). The gutter spike and ferrule method of attachment is the easier of the two methods for the do-it-yourself homeowner to work with.

All joints between sections of gutter should be sealed with cement or mastic to ensure a tight leakproof joint. This sealer is commonly available in tube form and is most easily applied with a caulking gun after the gutters have been attached to the facia boards.

After you have determined the required footage of gutter, determine how many 10-foot lengths of downspout you will need. You must also give careful consideration to how many elbows you will need to complete the job. Downspouts are held to the sidewall with downspout straps spaced about 6 feet apart for long runs or, for single-story houses, one at the top and another at the bottom.

After you have purchased all of the gutter and downspout components necessary for the job, lay them out on the ground, approximately where they will be installed. Next, drive two nails half-way into the facia, one at each end of the intended run of the gutter. Remember that the gutter should drop about 1 inch in height for every 20 feet of length. After the nails have been located on the facia, strike a chalk line between the points. This chalk line will be your guide to aligning the gutters as you install them.

Hanging gutters is most easily accomplished with two workers, one at each end. If you can't find someone to work with, there is an alternative method that, while taking a bit longer, will enable you to install gutters alone. On the high side of the gutter run, make a loop of strong wire, at least 6 inches in diameter, and fasten this to the nail that was used for the chalk line. The loop serves as an extra pair of hands to hold one end of the gutter in approximate position while you work from the other end.

Before raising the sections of gutter up to the facia you should install end caps, if the section will be the end of the run, or inside or outside corners, if the section will have these junctions. The reason is that it is far easier to attach these components on the ground than while working on a ladder.

Raise the gutter into position, and align the top edge of the gutter with the chalk line. The gutter should not extend beyond the eaves of the house, so if cutting is necessary, it should be done on the ground. Cutting, by the way, can be done with a pair of metal shears or a hacksaw. It is important to have square edges on all cuts, so if necessary, use a miter box to help you make a straight cut (see Figure 6-2).

FIG. 6-2. Use a hack saw and miter box for straight cuts.

The gutter is positioned along the chalk line and nailed into place. Whether you are using gutter spikes and ferrules or strap hangers, the nails should ideally be driven into the end of the roof rafters for added strength. Space the nails about 2½ feet apart and, if using spikes and ferrules, don't overdrive the nails, as this may cause damage to the gutter. Work along the gutter, toward the high end of the run, until you have it securely fastened to the facia boards. Install all of the gutter lengths before any downspouts are attached. After all of the gutters have been fastened to the facia, go back over the work and apply the sealer to all joints. The idea here is to provide a watertight trough to catch and carry water off the roof to the downspouts. Apply the sealer to all slip joint connectors, inside and outside corners, end caps, and downspout connector joints. After you are satisfied that you have sealed all of the joints, you can begin installing the downspouts.

Downspouts

As it is the job of the gutters to collect water runoff from roof surfaces, it is the downspout that helps to get the water away from the house. Downspouts direct the flow of water from the roof, down and away from the house. They are connected to the gutter at an outlet with elbows. The purpose of the elbows is to direct the flow of water from the gutter, back under the eave, and into the downspout. In some cases the distance from the gutter to the sidewall will be over a foot, but in most instances the overhang will be less.

When the overhang distance is great, you will have to use a spacer (a piece of straight downspout) cut to make up the distance of the overhang. In any event, the elbows connect the downspout with the gutter.

The downspout should always be attached to the sidewall of the house. Nothing looks quite as foolish as a downspout that runs in midair from the gutter to the ground, as in Figure 6-3. In addition, the downspout will be stronger and less likely to be damaged if it is attached to the sidewall. Downspouts are attached to the sidewall with downspout straps. These straps are sold as flat pieces of metal which must be bent to the contours of the downspout and nailed to the sidewall. Most professionals use hot-dipped galvanized roofing nails to fasten this strap to the sidewall. Never use common steel nails as they will surely rust and stain the house. Downspout straps are spaced about 6 feet apart for long runs. For single-story houses, it is common practice to use only two straps on the downspouts, one about 1 foot below the elbow junction at the top, and another about 1 foot up from the bottom elbow.

The bottom of the downspout should have an elbow attached to the end to direct further the flow of water runoff away from the foundation of the house. Where an elbow finishes off the downspout, a splashblock should be installed to carry off the water. If roof-collected rain water is not diverted away from the house, it can seep in through the foundation walls and cause moisture problems in the basement or crawl space.

Some professional contractors make sure the connections between gutter, elbows, and downspouts are tight by securing the sections with sheet metal screws. Personally, I think this is a sound idea and always do this when installing gutters (see Figure 6-4).

After the gutter and downspouts have been installed shoot a stream of water up on your roof with a garden hose. The system should carry off the water with no leaks. If leaks present themselves during this test, they should be repaired at once.

FIG. 6-3. Downspouts, for best performance, should always be attached to the sidewall of the house. Photo above shows downspout installed incorrectly.

FIG. 6-4. To ensure a tight joint between elbow and outlet in the gutter use a sheet metal screw through the elbow.

Dry Wells

If your home is on flat ground a splash block probably will not carry the water runoff away from the house. In this case you will have to dig a dry well, into which the water can be directed.

A suitable dry well can be constructed using a 55-gallon drum, which can usually be obtained from a local garage or farm supply store. (If there is a charge it should be nominal.) In addition to the oil drum you will also need some 4-inch pipe (either asphalt composition vinyl or terra-cotta tile pipe) to connect the bottom of the downspout to the dry well.

Ideally, a dry well should be located at least 5 feet from the foundation. In my opinion, the further away from the house the dry well, the better. You will have to dig a hole for the dry well. If you are using a 55-gallon oil drum, dig a hole deep enough so that the top of the drum will be at least 1 foot below the surface. If you are working in rocky soil you will find a pick-ax and stone bar helpful. If many rocks are present, you may have to rent a portable jack hammer, or possibly have a backhoe brought in to do the job for you. You will also have to dig a trench to connect the downspout with the top of the dry well. This trench should be deep enough so that the top of the connecting waste pipe will be at least 1 foot below the surface, and sloped toward the dry well. Line the bottom of the trench and hole with about a 2-inch layer of small stones or gravel to help drainage.

After the hole and connecting trench have been dug, and lined with a layer of stone, you can cut out the top and bottom of the drum. You must also make a hole in the side of the drum through which the waste pipe will enter. In addition, make about twenty to fifty holes through the sides of the drum to let the water seep out into the soil.

The perforated drum is set into the hole and connected to the downspout with the waste pipe. Then the drum in the hole is filled with stone, gravel, and rocks. Next, a lid must be built and laid over the top of the drum. I have found the easiest type of lid to make is one made from 2 × 6 or 2 × 8-inch lumber. After the lid has been set on top of the drum, I cover it with a sheet of saturated asphalt felt paper. Then the hole and trench are backfilled with the soil from the original digging.

FIG. 6-5. You may have to rent heavy equipment for digging in rocky soil when installing a dry well.

If you were careful when first breaking ground you should have pieces of sod to replace over the hole. If not, you can plant grass seed over the area and in a few months the digging will have been concealed by grass.

It is important, if your water runoff goes into a dry well, to have some type of screen or strainer in the gutter to prevent debris from clogging the system. The simplest type of downspout protector is called a *wire strainer,* which resembles a wire lightbulb protector because of its basket-like shape. The strainer is forced part way down into the outlet section of the gutter. The main problem with the wire strainer is that leaves and other debris back up against it and have to be removed because they will prevent most of the water from running off quickly. (See Figure 6-6.)

Another type of strainer, *gutter screening,* is actually a screen that is set into the top of the gutter. It is available in widths to match gutters. These screens snap into the top lip of the gutter on one edge and are fastened under the first course of shingles or just slightly below. This screening may be worthwhile for you if you

FIG. 6-6. A strainer, placed in the outlet hole of the gutter, will prevent debris from clogging the downspout.

live in an area with a great number of deciduous trees. Heavy rainfall, however, will often run right over the screening and off the edge of the gutter. The screening must also be cleaned at least once a year, as all gutter systems should.

In areas with many trees, you should climb up and inspect your gutters and roof area for debris every fall. Often fallen leaves and twigs will build up and prevent the free runoff of rain water. If valleys are present—where two roofs join, for example—a buildup of leaves will usually occur. Where valleys end at gutters is another potential problem area that should be given some attention. Most of this accumulation of leaves and twigs can be swept off the roof. You may also find it helpful to use the garden hose to wash out the gutters. The pressure from the water will usually be enough to do the job.

In areas in which ice and snow are a common winter occurrence, it is good practice to provide some form of protection from ice dams, which can cause damage to your gutter/downspout system. Ice dams occur, most commonly, where the eaves overhang the sidewalls of the house. One method of preventing ice dams involves installing flashing (the width of the eave overhang) over the eaves. The flashing method is discussed in Chapter 4, Reroofing. Another method of preventing ice dams is to install heat cables.

Heat cables are insulated wires, with a thermostat, that actually heat up (about 30°C.) when the surrounding temperatures drop below freezing. Heat cables are often wound around incoming water lines in unheated crawl spaces to prevent water pipes from freezing. These cables can also be attached to the eaves, gutters, and downspouts to prevent ice buildup in these areas. Some provision must be made to supply electrical current to the cable. A temporary solution is to run an extension cord to the heat cable, but a much more efficient operation is possible if an exterior receptacle is installed in the soffit or high on the sidewall of the house.

Heat cables are commonly installed along the eaves with clips (supplied with the heat cable kit) to the edges of shingles and gutter. The cables should be positioned so that one edge loops down the shingles and into the gutter. The cable should extend up the roof the width of the eave and extend along the roof in a general "W" pattern from one end of the roof to the opposite end. It is also common practice to drop one end of the cable down the downspout to prevent ice buildup there. Cables should not be shortened or allowed to cross over one another.

Once the heat cables have been properly installed and hooked up to an electrical source, you should not be bothered with ice problems. Heat cables use very little electricity and are worth the small investment to know that your roof will be free of the damaging effects of ice dams.

7

EXTERIOR PAINTING

Painting is one very good way to restore and protect the exterior of your home. Most homes, with the obvious exceptions of masonry, are painted. Even stone houses often have a wooden trim that must be painted periodically to keep it looking fresh and new. Once a house has been properly painted with a quality paint, the finish should last for a minimum of eight years. Fifteen years is not an uncommon life for a paint job in some parts of the country.

Several factors can affect the life of the paint you put on the exterior of your home. The quality of the paint is certainly the most important consideration; various types of paints will be discussed later in this chapter. Surface preparation is another important point, for even high quality paints will not adhere well or last long on an exterior surface in need of some type of remedial action. The third, and equally important, factor that will determine how long a paint job lasts is the care devoted to applying the paint; the best paint in the world will not last long if it is applied wrong.

TYPES OF EXTERIOR PAINTS

Exterior paints fall into two broad categories (neither of which includes clear coverings such as varnish, polyurethane, or stains): oil and alkyd base, and latex. Oil and alkyd base paints are lumped together simply because cleanup of painting tools and equipment (as well as the painter) and thinning must be done with a liquid other than water, usually a solvent such as mineral spirits or turpentine.

Oil-and Alkyd-Base Paints

Oil-and alkyd-base paints have been in use for many years and are popular with professional painters. These paints are made with drying oils or drying oils combined with an alkyd resin. The basic difference between an oil-base paint and an alkyd-base paint is that the former produces a generally flat type of finish. If a glossy finish is desired, an enamel should be used. Alkyd paints, on the other hand, are available in three types of finishes: flat, semigloss and high-gloss alkyd enamel.

Both oil-and alkyd-base paints provide excellent brushing and penetrating properties. They generally adhere well to previously painted surfaces and are resistant to blistering. Drying times vary but are generally about twelve hours.

Latex Paints

Latex paint is an easy paint for the do-it-yourselfer to work with and professional looking results are easily obtained. Latex paints have been developed and improved to the point where they are equal to and in some ways better than traditional oil-base paints. They are resistant to weathering and yellowing, and seem to have a better color retention.

Because latex paints have a water base they dry quickly, usually within an hour. They can be applied in damp weather and even over a slightly damp surface, so working with latex paints is much more flexible than with oil-base paints. Also, cleaning of paint tools and the painter can be done simply with warm soapy water.

Latex paint can be applied with brush, roller, or spray equipment to most surfaces including those which have been previously painted (even over oil paint), stucco, painted concrete, and other masonry and wood surfaces. Latex paint forms a type of flexible skin over the exterior of the home. This skin actually breathes and allows moisture to escape from the walls of the house. Such breathing action helps to lessen the chances of peeling and blistering of the paint in the future.

About the only time a latex paint cannot be used is over a surface with many coats of oil-base paint. It seems that oil-base paints never really harden but instead tend to flow over the years. When a latex paint is applied over a surface such as this, the latex paint will crack and peel. Another thing to keep in mind is that latex paints should not be applied when temperatures are below 10°C.

Transparent Finishes

For transparent finishes, there are the time-tested varnish and relatively new polyurethane. Varnish is simply a solution of resins in a drying oil. It contains no pigment. Varnish dries and hardens by evaporation of the oils or solvents that it is composed of. Spar varnish will provide an excellent exterior finish that is impervious to moisture, for it is hard and glossy. Varnish will not change the tone of the wood, nor will it turn yellow with age.

Polyurethane is a one-component synthetic finishing material that gives outstanding resistance to abrasion, weathering, water, oils; in fact, almost everything. One point about polyurethane, however, is that this finish tends to yellow with age and thereby changes the tone of the wood slightly.

PREPARATION FOR PAINTING

The foundation of every good paint job begins with a thorough surface preparation of the new or previously painted surface. If the paint is to provide the service and performance it was designed for, the surface to which it will be applied must be clean, dry, free of deteriorated old paint, and in sound condition. Loose or cracked old paint, dirt, scale, oil, stains, grease, rust, mildew, chemical deposits, and other foreign matter must be completely removed. All problem areas as well as all bare wood must be given a coat of primer to protect the wood and prevent problems from recurring. In addition, any areas in need of repair (rotten sections and holes, for example) must be remedied before the finish coat is applied. Areas around windows and doors should be checked and recaulked if necessary. Window putty should also be checked and replaced where not in sound condition.

Surface preparation will vary, depending, of course, on the general condition of the house you are painting. Usually one day for surface preparation is sufficient. Assuming that no major repairs are necessary, the main tools that are required for surface preparation are a wire brush, paint scraper (I find that a 4-inch wide, stiff putty knife works best), sandpaper, caulking gun, and a few tubes of quality caulking, nail set, hammer, window putty (if required), exterior spackle (for filling small nail holes), extension ladder long enough to reach the peaks of your house, a gallon of primer, and a paintbrush.

A few words about primers might prove helpful at this point. I personally prefer to use an oil-base primer, even when I will be giving a finish coat of latex paint. My main reason is that I feel oil base primers penetrate the wood better and I think that they mask stains and other problem areas better than a latex base primer.

It is suggested that you begin surface preparation on an end of the house, setting the extension ladder up against the peak of the house and scraping the trim first. Usually, paint is peeling or blistering and you should scrape it off with the putty knife. If you are right-handed, you will probably find it easier, in the long run, to scrape from right to left. Keep your eyes open for protruding nails (which you should reset), damaged boards (which should be replaced) and any other problem areas that will need attention.

As you work under the eaves, scrape off any wasp or bee nests and remove bird nests. Needless to say, you should be extremely careful when working around wasp or bee nests; according to a government report, more people are killed every year by bees and wasps than by poisonous snakes. Try to remove these nests in the early morning when the air is still and cool, rather than in the heat of the day when the insects will be more active. You can spray these nests first with a suitable flying insect bomb to be on the safe side.

If trees or bushes are close to the house, you will have some pruning to do as part of your surface preparation. Any branches that come close to or touch the house must be trimmed. If you don't do this selective pruning, the branches will rub against the house when the wind blows, and cause damage to the paint job and possibly the house itself.

TROUBLE SPOTS

Certain problems with existing paint coverings are easily identified. You should be familiar with these problems, so that you can correct them and prevent them from recurring.

Blistering Paint

Blistering paint (as shown in Figure 7-1) is a common problem that is usually caused by excess moisture on the inside of the house and poor or inadequate ventilation as well as insufficient insulation on the inside. The daily evaporation for an average size home is around 25 quarts of water. Water vapor from activities such as cooking, bathing, dishwashing, and laundry must pass from the inside of the home to the outside atmosphere. If the house is not properly ventilated, this water vapor tries to pass through the walls. If the outside of the home is covered with a coat of paint—as most homes are—then the paint will blister.

FIG. 7-1. An example of blistering paint, commonly caused by excess moisture escaping from inside the house.

To remedy a blistering paint problem you must scrape off the blisters and spot prime the area. The real solution, however, is to provide more ventilation inside your home. This can be accomplished by adding extra or larger attic louvers, exhaust fans, or possibly installing a dehumidifier. For more information on ventilation, see Chapter 12, Ventilation and Insulation.

Peeling Paint

Peeling paint is usually caused when paint is applied over a greasy or oily surface. The surface should have been primed with a good oil base primer after it was first cleaned to remove the oil or grease. Peeling will also result when an oil base paint is applied over a damp surface. The solution to peeling paint is to scrape the area, sand thoroughly, and then prime with an oil base primer. Make sure that the surface is dry first, however, or the problem will not be sufficiently corrected.

Excess Chalking

Excess chalking occurs when paint is applied in the rain, fog, mist, or very humid weather. It can also result from a low quality paint or a paint that was applied too thin. All paints will chalk to a certain extent but if, when you brush the surface with your fingertips, they look as if you have just dipped them in talcum powder, the existing paint is excessively chalking, as in Figure 7-2. The solution is to remove the chalk with a stiff wire brush or sandpaper; then, apply a quality primer to the area.

Alligatoring

Alligatoring (see Figure 7-3) happens when a low quality paint has been used; when there has been insufficient drying time between coats; or when a hard coating, such as latex paint, has been applied over a soft, oil base paint. The best solution is to scrape and thoroughly sand the area until smooth. Then apply a good quality oil base primer to the area and allow it to dry overnight before applying the finish coat.

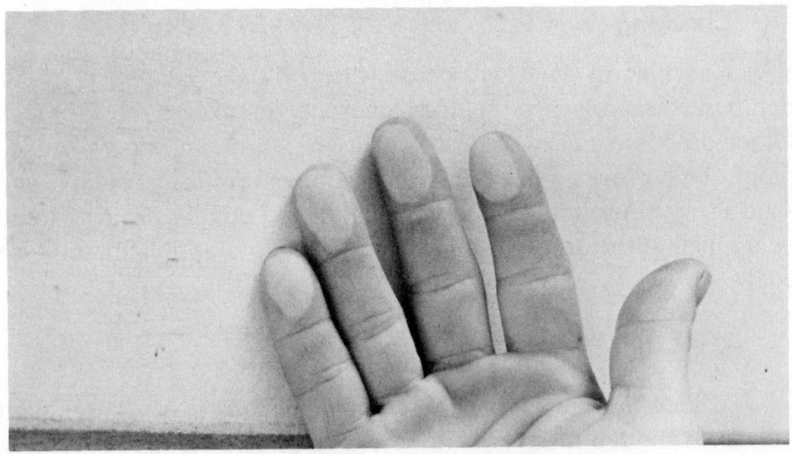

FIG. 7-2. Brush your fingertips over a painted surface; if this results in a residue, the paint is chalking excessively.

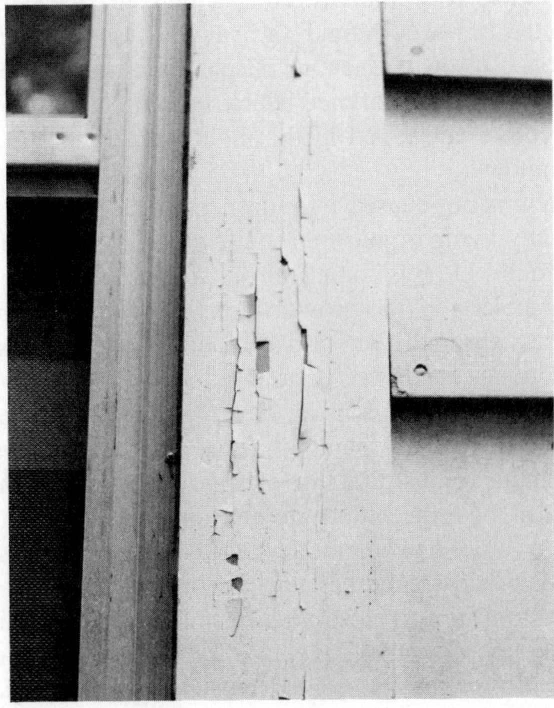

FIG. 7-3. An example of alligatoring exterior paint.

Checking

Checking of paint will occur when oil paint is applied over a damp surface or when paint is unevenly or excessively applied. Other probable causes are low quality paint, or improperly mixed paint. To correct a checking paint problem, you must scrape and sand the area until it is smooth. Then a good quality primer should be applied to the area and allowed to dry before applying the finish coat.

Mildew

Mildew is one of the most common causes of house paint failure. Although there does not seem to be any certain prevention against mildew when conditions for its growth are ideal, time, effort, and expense can be saved by a more thorough understanding of its causes and effects as well as how it can be controlled.

Mildew is a fungus that is visible as it grows on the surface of organic matter. It commonly attacks painted surfaces, especially those situated in warm, humid, or shady locations. Mildew appears as tiny spots of brown, black, or purple discoloration, resulting in a dirty, unattractive appearance which becomes progressively worse as dirt becomes entrapped in the mold web. Figure 7-4 is an example of mildew.

Mildew is not caused by paint; rather, it lives off paint. Mildew, like any living organism, requires food to live. It lives off the nutrients found in house paint, in the surface under the paint film, or in both places. If the growth of mildew is not stopped it will flourish, pass through the surface of the paint, and spread as far over the house as conditions permit.

Paint manufacturers have tried to solve the mildew problem for years by developing paints that are mildew resistant. Mildew-resistant paints are just that: resistant to the actions of mildew. But no paint can be expected to do its job unless the surface to be painted is clean of existing mildew and, in extreme cases, sterilized. Since mildew will sometimes appear visually as a dirt collection, it is best to test the suspected area for mildew before painting.

A very simple and effective test for mildew involves placing a few drops of common household bleach on the area you suspect. If the drops of bleach cause the area to lose its blackish or brownish appearance, then there is reason to believe that mildew is

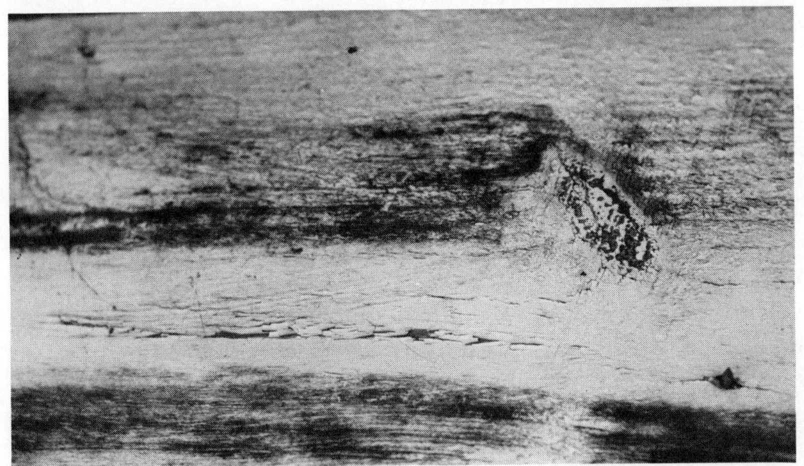

FIG. 7-4. Mildew shows up as dark areas on painted surfaces.

present; the area should then be sterilized before painting for best results. If, however, the drops of bleach leave the area black or brown, then chances are very good that the problem is simply dirt. Houses in urban areas, close to major highways or airports, will have blackish or brownish areas that at first appear to be mildew but are actually airborne dirt from the exhausts of automobiles and aircraft. If the problem is simply dirt, you should clean the area with some type of household cleaner. Whether mildew or dirt, the area must be cleaned if you want the paint job to last.

I have found that the best way to sterilize a mildewed area is to mix up a solution of 3 quarts of warm water, 1 quart of household bleach, ⅔ cup of trisodium phosphate (available in paint stores), and ⅓ cup of laundry detergent. Scrub the solution on the mildewed area with a medium-soft brush. Next, using a garden hose and plenty of water, spray the area clean. After it has dried, prime the area with a mildew-resistant oil base primer. Then, paint the area the same as the surrounding area.

The sterilizing solution is powerful stuff. You should wear goggles to protect your eyes, rubber gloves to protect your hands, and protective clothing, such as a hat, jacket, and an old pair of pants. Work carefully and keep children and pets away. Avoid splashing this cleaner on shrubs and grass.

Although there is still no positive and assured means of preventing mildew growth on paint film under conditions that are ideal for its growth, the above sterilizing solution will help. If mildew is a serious problem you should apply only paints that contain a mildewcide. If you do not, the mildew problem will reappear soon.

SURFACE PREPARATION: RECAULKING

Other areas of surface preparation include caulking around windows, doors, chimneys, and any other breaks in the body of the house. If repairs are necessary the amount of work and time involved will be determined by the area in need of repair. Possible examples are rotten facia boards, broken or missing siding, deteriorated trim around windows and door frames, or damage by insects and small animals.

As you work down from the peak of the house, keep your eyes open for protruding nailheads. These should be driven back into place with a hammer and countersunk with the aid of a nail set. For truly professional looking results you should fill these nail holes with a suitable filler such as exterior spackle or wood putty. When the filler dries it should be sanded smooth, with the grain of the wood, and then spot primed.

Check the trim around window and door frames, which will have a bead of caulking around the entire frame. Most of these areas will have to be recaulked, as old caulking tends to dry out and crack with age. Caulking should be applied to a clean surface and allowed to harden before painting (see Figure 7-5). If the caulking is latex based, however, latex paint can be applied over it immediately without waiting for the caulk to harden.

New caulking is most easily applied with the aid of a handheld caulking gun and a tube of caulking. Many different types of caulking are available and it seems that new types of caulking are developed every year. Check with your local paint store to find the best type of caulking for your home and your geographical area.

As you apply new caulking around window frames, check the condition of the glazing compound around each pane of window glass. Time and the elements will cause the glazing compound to dry out and crack. The result is a pane of glass that is not held tightly in its frame. When the wind blows, the pane of glass will move, slightly at first, until the putty falls out. A poorly glazed window will not efficiently keep out cold air, insects, or moisture, and therefore should be replaced.

FIG. 7-5. Part of surface preparation involves recaulking window and door frames.

You must first remove all of the dried out and cracked putty. The edge of a putty knife is the best tool for this. After the old putty has been removed, the area should be brushed clean (I always use an old paintbrush) and new glazer points installed, where necessary, to help hold the window pane in place.

Just prior to installing new window putty some professional painters like to wipe the inside of the window frame with turpentine. This tends to take some of the dryness out of the wood and make the glazing compound adhere better.

To reglaze an average sized window, I roll a wad of premixed window putty, about the size of a golf ball, between my hands until it resembles a small snake, slightly longer than the section I plan to fill. Next, I place this length of putty into the window frame against the glass and press it into place with my fingers. After one side of the frame has been covered I place my putty knife so that one corner rests against the glass while the flat part of the knife rests on the outside edge of the frame. Then I pull the putty knife toward me, keeping constant downward pressure against the new putty. The new putty will be pressed into position between the glass and the frame. I continue to remove and replace window putty in this fashion until the entire window is completed.

Glazing compound—or window putty, as it is commonly called—is available in two colors: white and black. Be sure to buy the color that most closely resembles the trim around your windows, as it can then be covered with one coat of trim paint.

It is probably easiest to work on one side of the house at a time. Complete all of the scraping, sanding, and priming first, as this work is the most time consuming part of surface preparation. Then do all of the recaulking and window glazing on that side. When all of this work has been completed, as well as any necessary repairs, move on to the next side of the house, and continue the surface preparation until, finally, all sides of the house have been finished.

One general rule that is followed by all successful painters when doing surface preparation or finish painting is to "follow the sun." By following the sun, you are assured that the area you are working on has been dried by the sun and that the sun's direct rays will not beat down on the freshly painted work.

Surface preparation is an important part of a painting job. Work carefully and diligently until all sides of the house have been thoroughly worked over. Then, after all of the preliminary work has been completed, you can begin painting the finish coat.

PAINTING TOOLS

Professional looking results require proper painting tools. Your main tool will, of course, be a paintbrush. For most trim work—window frames and doors, for example—I prefer a 2- or 3-inch-wide sash brush. Sash brushes have longer handles than most other types of brushes and enable the user to obtain straight lines and do accurate detail work. For large areas, such as the sidewalls of the house, I prefer a 4-inch-wide brush that is about 1 inch thick. Brushes larger than this, while able to hold more paint and cover large areas quickly, tend to become heavy rather quickly; they are thus much more tiring to work with for long periods. (See Figure 7-6.)

For large, flat areas, such as asbestos shingle sidewalls and some cedar shingles, I use a roller. With the right roller cover (technically known as a *roller sleeve*) almost anyone can cover almost any surface with lightning speed. It is not unusual for one person to paint an entire house in less than one day using the proper roller. In general, the best rule to follow when selecting a roller is

FIG. 7-6. Two types of exterior paintbrushes: sash brush (top) and 4-inch-wide wall brush.

"the smoother the surface, the shorter the nap—the rougher the surface, the longer the nap." *Nap* is the hair-like covering on the roller sleeve. Roller covers are available for just about any type of surface, from ¼-inch, very short napped rollers to ¾ to 1-inch-long napped rollers. Figure 7-7 shows two examples of roller sleeves.

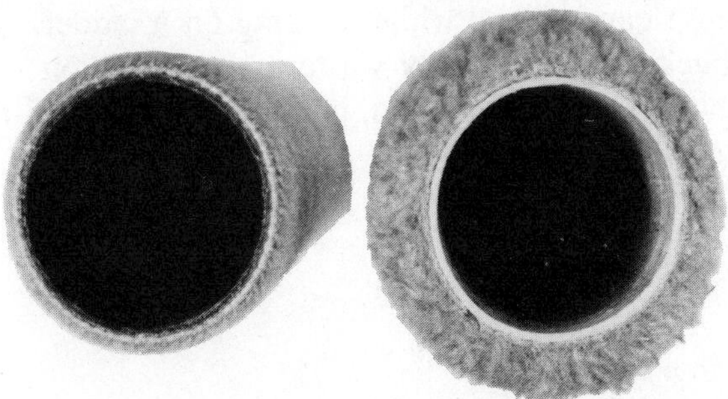

FIG. 7-7. Short nap roller (left) for smooth areas and long nap roller (right) for covering coarse textured surfaces.

The standard length of a roller is 9 inches, although rollers are available in 36-inch lengths. A strong roller handle is necessary when using a roller to paint a house. The amount of strain that is put on a roller handle will quickly bend an inexpensive roller handle. Buy a good roller handle and it will last for years.

You will also need an extension handle for the roller; in fact, you should never use a roller without an extension handle. You can't apply the necessary pressure by hand-holding a roller. I have found that a 6- to 8-foot roller handle extension works about the best for most types of work.

Before you begin the actual painting of the house you should cover shrubs, walks, porch flooring, and stairs or any other area that may be damaged by accidental paint droppings. The best thing to use is a painter's drop cloth, but these are expensive and there are alternatives. Old sheets are handy, although if a large quantity of paint is spilled on these, they will leak. A better alternative is a sheet of plastic. Several companies sell plastic drop cloths; if you buy these, make sure they are heavy plastic or they won't last long.

Dress properly when doing exterior painting. Appropriate dress includes a hat to protect your hair, a long-sleeved shirt, and long pants. If you spend a lot of time on a ladder you might consider wearing a pair of heavy work shoes or possibly boots. (See Chapter 1, Asphalt Roofing, for a discussion on boots for use on ladders.) Sunglasses will protect your eyes from paint splatters.

When working up on a ladder, you should probably carry only one quart of paint. It is usually impossible to paint more than this quantity of paint when working up on a ladder. A plastic paint bucket with a wire hook (for attaching the paint bucket to the ladder rungs) can be used while working on a ladder. Also, if you drop the bucket you will only waste a small portion of the paint rather than an entire gallon. And, in the event of a spill there is less paint to clean up.

PAINTING PROCEDURES

Windows and Doors

Begin painting a house at the highest part; start with the trim work. Next, after all of the trim on one side of the house has been painted, paint the window and door frames.

Windows are the most time consuming part of any painting job, because of the detail. Begin painting window frames with that part of the frame that is closest to the actual windowpane, and work outward, toward the trim or molding around the window. (As mentioned earlier, a small 2- or 3-inch sash brush will make this type of detail painting easier.) Window frame paint should not be spread on too thickly or the window will be very difficult to operate. Brush the paint on uniformly and smoothly. The last part of the window frame to be painted should be the trim around the outermost part of the window frame.

Next, paint all of the doors, door frames, and trim. Like most other parts to be painted, start painting doors at the top and work downward. As with surface preparation, work on one side of the house until it is completed. When all sides of the house have had a coat of trim paint, go back to the starting point and begin painting the body of the house.

Body

After all the detail work is done, you are ready to paint the body of the house. Begin, again, at the highest point and paint the body color in a 6- to 8-inch band beginning where the body of the house meets the trim. If you don't plan to use a roller on the large flat areas, then you can do all of the painting of the body from where you stand on the ladder. If you do plan to use a roller, however, simply paint with a brush all of those areas that cannot be painted with the roller—for example, the areas close (within 6 inches) to window and door frames, and where the body of the house meets the trim. After all of these areas have been given a coat of body paint, begin to apply paint with a roller to the body of the house.

Before you begin rolling paint on your house there are a few things that you should know about proper roller use. First, the paint must be mixed well; this is best done by "boxing" the paint. *Boxing paint* is a term that means that several gallons of paint are mixed together, before they are spread over the surface of the house. Paint tone and colors have a tendency to be a bit different, especially between batches of paint. It is not uncommon to find a slight color variation between gallons of the same batch, however. By mixing several gallons of paint together, you will come up with a house paint that is uniform in color. A 5-gallon plastic bucket is best for boxing paints. Pour about 3 gallons of paint into the 5-gallon bucket, stir well, and then pour the mixed paint back into the original containers. Boxing paint is usually necessary only when more than 3 gallons of paint are used, as on the body of the house. It is generally not a good idea to mix paint from different makers as the paints may have different formulas.

Pour about ½ gallon of paint into a paint tray and begin rolling the roller down into the paint. Roll back and forth, forcing paint into the nap of the roller cover. You will have to roll quite a bit, especially with a new, dry roller cover. A roller works most effectively when it is completely and evenly saturated with paint. Therefore, you should take extra time, especially on the first fill, to ensure that the paint is worked well into the nap on the roller cover. When you think you have enough paint on the roller cover, lift it out of the tray. If paint drips off the cover, you have too much paint and the excess should be rolled off inside the tray.

Begin rolling on the body color in an upward direction; this will help to avoid dripping paint. You should apply with an even pressure as you roll over a surface. Roll upward, then downward, in straight lines. The best coverage can be obtained by limiting your coverage. An area of about 6 feet by 6 feet is probably optimal for each roller full of paint.

As you work, start in a dry area (one that has not been painted yet) and work toward the previously painted area. Don't roll too fast, as this action will cause paint to spatter. Smooth, even, fluid strokes are best. One common mistake is to use too much pressure on the roller handle. This will result in poor coverage (paint too thin) and also tends to mat the nap on the roller cover, thereby reducing the paint holding capacity of the roller.

As you work up to areas around window and door frames that have been trimmed out with the body color, work carefully to avoid spattering paint over the finished trim. After you have finished one side of the house, look over the work before moving on to another side of the house. One of the most common complaints about rollers is that they leave "holidays." *Holidays* are areas that are not covered sufficiently, leaving the original house body color to show through. It is probably easiest to look over the side just painted, and, with a paintbrush in hand, touch up these holidays as you see them.

If you are painting a shingle house you may find that the roller did not cover the area where one shingle overlaps another. Check these areas over and touch up where necessary with a paintbrush.

After the first side of the house has been painted to your satisfaction, move on to the next side and begin again. Remember that you should follow the sun, as you move around the house.

If you are painting a house that has textured stucco or hand-split cedar shakes, it will not be possible to use a roller, so you will have to use a paintbrush. Begin at the highest point on the house and paint downward. When painting the body of a house with a brush, stand in one place and paint as much of an area as possible before moving the ladder. Painting from right to left, you can probably cover an area of about 30 square feet. When painting shingles, it is best to paint each row of shingles, forcing the bristles of the brush, and the paint, up under the edges of the upper courses of the shingles. Painting downward it will take at least three hours to paint the side of an average sized house. That same area can usually be covered with a roller in about an hour or less, if a roller can be used.

When the entire house has been painted, you should go back over the work and check for holidays and misapplied paint. Touch up where necessary. When you have finished all of the touch-ups, and there will be some, you can expect to get a minimum of eight years of service for your efforts. You should, however, check over the exterior of your home every spring and fall, and touch up any problem areas before they get serious. By doing this it is possible for a paint job to last up to fifteen years.

ADDITIONAL PAINTING TIPS

The following pointers that professional painters use can help you achieve long-lasting results.

First, unless you are using a latex paint, you should not paint on a damp day. Moisture on the painting surface may prevent a good bond. If the humidity is high, check the surface before starting to paint. If you can feel a film of moisture on the surface, it would be wise to wait for a drier day.

Exterior painting is not recommended if the temperature is below 10°C. or above 35°C., since you may not be able to get a good bond. This is especially important if you are using latex paint.

The tendency of wood to expand and contract during changes in temperature and humidity makes it imperative that a good wood primer be applied to provide the necessary base for the finish coat of paint. Surfaces such as wood siding, porches, trim, shutters, sash, doors, and window frames should be primed with an exterior primer intended for wood. Primer should be applied with a brush, only to clean, dry surfaces.

Painted wood usually does not need priming unless the old paint has cracked, blistered, or peeled down to the bare wood. Defective paint must be removed by scraping or wire brushing down to the bare wood and then primed.

New masonry surfaces should be primed with an exterior latex paint, preferably one specifically designed for masonry. Common brick is sometimes sealed with a penetrating type of clear, exterior varnish to control efflorescence and spalling (flaking or chipping of the brick). This varnish withstands weather, yet allows the natural appearance of the brick to show through.

Old masonry painted surfaces that have become a little chalky should be painted with an exterior oil primer to rebind the chalk. If there is a lot of chalk, it should be removed with a stiff brush or by washing with a household washing soda or trisodium phosphate mixed with water.

Galvanized steel surfaces, such as gutter and downspouts, should be primed with recommended special primers, because conventional primers usually do not adhere well to this type of metal. A zinc-dust or zinc-oxide type of primer works best on galvanized steel. Exterior latex paints are sometimes used directly over galvanized surfaces but oil-base paints are not.

Unpainted iron and steel railings will rust when exposed to the weather. Rust, dirt, oils, and loose paint should be removed before painting these surfaces. A wire brush or power cleaning tool will speed up the work. The surface should then be primed with an anticorrosive primer before painting.

A good paintbrush is an expensive tool, and it will last for many years if you invest the necessary time and effort to take care of it properly. Clean brushes as soon as possible after use with a paint thinner or special brush cleaner. A paint supply store is the best place to find out what to use for cleaning your brushes. Use turpentine or mineral spirits to remove oil base paints, enamels,

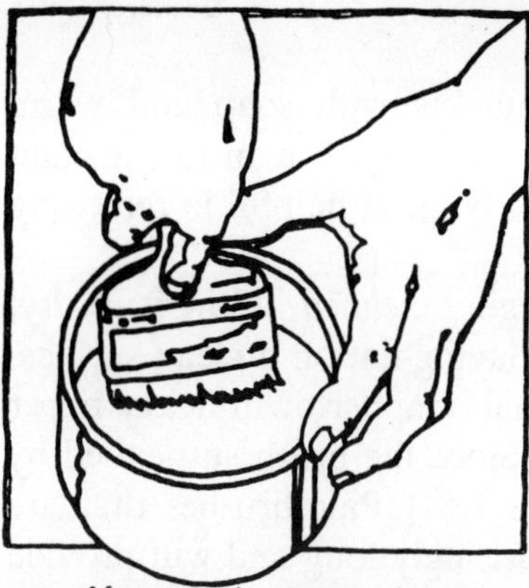

1 After removing excess paint with scraper, soak brush in proper thinner, work it against bottom of container.

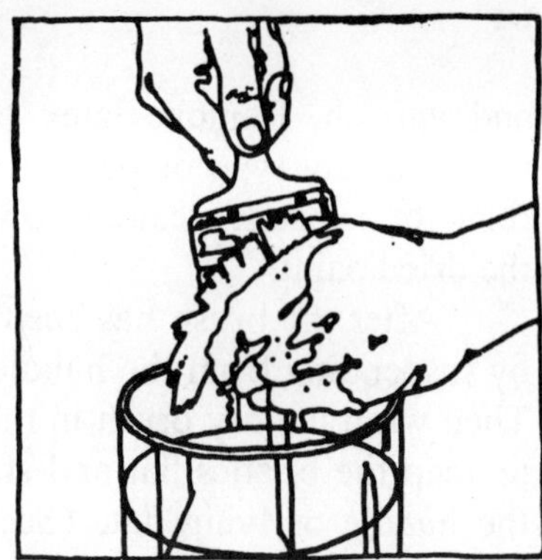

2 To loosen paint in center of brush, squeeze bristles between thumb and forefinger, then rinse again in thinner. If necessary, work brush in mild soap suds, rinse in clear water.

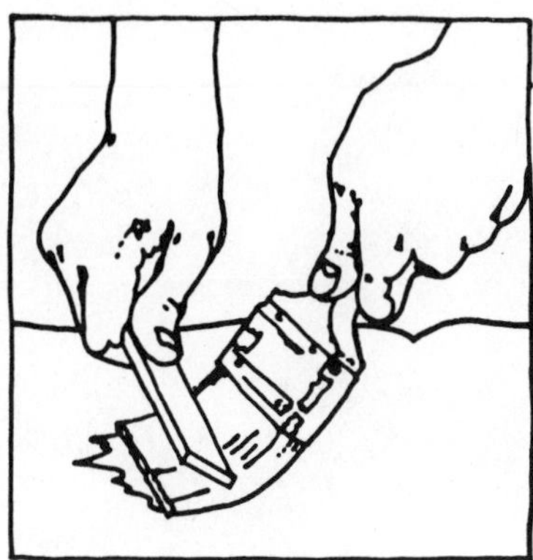

3 Press out water with stick.

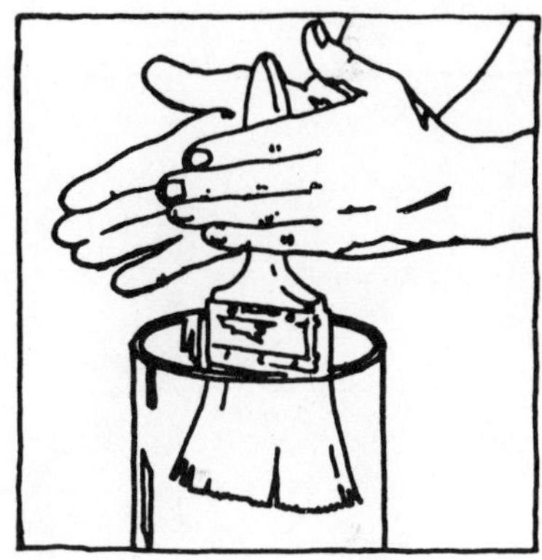

4 Twirl brush — in a container so you won't get splashed!

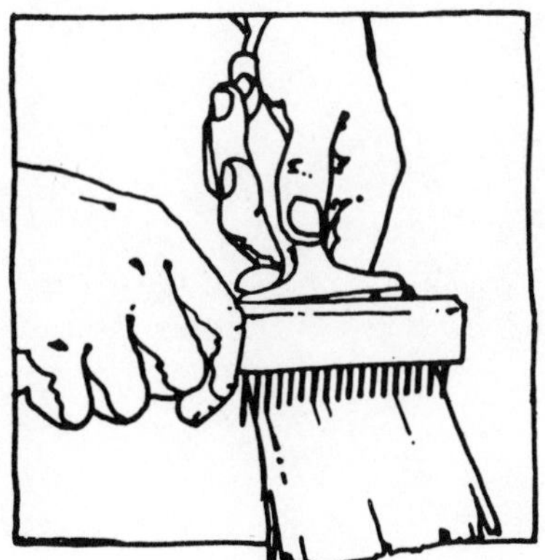

5 Comb bristles carefully — including those below the surface. Allow the brush to dry by suspending from the handle or by laying it flat on a clean surface. Then wrap the dry brush in the original wrapper or in heavy paper to keep the bristles straight. Store suspended by handle or lying flat.

FIG. 7-8. Proper procedure for cleaning brushes.

and varnish. Remove latex paints quickly with soap and warm water. If any type of paint is allowed to dry on a brush, a paint remover or brush cleaning solvent will be most helpful in removing the dried paint.

After the brush has been thoroughly cleaned, allow it to dry, by suspending from the handle or by laying flat on a clean surface. Then wrap the dry brush in the original wrapper or in heavy paper to keep the bristles flat and straight. Store the brush suspended by the handle or lying flat. (See Figure 7-8.) Paintbrushes that are cared for in this manner will last surprisingly long and will provide a lifetime of service.

8 WOODEN SIDING

Wood, in one form or another, covers more home exteriors than does any other single type of exterior wall covering. Wood is a good choice for exterior sidewalls because it is relatively inexpensive, easy to work with, and, if installed properly and maintained, will provide a lifetime of service.

Exterior wall coverings are usually installed over sheathing but can be attached directly to the framing members. In the latter case, the siding serves as both sheathing and finish covering. This type of application is usually only used in the more temperate areas of the country. Where greater temperature fluctuations are common, a house is first sheathed and then a finish sidewall covering is attached.

TYPES OF SIDING

In addition to cedar shingles and shakes (discussed in Chapters 2 and 10), two basic types of wooden siding are used in this country: siding that is installed vertically and siding that is installed horizontally. Of course, some types may be used in either manner if adequate nailing areas are provided. Following are descriptions of each of the general types of exterior sidewall coverings. (See Figure 8-1.)

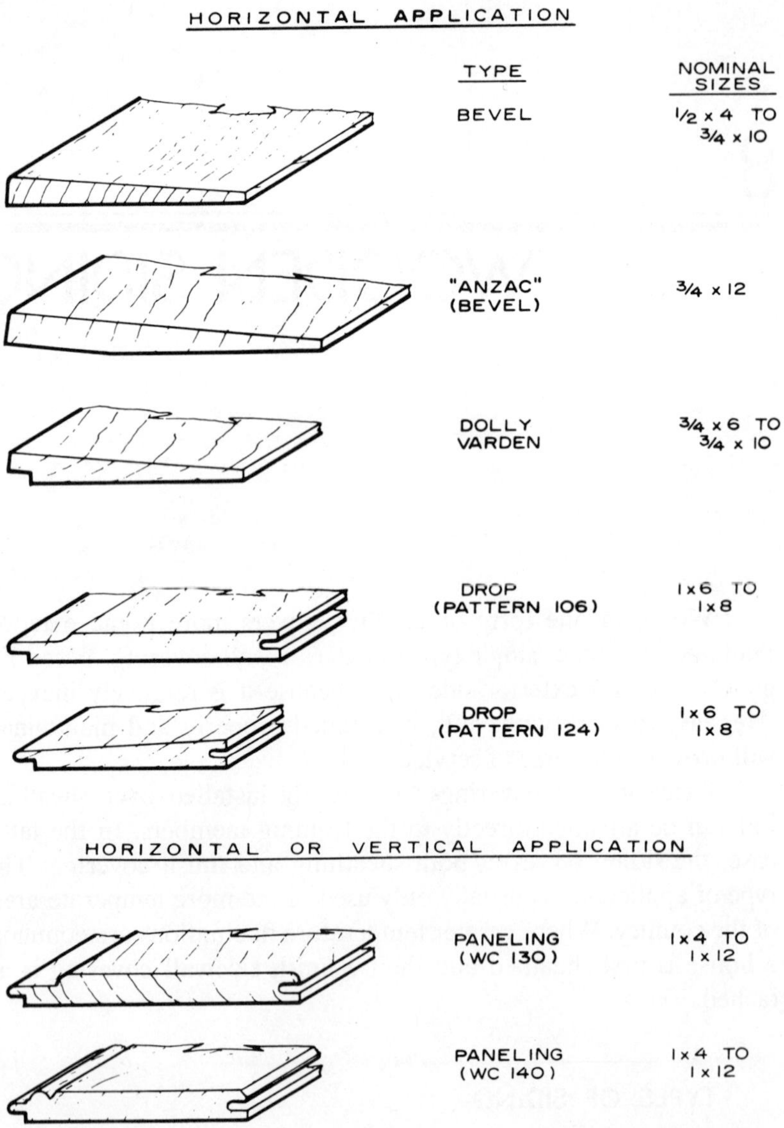

HORIZONTAL APPLICATION
TYPE
NOMINAL SIZES
BEVEL
1/2 x 4 TO 3/4 x 10
"ANZAC" (BEVEL)
3/4 x 12
DOLLY VARDEN
3/4 x 6 TO 3/4 x 10
DROP (PATTERN 106)
1 x 6 TO 1 x 8
DROP (PATTERN 124)
1 x 6 TO 1 x 8
HORIZONTAL OR VERTICAL APPLICATION
PANELING (WC 130)
1 x 4 TO 1 x 12
PANELING (WC 140)
1 x 4 TO 1 x 12

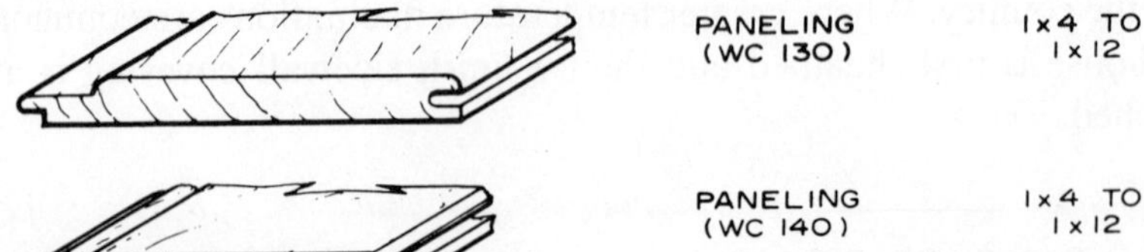

FIG. 8-1. Examples of several types of vertical and horizontal siding.

Bevel Siding

Plain bevel siding can be obtained in sizes from ½ × 4 inches to ½ × 8 inches and also in sizes of ¾ × 8 and ¾ × 10 inches. "Anzac" siding is ¾ × 12 inches in size. Usually the finished width of bevel siding is about ½ inch less than the listed size. One side of "anzac" siding has a smooth planed surface; the other has a rough sawn surface. For a stained finish, the rough or sawn side is exposed to the weather because wood stain is most successful and longer lasting on rough wood surfaces.

Dolly Varden Siding

Dolly Varden siding is similar to true bevel siding except that shiplap edges are used, resulting in a constant exposure distance. Because it lies flat against the studs, it is sometimes used for garages and similar buildings without sheathing. Diagonal bracing is then needed to provide racking resistance to the wall.

Other Horizontal Sidings

Regular drop sidings can be obtained in several patterns. Siding with matches or shiplap edges can be obtained in 1 × 6 and 1 × 8 inch widths. This type of siding is commonly used for lower-cost dwellings and for garages, usually without the benefit of sheathing. Tests conducted at the Forest Products Laboratory have shown that the tongued-and-grooved (matched) patterns have greater resistance to the penetration of wind-driven rain than do the shiplap patterns when both were treated with a water repellent preservative.

Fiberboard and hardboard sidings are also available in various forms. Some have a backing to provide rigidity and strength while others are used directly over sheathing. Plywood horizontal lap siding, with medium density overlaid surface, is also available as an exterior covering material. Commonly ⅜-inch thick and 12 to 16 inches wide, it is applied in much the same manner as conventional wooden siding, except that a shingle wedge is used behind each vertical joint.

A method of siding application, popular for some architectural styles, utilizes rough sawn boards and battens applied vertically. These boards can be arranged in several ways: (1) board and batten, (2) batten and board, and (3) board and board. As in the vertical application of most siding materials, nominal 1-inch thick sheathing boards or plywood sheathing (⅝- or ¾-inch thick) should be used for nailing surfaces. When other types of sheathing materials or thinner plywoods are used, nailing blocks between the studs commonly provide the nailing areas. Nailers of 2 × 4

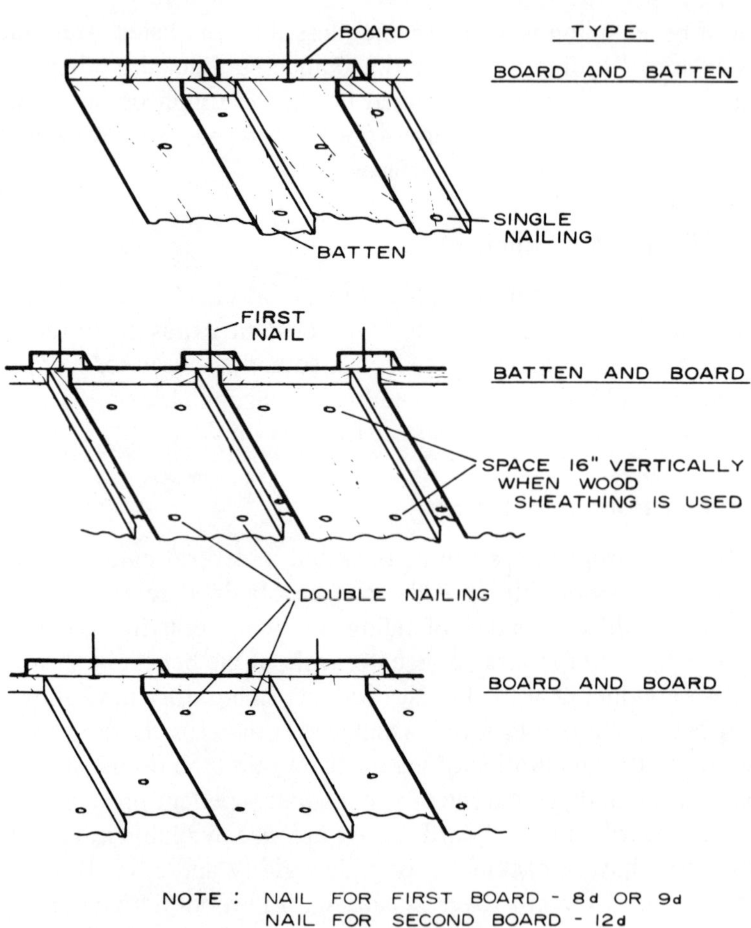

FIG. 8-2. A few examples of vertical board siding.

inches, laid horizontally and spaced 16 to 24 inches apart vertically, can be used over nonwood sheathing. However, special or thicker casing is sometimes required around doors and window frames when this system is used. It is good practice to use a building paper over the sheathing before applying the vertical siding.

A number of siding or paneling patterns can be used horizontally or vertically. These are manufactured in nominal 1 inch thicknesses and in even widths from 4 to 12 inches. Dressed, matched, and shiplapped edges are available. The narrow and medium width patterns will likely be more satisfactory when there are moderate moisture content changes. Wide patterns are more successful if they are vertical grain to keep shrinkage to a minimum. The correct moisture content is also important when tongued-and-grooved siding is wide, to prevent shrinkage to a point at which the tongue is exposed.

Treating the edges of both drop and the matched and shiplapped sidings with water repellent preservative usually prevents wind-driven rain from penetrating the joints if exposed to the weather. In areas under wide overhangs, or in porches or other protected sections of the house, this treatment is not as important. Some manufacturers provide siding with this treatment applied at the factory.

FINISH COVERINGS

Quite a large selection of sheet materials are now available for finish coverings on exterior walls. These include plywood in a variety of face treatments and species, paper overlaid plywood, and hardboard. Plywood or paper overlaid plywood is sometimes used without sheathing and is known as *panel siding,* with ⅜-inch thickness considered the minimum for use over framing members spaced 16 inches on center. However, from the standpoint of stiffness and strength, better performance is usually obtained by using ½- or ⅝-inch thickness.

These 4 × 8 foot and longer sheets must be applied vertically with intermediate and perimeter nailing to provide the desired rigidity. Most other methods of applying sheet materials require some type of sheathing beneath. When horizontal joints are necessary, they should be protected by simple flashing.

An exterior grade plywood is the only type that should ever be used for siding. These can be obtained with surfaces that have been grooved, brushed, and saw textured. These surfaces are usually finished with some type of stain. If shiplap or matched edges are not provided, some method of providing a waterproof joint should be used. This often consists of caulking and a batten at each joint and a batten at each stud if closer spacing is desired for appearance. An edge treatment of water repellent preservative will also aid in reducing moisture penetration. Allow 1/16-inch edge and end spacing when installing plywood in sheet form.

Exterior grade particle board might also be considered for panel siding. Normally, ⅝-inch thickness is required for 16-inch stud spacing and ¾-inch for 24-inch stud spacing. The finish must be with an approved paint and the stud wall behind must have corner bracing.

Paper overlaid plywood has many of the advantages of plywood with the addition of providing a very satisfactory base for paint. A medium density, overlaid plywood is most commonly used.

Hardboard sheets used for siding are applied the same way as plywood; that is, by using battens over vertical joints and at intermediate studs. Medium density fiberboards might also be used in some areas as exterior coverings over certain types of sheathing (see Figure 8-3).

Many of these sheet materials resist the passage of water vapor. Hence, when they are used it is important that a good vapor barrier, well installed, be employed on the warm side of the insulated walls. (See Chapter 12, "Ventilation and Insulation.")

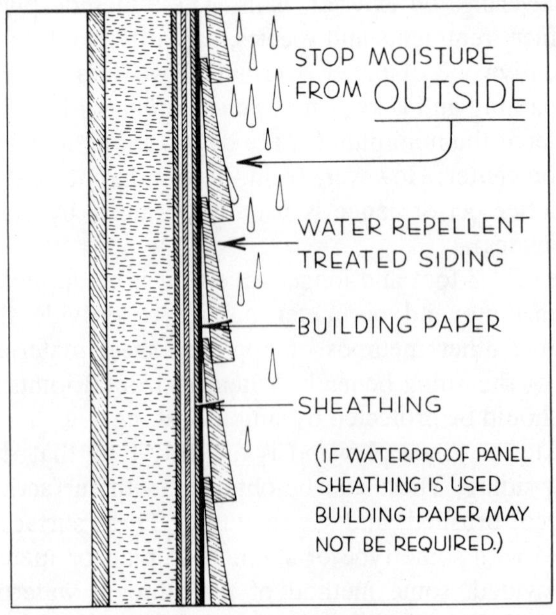

Courtesy of California Redwood Association

FIG. 8-3. To bar moisture, siding should be treated with a water repellent and backed with sheathing covered with water-repellent building paper.

FASTENERS

Successful performance of various siding materials is also dependent on the type of fasteners used. Nails are the most common means of fastening, and it is poor economy indeed to use them sparingly. Corrosion resistant nails—galvanized or made of aluminum, stainless steel, or similar metals—may cost more, but their use will ensure spot-free siding under adverse conditions.

Two types of nails are commonly used with siding: the finishing nail, which has a small head and the siding nail, which has a moderate-sized head (see Figure 8-4). The small head finishing nail is set (driven below the surface with the aid of a nail set) about 1/16-inch below the surface of the siding, and the hole is filled with putty after the prime coat of paint has been applied. The flathead siding nail, most commonly used, is driven flush with the face of the siding and the head later covered with paint.

Ordinary steel wire nails tend to rust in a short period of time and cause a disfiguring stain on the face of the siding. In some cases, the small headed nails will show rust spots through the putty and paint. Noncorrosive nails, which will not cause rust, are readily available.

Siding to be finished with a clear, water-repellent preservative or stain should be fastened with stainless steel or aluminum nails.

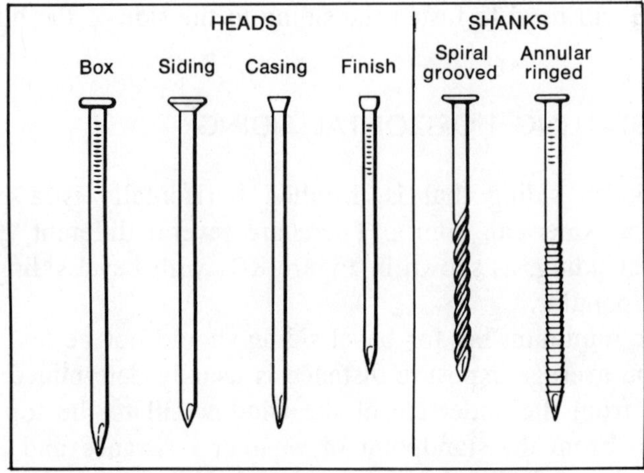

FIG. 8-4. Examples of the common types of nails used for attaching most types of wooden exterior siding.

In some types of prefinished sidings, nails with color-matched heads are available.

In recent years, nails with modified shanks have become quite popular. These include the annularly threaded shank nail and the helically threaded shank nail. Both have greater holding power (up to 400 times) and for this reason, a shorter nail is often used.

Exposed nails should be driven just flush with the surface of the siding. Overdriving may not only show the hammer mark, but may also cause objectionable splitting and crushing of the wood. In sidings with prefinished surfaces or overlays, the nails should be driven so as not to damage the finished surface.

ESTIMATING MATERIALS

To estimate the required number of board feet of wooden siding for the job you are doing, it will be necessary to measure the length and height of the area. Obviously, this must be done for all sides of the house. This square-foot figure is then multiplied by a conversion factor to give the required number of board feet. Common conversion factors are listed in Table 8-1. This factor allows for width loss in dressing or lapping. You must add to your estimate an additional 3 to 5 percent to allow for end cutting and matching on the job.

Table 8-2 will give you an idea of the number of pounds of nails you will need to fasten the siding to the side of the house.

INSTALLING HORIZONTAL SIDING

Wooden siding that is installed horizontally is a popular choice for American homes. There are several different types of horizontal siding, as shown in Figure 8-1, with bevel siding being the most popular.

The minimum lap for bevel siding should not be less than 1 inch. The average exposure distance is usually determined by the distance from the underside of the window sill to the top of the drip cap. From the standpoint of weather resistance and appearance, the butt edge of the first course of siding above the window should coincide with the top of the window drip cap. In many one-

TABLE 8-1

Estimating Siding (Multiply length × width × area factor)

	Nominal Size	WIDTH Dress	WIDTH Face	AREA FACTOR*
SHIPLAP	1 x 6	5½	5⅛	1.17
	1 x 8	7¼	6⅞	1.16
	1 x 10	9¼	8⅞	1.13
	1 x 12	11¼	10⅞	1.10
TONGUE AND GROOVE	1 x 4	3⅜	3⅛	1.28
	1 x 6	5⅜	5⅛	1.17
	1 x 8	7⅛	6⅞	1.16
	1 x 10	9⅛	8⅞	1.13
	1 x 12	11⅛	10⅞	1.10
S4S	1 x 4	3½	3½	1.14
	1 x 6	5½	5½	1.09
	1 x 8	7¼	7¼	1.10
	1 x 10	9¼	9¼	1.08
	1 x 12	11¼	11¼	1.07
PANELING PATTERNS	1 x 6	5 7/16	5 1/16	1.19
	1 x 8	7⅛	6¾	1.19
	1 x 10	9⅛	8¾	1.14
	1 x 12	11⅛	10¾	1.12
BEVEL SIDING (1″ lap)	1 x 4	3½	3½	1.60
	1 x 6	5½	5½	1.33
	1 x 8	7¼	7¼	1.28
	1 x 10	9¼	9¼	1.21
	1 x 12	11¼	11¼	1.17

*Allowance for trim and waste should be added.

Courtesy of Western Wood Products Association

TABLE 8-2

Nail Requirement Computation Chart

nail size specification						
Size	Length (Inches)		Siding Nails (Count per lb.)		Approx. lbs. Per 1,000 B.F. of Siding	
	*	**	*	**	*	**
6d	1⅞″	2″	566	194	2	6
7d	2⅛″	2¼″	468	172	2½	6½
8d	2⅜″	2½″	319	123	4	9
10d	2⅞″	3″	215	103	5½	11

*Aluminum **Hot Dipped Galv.

Courtesy of Western Wood Products Association

story houses with an overhang, this course of siding is often replaced with a frieze board. It is also desirable that the bottom of a siding course be flush with the underside of the window sill. However, this may not always be possible because of varying window heights and types that might be used in a house.

One system used to determine the siding exposure width so that it is about equal both above and below the window sills is described below. Divide the overall height of the window frame by the approximate recommended exposure distance for the siding used.

Horizontal Siding Exposure

Width of Siding (inches)	Standard Exposure (inches)
6	4
8	6
10	8
12	10

This will result in the number of courses between the top and the bottom of the window. For example, the overall height of our sample window, from the top of the drip cap to the bottom of the sill is 61 inches. If 12-inch siding is used, the number of courses would be $61/10 = 6.1$ or six courses of siding. To obtain the exact exposure distance, divide 61 by 6 and the result would be 10$\frac{1}{16}$ inches. The next step is to determine the exposure distance from the bottom of the sill to just below the top of the foundation wall. If this is 31 inches, three courses at 10$\frac{1}{3}$ inches each would be necessary. Thus, the exposure distance above and below the window would be just about the same as the exposure around the window.

When this system is not satisfactory because of large differences in the two areas, it is preferable to use an equal exposure distance for the entire wall height and notch the siding at the window sill. The fit should be as tight as possible to prevent the entry of moisture.

Bevel siding (as well as all other types of horizontal siding) is installed beginning with the bottom course. This first course is normally blocked out with a starting strip the same thickness as the top of the siding board. The starting strip is nailed to the sheathing or framing members at a point where the first course lower edge will begin. Each succeeding course overlaps the upper edge of the course below. Siding should be nailed at each stud location or on 16-inch centers. When plywood or wood sheathing or spaced wood nailing strips are used over nonwood sheathing, sevenpenny or eightpenny nails (2¼ and 2½ inches long) may be used for ¾-inch thick siding. However, if gypsum or insulation board sheathing is used, the tenpenny nail is recommended to penetrate the stud, as these types of sheathing have very little nail holding power.

The lowest edge of the siding should be at least 6 inches above ground level. The high humidities and free water, which are often present at the base of a foundation because of landscaping, can cause finish difficulties and structural problems (see Figure 8-5).

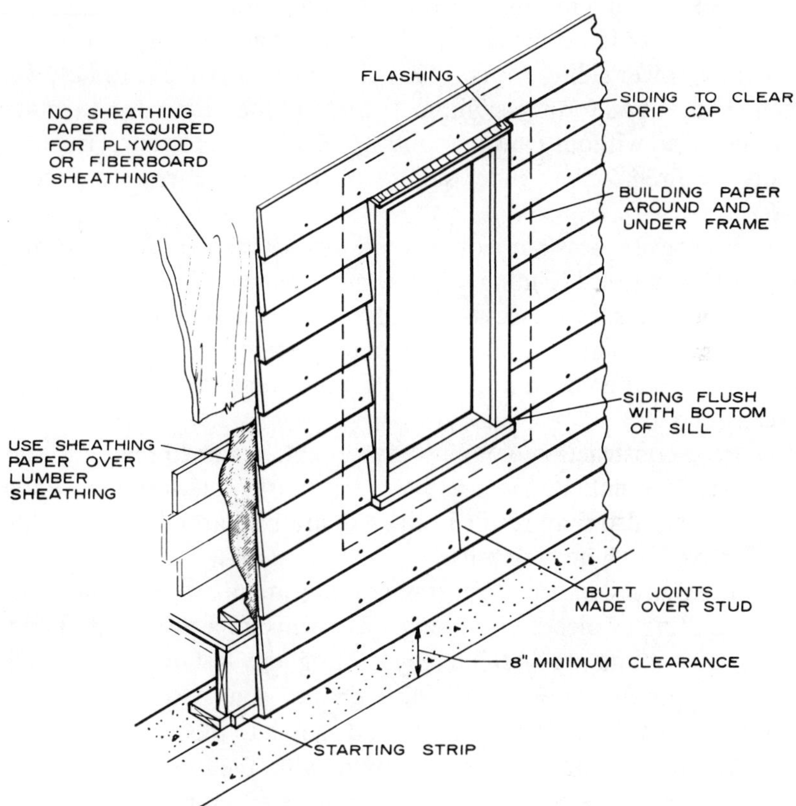

FIG. 8-5. Bevel siding installation.

It is particularly important that the end grain at the bottom of vertical siding be given a water-repellent treatment. The use of a drip cap at the lower edge of the siding will help direct water away from the foundation. It is also desirable to have the earth adjacent to the wall sloping away from the house, to assist drainage.

A water-repellent building paper should be applied to board sheathing. If no sheathing is used, the building paper should be placed across the studs. If weatherproof panel sheathing such as plywood is used, the building paper may be omitted. The purpose of the building paper is to block water and wind penetration, not to serve as a vapor barrier. Thus, there is no danger of entrapping moisture within the walls. The paper should have a permeability of at least five perms.

It is structurally desirable to back up the thinner siding patterns with sheathing. In colder climates, sheathing is advisable even with thicker siding for the added insulation it provides.

Nails should be driven far enough up from the butt to miss the top of the lower siding course. This clearance distance is usually ⅛ inch. This allows for any slight movement of the siding due to moisture changes without causing splitting. Such an allowance is especially required for the wider sidings of 8 to 12 inches (see Figure 8-6).

Whenever possible you should avoid butt joints. Use the longer sections of the siding under windows and on longer stretches. Try to use the shorter sections of the siding for the areas between windows and doors. If you have to make butt joints, make sure that the joint is centered on a stud and that all joints are staggered between rows.

Poor construction detailing may enable water to seep into the siding and, eventually, cause paint or finish deterioration. Poor construction also may result in inadequate insulation, causing discomfort and high heating bills.

With any siding pattern, tight fitting joints are essential. Accurate cutting of pieces is the only way to ensure a proper fit. Tight fitting butt joints are obtained by cutting the last board of each course approximately 1/16 of an inch too long. Bow the piece slightly, to get the ends in position, and snap into place.

Mitered corners, sometimes used with the thicker patterns, should be cut in a miterbox. Nail the mitered ends to the corner post and not to each other.

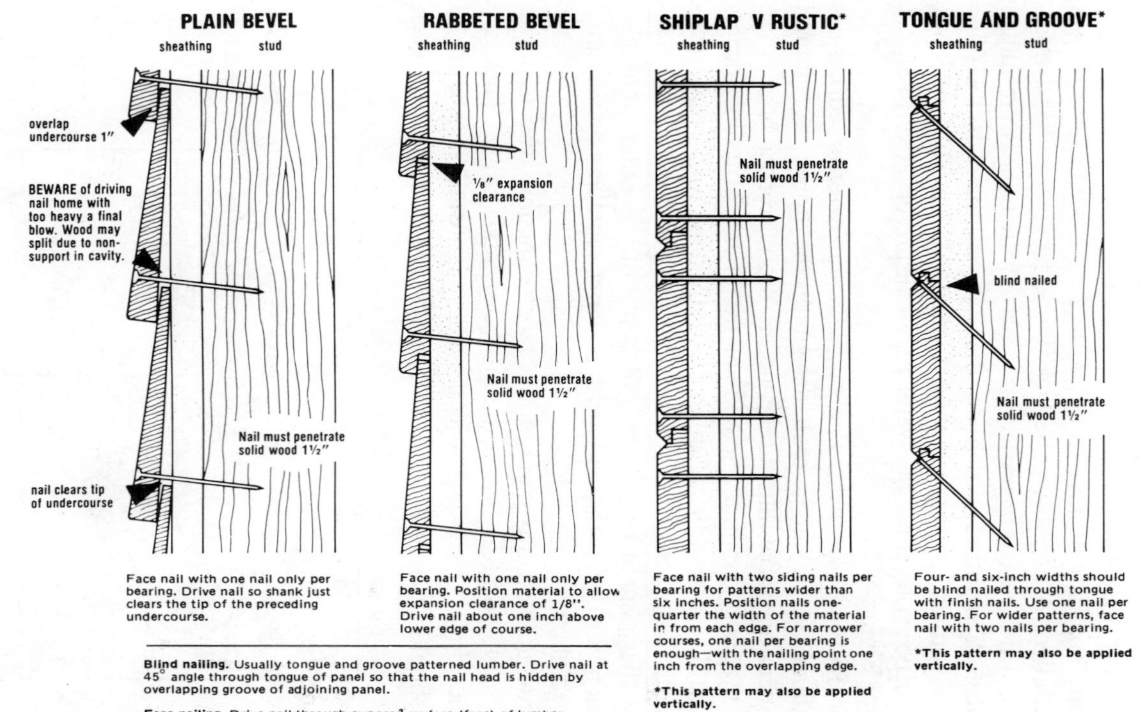
PLAIN BEVEL
sheathing
stud
overlap undercourse 1″
BEWARE of driving nail home with too heavy a final blow. Wood may split due to non-support in cavity.
Nail must penetrate solid wood 1½″
nail clears tip of undercourse
Face nail with one nail only per bearing. Drive nail so shank just clears the tip of the preceding undercourse.
RABBETED BEVEL
sheathing
stud
⅛″ expansion clearance
Nail must penetrate solid wood 1½″
Face nail with one nail only per bearing. Position material to allow expansion clearance of 1/8″. Drive nail about one inch above lower edge of course.
SHIPLAP V RUSTIC*
sheathing
stud
Nail must penetrate solid wood 1½″
Face nail with two siding nails per bearing for patterns wider than six inches. Position nails one-quarter the width of the material in from each edge. For narrower courses, one nail per bearing is enough—with the nailing point one inch from the overlapping edge.
*This pattern may also be applied vertically.
TONGUE AND GROOVE*
sheathing
stud
blind nailed
Nail must penetrate solid wood 1½″
Four- and six-inch widths should be blind nailed through tongue with finish nails. Use one nail per bearing. For wider patterns, face nail with two nails per bearing.
*This pattern may also be applied vertically.
Blind nailing. Usually tongue and groove patterned lumber. Drive nail at 45° angle through tongue of panel so that the nail head is hidden by overlapping groove of adjoining panel.
Face nailing. Drive nail through exposed surface (face) of lumber.

Courtesy of California Redwood Association

FIG. 8-6. Recommended nailing methods for various types of horizontal siding.

If corner boards are used, siding ends should butt snugly to the boards. Metal corner caps are sometimes used to finish off corner joints of bevel sidings.

Many boards will have to be cut to length while the siding is being installed. All freshly cut edges should receive a liberal treatment of a water-repellent preservative before the boards are nailed into place. A paintbrush will do the job but the work will go quicker if you use a small finger-activated oil can (buy one just for this purpose) to apply the water-repellent preservative to all cut edges (see Figure 8-7).

The method of finishing wood siding at exterior corners is often influenced by the overall design of the house. A mitered corner effect on horizontal sidings or the use of corner boards are perhaps the most common methods of treatment. Mitering corners of bevel and similar sidings, unless carefully done to prevent openings, is not always satisfactory. To maintain a good joint, it is necessary that the joint fit tightly the full depth of the miter. It is also good practice to treat the ends with a water-repellent preservative as outlined above.

Metal corners are perhaps the most common way to finish off an outside corner when installing horizontal siding. They are easily placed over each corner as the siding is installed. The metal corners should fit tightly without openings and be nailed on each

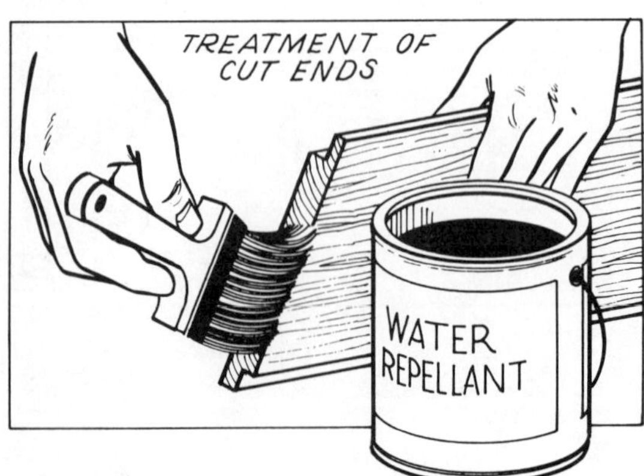

Courtesy of California Redwood Association

FIG. 8-7. Ends of boards that are cut to length while the siding is being fastened in place should also receive treatment with a water repellent.

side to the sheathing or corner stud beneath. If made of galvanized iron, they should be cleaned with a mild acid wash and primed with a metal primer before the house is painted to prevent early peeling of the paint. Weathering of the metal will also prepare it for the prime coat of paint.

Corner boards of various types and sizes may be used for all horizontal sidings. They also provide a satisfactory termination for plywood and similar sheet materials. Vertical application of matched paneling or of boards and battens (which will be covered later) are terminated by lapping one side and nailing into the edge of this member as well as to the nailing members underneath. Corner boards are usually 1⅛ or 1⅜ inch material and for a distinctive appearance might be quite narrow. Plain outside casing commonly used for window and door frames can also be adapted for corner boards (see Figure 8-8).

When siding returns against a roof surface, such as at a dormer, there should be a clearance of about 2 inches. Siding cut tight against the shingles retains moisture after rains and usually causes paint peeling at some later time. Shingle flashing extending well up on the dormer wall will provide the necessary resistance to entry of wind-driven rain. Here again, a water-repellent preservative should be used on the ends of the siding before it is installed at the roof line (see Figure 8-9).

Interior corners are butted against a square corner board of nominal 1¼ or 1⅜ inch size, depending on the thickness of the siding being installed.

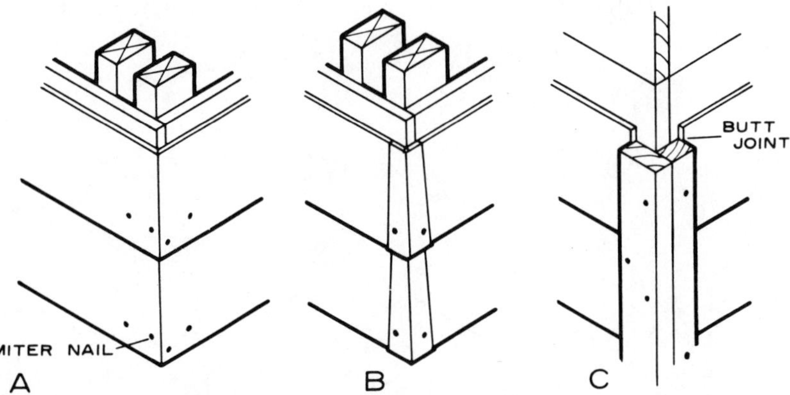

FIG. 8-8. Different outside corner treatments: (A) mitered; (B) capped; and (C) butt joined.

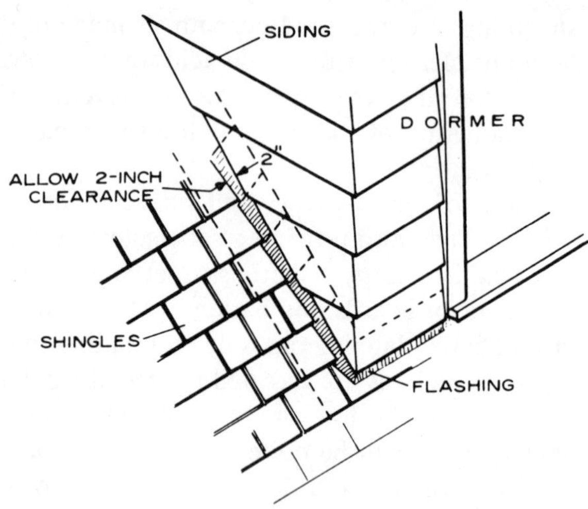

FIG. 8-9. Install metal flashing where siding meets a roof surface.

One popular method of installing wooden siding is called the board and batten method. Since the framing members run vertically, it is necessary to install blocking between the studs to serve as nailers. Blocking may be eliminated if plywood sheathing is used to cover the frame of the house (see Figure 8-10).

The first boards are attached vertically with eightpenny or ninepenny nails, driven into the sole plate, top plate, and any blocking that may have been installed. Spacing for the boards (which are commonly 8, 10 or 12 inches wide) should be about ½ to ¾ inch. Later, the battens will be installed over these spaces. Do

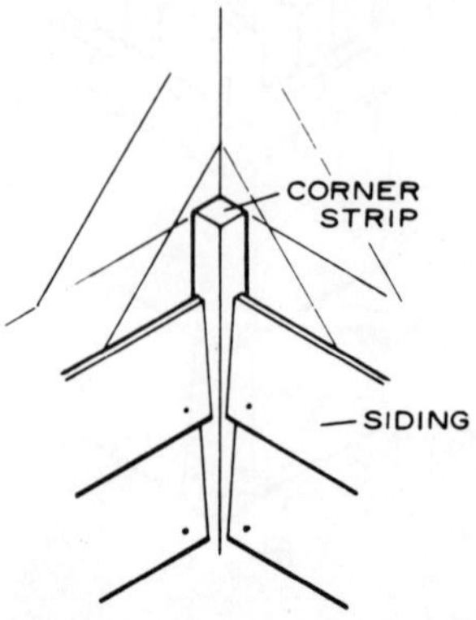

FIG. 8-10. Inside corner treatment.

not rely on sight alone to position the boards to the wall: use a level, especially on the first board. Later, boards can be positioned by using a spacer (1 × 2, for example, on edge), which is placed between the previously installed board and the board to be installed.

Nailing is important when installing board and batten siding. For boards up to 8 inches in width, drive one nail in the center of the board, at each nailing location. For boards wider than 8 inches, it is better to use two nails, spaced approximately 2 inches apart. Wider boards have a tendency to cup as they age, and double nailing seems to prevent this somewhat (see Figure 8-11).

Battens or top boards are centered over the spaces between the board below. These battens should be nailed with nails that are long enough to pass through the batten, the space between the boards, and about 1½ inches into the sheathing or blocking below. Nails of the top board or batten should always miss the under-

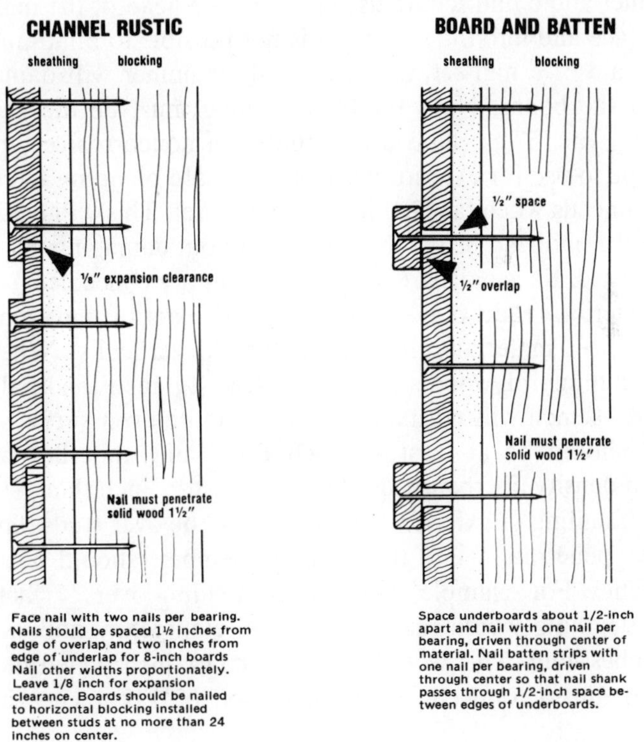

CHANNEL RUSTIC
sheathing
blocking
1/8" expansion clearance
Nail must penetrate solid wood 1½"
Face nail with two nails per bearing. Nails should be spaced 1½ inches from edge of overlap and two inches from edge of underlap for 8-inch boards Nail other widths proportionately. Leave 1/8 inch for expansion clearance. Boards should be nailed to horizontal blocking installed between studs at no more than 24 inches on center.
BOARD AND BATTEN
sheathing
blocking
½" space
½" overlap
Nail must penetrate solid wood 1½"
Space underboards about 1/2-inch apart and nail with one nail per bearing, driven through center of material. Nail batten strips with one nail per bearing, driven through center so that nail shank passes through 1/2-inch space between edges of underboards.

Courtesy of California Redwood Association

FIG. 8-11. Nailing suggestions for vertical siding (overhead view).

boards and not be nailed through them. In such applications, double nails should be spaced closely to prevent splitting if the board shrinks. It is also good building practice to use sheathing paper, such as 15-pound asphalt saturated felt, under the vertical siding.

Other types of wooden siding that may be installed vertically include square edged (which is board and batten), tongued-and-grooved, channeled and V-joint. All of these are installed in basically the same manner with variations in nailing. Some types are face nailed, as described for board and batten siding, while other types, such as tongue-and-grooved, are blind nailed. Usually boards of widths of up to 6 inches are blind nailed, while boards of wider widths (over 8 inches) are face nailed, usually with two nails at each nail location.

To blind nail, nails are driven at a 45 degree angle through the tongue of the board. After the nail has been driven almost flush, a hammer and a nail set are used to drive the head of the nail below the surface and into the tongue. It is not possible to blind nail without the aid of a nail set; the head of the hammer will damage the edge of the board. Nails for blind nailing must be the casing or finishing type. These nails are available in noncorrosive types, the only type to use for exterior work. (If you are planning to countersink nailheads when face nailing, use a nail set. This will enable you to sink the nailhead below the surface without damaging the surface of the board. Face nails are seen; blind nails are concealed.)

Exterior grade plywood, prefinished exterior sheathing, and similar sheet materials are usually applied vertically. When used over sheathing, plywood should be at least ¼ inch thick, although 5⁄16 and ⅜ inch will normally provide a more even surface. Hardboards should be at least ¼ inch thick and materials such as medium density fiberboard should be at least ½ inch thick.

All nailing of exterior plywood should be over studs, and total effective penetration into the framing members should be at least 1½ inches. For example, ⅜ inch finish siding over ¾ inch thick wood sheathing would require about an eightpenny nail, which is 2¼ inches long. This would result in a 1⅛ inch penetration into the stud, but a total effective penetration of 1⅞ inches into the wood.

Plywood should be nailed at 6-inch intervals around the perimeter and 12 inches at intermediate members. Hardboard siding should be nailed at 4 and 8 inch intervals. All types of sheet materials should have a joint caulked with mastic unless the joints are overlapping or are the matched type or if battens are installed. A strip of 15-pound asphalt saturated felt under uncaulked joints is a good alternative.

GENERAL COMMENTS

As mentioned earlier, square cuts are necessary for tight, water-resistant joints. You should use a miter box to help you achieve cuts with square edges. When you have to make a cut on a piece of plywood sheathing, it will be easier to mark the cut if you use a chalk line. Measure both ends of the sheet and then strike a chalk line between the two marks. I prefer to use a special, fine-toothed blade (designed for cutting laminated wood) for cutting plywood.

Installing siding will be much easier to accomplish if you use a level and enlist the aid of a good friend. Nailing a 16-foot-long piece of bevel siding is almost impossible for one person. Nailing the board while keeping it level is best accomplished with two people.

It is common practice to put some type of finish on all wooden exterior siding. Painting is discussed in Chapter 7; however, some helpful points will be mentioned here.

If you are installing redwood siding, the simplest and most economical treatment is no treatment at all. If redwood is allowed to weather naturally, the colors and textures of the wood will go through two stages. The first stage is a darkening of the wood. As time goes on, this darkening may be rinsed away by rain and the redwood will eventually weather-bleach to a soft, driftwood gray. These changes usually take place in a damp or humid climate. In drier climates, however, unfinished redwood may not darken. Instead, the wood will gradually turn a silvery tan, becoming lighter in color as the natural weathering continues.

Water-Repellent Finishes

The California Redwood Association recommends the use of a water repellent in favor of other natural finishes. Although this obviously will cost more than not treating the wood at all, water repellents offer very definite advantages.

A water-repellent finish will not alter the rich, natural grain and texture of redwood. One of its biggest advantages, however, is that this finish modifies the effects of weathering, eliminating the dark stages that redwood sometimes goes through. It also slows down the fading process. The wood gradually changes from its reddish-brown color to a buckskin tan, at which it will stabilize for a period of time. Areas exposed to falling water and sun may eventually bleach to the driftwood gray of naturally weathered wood.

Quality water repellents contain a mildewcide to prevent the growth of mildew. Without such protection, mildew can cause discoloration of large areas on any type of wooden siding.

Bleaches

Bleaches are another type of natural treatment for redwood siding. Next to leaving redwood unfinished, the bleaches probably come the closest to truly carefree performance. By reacting chemically with the wood, bleaches hasten redwood's natural color changes and produce a permanent driftwood gray appearance. Besides being much faster than natural weathering, bleaches provide a more uniform color and eliminate the darkening that often occurs in the early stages of redwood's weathering.

Stains

For many people the pigmented stains strike a happy balance between the color contrast offered by paints and the more natural effects of a bleach or a water repellent. Stains are flat or dull in appearance. They are a breathing type of finish, and do not form a film on the surface. Stains are available in a number of colors, ranging from various natural shades to greens, tans, charcoal browns, and blacks.

Stains are available in two basic types. Light-bodied penetrating stains do not obscure the grain characteristics of the wood but do present a uniform appearance. Heavy-bodied stains have greater hiding power, and tend to look more like paint than a natural finish. When first applied, they will obscure the grain but not the texture of the wood. The character of the wood will, however, become more noticeable as the finish weathers. (For more detailed information on paint and painting see Chapter 7, Exterior Painting.)

9

ALUMINUM AND VINYL SIDING

Improving the general appearance of the exterior of your home is one very good reason for re-siding with aluminum or vinyl siding. If your existing siding is timeworn, and painting seems to be only a temporary improvement, then you should consider covering all exterior surfaces with a finish that will last and endure. Although the cost of re-siding will be more than a paint job, you can easily expect your home to look new (from the outside) for a very long time with only a small amount of periodic maintenance. However, if you think that once you have installed new aluminum or vinyl siding you can forget about it, you are mistaken; no siding product is maintenance free. To keep your siding looking new, you must wash your home about once a year, much the same as you must wash your automobile. (More on maintenance later in this chapter.)

Protecting your investment in your home is another good reason for re-siding with aluminum or vinyl siding. Most people do not make improvements on their home in the hopes of generating income; but it is a fact that if your home is neat and fresh looking, you will be able to realize a greater price if you should ever decide to sell. Also, by re-siding your exterior walls, you will be increasing the insulation of your home, and in these times of increased heating and cooling costs, anything that improves the heat holding ability of your home is an investment that can certainly pay off with lower heating costs. At the time of this writing there is a possibility that some sort of Federal legislation is in the works that would permit a tax break for homeowners who increase the insulation in their home. The best place to check for details would be at the lumberyard or insulation dealer where you plan to purchase the materials.

Although it is true that the bulk of heat loss from a home is through the roof—heat rises—heat also escapes from the sidewalls of a home. Insulative value in a home is measured by the "resistance value" of a wall, floor, or ceiling. Resistance value depends on a combination of wall material thickness and existing insulating materials; it is commonly referred to as "R-value," and in effect means the area's ability to hold back heat or cold. To illustrate: the R-value of a common building brick wall is rated at 0.20, and the R-value of a standard (2 × 4 stud) uninsulated wall is 4.16. Adding aluminum siding, with ⅜-inch foil-backed foam insulation backer, will increase the R-value of a wall by approximately 3.00.

In older homes, built prior to World War II, chances are good that no insulation was used between the wall studs. Homes built in the 1950s were the first to have some type of insulation—generally speaking, of course. Homes built from the 1960s on have been commonly insulated with full aluminum foil-backed batt or blanket type insulation.

To be sure, there are other ways of adding insulation to exterior walls: the blown-in type is one example. Holes are drilled between the studs, high on the exterior walls, and a special insulating wool, fibrous material, or foam is blown into the wall cavity. This method is beyond the capabilities of the do-it-yourself homeowner because of the necessary investment in equipment. Also, the exterior walls must be patched after the insulation has been added.

Installing either aluminum or vinyl siding that has backer boards of foam insulation is probably the best method for the homeowner. Few tools are needed and the siding is not too difficult to install. The added benefits of having a new look while at the same time increasing the R-value of the home are appealing advantages to re-siding with aluminum or vinyl.

Although installation of aluminum siding and vinyl siding is similar, the two materials differ somewhat in characteristics. Let us examine the distinctions between the two types.

CHARACTERISTICS OF ALUMINUM SIDING

Aluminum (and steel, although less popular and not as widely used) was first used as an exterior wall covering in the 1950s. In the building industry, aluminum is synonymous with low maintenance and long life. Aluminum, by itself, however, unless anodized, is subject to pitting and other forms of unattractive oxidation. For this reason, just about all aluminum siding products have a factory applied finish. These finishes may be in the form of the common baked-on enamel or a thin coating of some plastic material. These finishes protect the aluminum and are, in fact, the sole defense between the elements and the aluminum. Quite a bit of research and development has gone into perfecting durable finishes for siding; the present offerings by the larger companies are the results of years of work by scientists. Unfortunately, even these sophisticated finishes will not last forever and are subject to chalking and fading as time goes by. Generally speaking, the more expensive the siding the more durable the finish: you pay more for a better product.

Standard thickness of aluminum siding is 0.024 gauge for flat sections over 5 inches and without any backing. Narrower widths and siding with factory attached backing is commonly 0.019 gauge. Backing, incidentally, is what gives the siding its insulative properties, for aluminum siding with no backing will do little to increase the R-value of your home.

Some aluminum siding is flat finished, as were the first types back in the 1950s. Increasing in popularity, however, are those finishes that are embossed with a grain pattern to simulate natural wood (see Figure 9-1). Many different colors are available, depending on your geographical location. Light pastel colors are most common, but darker colors are sometimes available.

Aluminum siding is most commonly attached horizontally on the exterior wall, but a few companies offer a line of aluminum siding that is attached vertically. Matching soffit coverings, inside and outside corners, window and door trim, and vents are also available. Standard panel length is 12 to 13 feet.

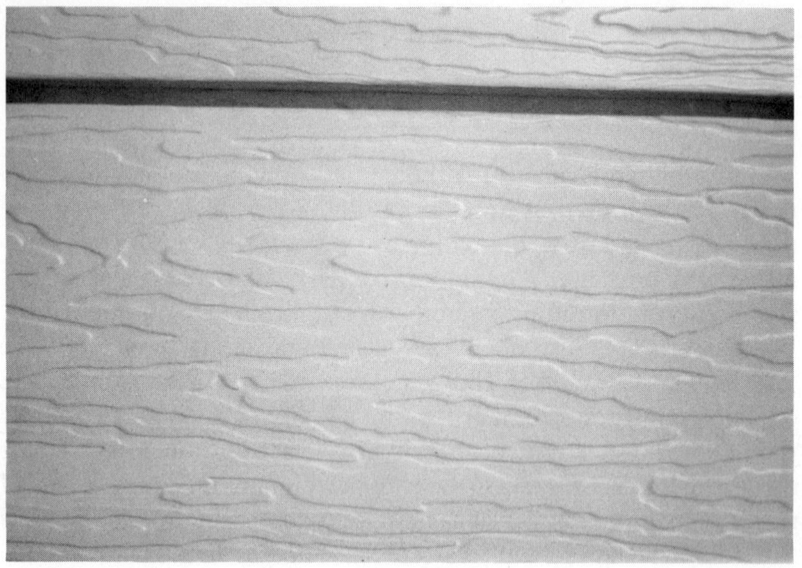

FIG. 9-1. An example of the simulated wood grain pattern available in both aluminum and vinyl siding.

CHARACTERISTICS OF VINYL SIDING

Vinyl siding is relatively new to the exterior wall-covering industry, but it has been well received, and is by now established as a viable material. Installation is similar to aluminum siding but most carpenters find it easier to work with than aluminum. Vinyl siding, as with aluminum, can be cleaned—and, in fact, should be—easily with a garden hose. Vinyl is not subject to rust, mildew, or those little accidents that can happen when installing metal siding.

Colors, although limited to fewer than about a dozen, are more appealing than the same colors in aluminum, perhaps because the color runs throughout the panel rather than being factory applied to the surface. Vinyl can be painted, however, in case you decide to change the color of your home at some time in the future.

When vinyl wall coverings were first introduced they were a bit more expensive than the same product made from aluminum. Now, however, the two are competitive in price because of the overwhelming acceptance of vinyl.

One shortcoming that has become apparent about vinyl siding could be a problem in the colder areas of the country. Vinyl becomes brittle when outside temperatures drop below freezing and is therefore likely to develop cracks when struck. Although such a problem is possible, vinyl (and aluminum) siding is easier to repair than, say, wooden siding. A special hooked tool is used to remove the damaged panel and then a new panel is installed.

Aluminum siding and vinyl siding are about the same in many respects: price, installation techniques, maintenance, and durability. Before you decide which type you want on the outside of your home you should investigate both types made by several different manufacturers. From talking to salespersons and even contractors, you will quickly become aware of the benefits of the two different types of siding. After all, salespeople are in business to sell, so they may not point out the disadvantages or shortcomings of their product. By talking to several different manufacturers' representatives you can get a clearer picture of what is available, how easy (or hard) it is to install, and how long you can reasonably expect the siding to maintain its new look. Once you have all the relevant information, make your final purchase decision: aluminum or vinyl.

SURFACE PREPARATION

As with any remodeling project, the finished results can only be as good as the surface preparation—this holds as true for painting as for re-siding with aluminum or vinyl. Needless to say, the condition of the outside of your home will determine the extent of surface preparation. Before you can expect to obtain professional looking results, you must have a surface that is as square as possible, free of rot or mildew, and in sound condition.

Before a professional re-sider begins installing new siding, he will go over the entire house and nail down any loose existing siding. He will also nail down any cupped or warped siding unless it is very bad, in which case he will remove the culprit and replace with some replacement material. Any unevenness must be corrected as much as possible. Depressions will be filled, if they are great, and boards that are bulging will be cut in the center and nailed back to a level position. Shims (using cedar shingles) may be used to raise depressed areas as well.

In some cases when the existing siding is excessively bowed, warped, and out of alignment, the only solution is to apply furring strips vertically over the entire house. This is almost standard practice when the existing siding is cedar shingles or beveled siding. The furring strips (1 × 2″ lumber) are attached, spaced about 16 inches apart on unbroken walls, around the four sides of windows and three sides of door frames. Occasionally, the attachment of furring strips around window and door frames can present a problem because the existing window or door frame is not of sufficient projection to overhang the siding when it is installed. The common solution for this problem is to attach furring strips to the frame of the window or door itself and then cover these with specially designed window and door frame caps. Most of the larger aluminum and vinyl manufacturers produce this cap material.

You may also have to attach some sort of blocking where the sidewalls join the overhang of the roof. All of this preparatory work should be completed before you begin installing the horizontal panels of siding.

If you are planning to cover the facia, soffit, and eaves of the house, this work should be done before the sidewall siding is attached. After all of the existing siding has been nailed down, shimmed out, or furring strips have been installed, and after all of the window, door frames, facia, soffit, and eaves have been covered with cap you can begin installing the full lengths of siding to the house.

INSTALLATION

Although it is not possible to give specific details for re-siding with either aluminum or vinyl siding, general comments can be made. Each manufacturer produces a line of siding that is similar to all of the other makers' offerings. But slight differences do occur, and therefore directions for installation are slightly different. Some manufacturers, for example, recommend that the sidewalls of the house be covered first with perforated aluminum faced paper before the siding is installed, while other makers do not. Nevertheless, enough similarities do exist to give the basic installation procedures for all types of aluminum and vinyl siding.

After all of the walls of the house have been gone over and made as flat and sound as possible, or after furring strips have been attached over the sidewalls, you can begin the job of re-siding by covering the facia, soffit, and eaves with special trim. The most common material for covering these areas is aluminum, even when the house will receive a new siding made of vinyl.

Several different variations are possible for covering the facia of a house. Some of the materials available have special slots or channels that will enable you to cover the eaves at the same time. These are commonly referred to as hook bottom, "J" channel, and "F" channel.

Begin by attaching undersill trim to the top of the facia board, all around the house. This undersill trim should be attached at the uppermost edge of the facia and nailed into place. Later, the facia cover will be pushed up and locked into place. First, however, the soffit is covered with aluminum panels (see Figure 9-2), cut at the site to fit over the existing soffit. After all of the soffit has been covered with the new material, the facia is installed (see Figure 9-3).

FIG. 9-2. First the soffit area is covered with special ventilating panels. Then the facia is covered with facia covering.

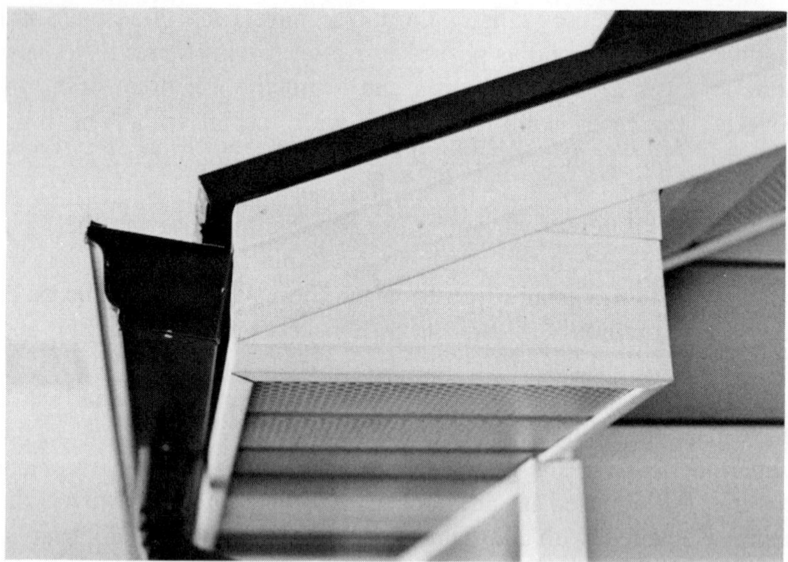

FIG. 9-3. Finished soffit, facia, and gable end, with gutter installed.

After the soffit and facia have been covered, you can begin installing "J" channel around window and door frames. Later, as you attach the siding to the sidewalls, the edges of the siding will fit and interlock into this window trim (see Figure 9-4).

FIG. 9-4. Special window and door trim is installed first and serves as a neat finish for the edges of panels.

Before you can actually begin installing the siding, you must strike a level chalk line around the entire bottom edge of the existing siding. This chalk line will be your guide for nailing the starter strip around the house.

One person can begin installing the panels on the sidewall but the work will be much easier if two workers are present. The first panel's bottom edge is interlocked with the bottom strip and the top of the first panel is nailed into place. Nails should be driven through the slots along the top edge of the panel, but should not be driven so the top edge of the panel is damaged. The top edge of the first panel (and succeeding panels) is where the second panel's bottom edge interlocks. Some contractors like to complete one wall of the house at a time, and this makes a lot of sense since all of the materials are close at hand (see Figure 9-5).

FIG. 9-5. Side view of a typical aluminum panel showing how the panels interlock. Note, also, insulation material on panel back.

After it has been cut, the top edge of the siding will fit into, and interlock with, the "J" channel around the bottom and sides of windows. The edge of the panel should not fit so tight that it must be forced into place. Seasonal changes in temperature will have an effect on the paneling; you should install the panels at joints so there is a little room for expansion and contraction.

Panels will obviously have to be cut. This is best accomplished with a pair of heavy-duty sheet metal shears. With cutting, the old carpenter's rule of "measure twice—cut once" will prove useful.

As the courses of siding rise up to the level of the rake you will have to make diagonal cuts. A tool called a sliding "T" bevel will help you to obtain the exact angle. A sliding "T" bevel is a tool with a rotating blade attached to a handle. The blade is laid against the angle and the handle is positioned so that the angle is duplicated. The blade and handle are then locked in this position with a set screw, and the angle is transferred to the sliding strip.

When you get to the peak of the house, the last panel is attached in the same manner as panels under windows—into "J" channels. The job progresses in this fashion until all sides of the house have been covered with the siding. Then corner caps are slid into place at all outside corners. The alternative is to use prefabricated corner posts, available for both inside and outside corners (see Figures 9-6 and 9-7).

If you work carefully, with some help, you should be able to completely re-side an average sized house in a few days.

MAINTENANCE

Periodic maintenance of the exterior of your home should be a standard practice, in the spring and then again in the fall. You should wash the siding with a strong stream of water from a garden hose. If stubborn spots or blemishes will not come off with the hose, you can try a mild solution of powdered automobile wash. Use a soft cloth and wipe the area, then spray with the garden hose. Strong detergents and abrasive cleaners should not be used because they will dull vinyl and possibly take the finish off aluminum sidings. Cleaning the siding can be part of periodic exterior maintenance, which should include checking the roof surfaces, cleaning

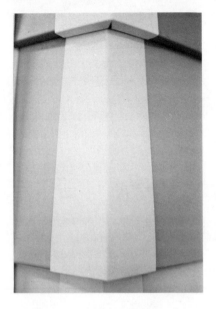

FIG. 9-6. An example of corner caps, which are slipped in between the panels to finish off outside corners.

FIG. 9-7. An example of prefabricated corner posts. Posts are installed first, then edges of the panels are fit into place.

gutters and downspouts, caulking, and selective pruning. All of these little tasks will go a long way to increasing the life of the exterior of your home.

10

SHINGLE SIDING

Many American homes have shingle siding in one form or another. The three types of shingle siding are asbestos, asphalt, and cedar shingles and handsplit shakes. Although installation is basically the same for all three, each has its own qualities and differs slightly from the others. For example, an exterior wall covered with asphalt shingles will endure for years but is more functional than aesthetically pleasing. On the other hand, an exterior wall covered with cedar shingles will also last for years, without any maintenance, and is also quite attractive (see Figure 10-1); however, cedar costs easily twice as much as asphalt.

So, the choice of an exterior wall covering is governed, in part, by the amount of money you can spend. The three types of shingle siding covered in this chapter range in price from modest to expensive.

ASBESTOS SHINGLES

Asbestos shingles probably cover more exterior sidewalls than any other type of shingle, probably because asbestos shingles are a relatively inexpensive finish wall covering. Asbestos shingles will last indefinitely with no maintenance. They are very brittle and

Courtesy of Red Cedar Shingle and Handsplit Shake Bureau

FIG. 10-1. Cedar shingles provide durability, superior insulation value, natural beauty, and are easy to install.

porous, two facts that make asbestos shingles slightly tricky to work with, and can cause the house to be on the damp side.

Because of their brittleness, asbestos shingles damage easily; care must be taken in their handling and storage. Even after they are installed on an exterior wall, asbestos shingles can be damaged easily. Anyone who as a child has thrown a ball against a house covered with asbestos siding knows just how easily these shingles can be broken.

Asbestos shingles are porous, which means that when they get wet, from rain or melting snow, the shingle is just as wet on the back, or wall side, as on the finish or exterior wall side. The fact that saturated asphalt felt paper is attached to the wall surface before the shingles are applied does not materially alter the passage of moisture into the house. This results in a humid house in damp weather. In addition, this porosity also causes a house to lose heat during the heating season as warm air escapes easily through asbestos shingles.

There are ways, to be sure, to prevent heat loss from inside and moisture passage from the outside: vapor barriers are the best.

Vapor barriers are discussed in detail in Chapter 12. You should understand vapor barriers and how they work before attempting any type of exterior siding.

Asbestos shingles are available in several different factory applied colors and finishes. Butts are straight or wavy and surfaces may be smooth or textured. The standard height is 12 inches and lengths range from 16 to 24 inches, the most popular size being 12 by 24 inches. Thicknesses range from $\frac{5}{32}$ to $\frac{3}{16}$ of an inch with the latter being the most commonly used.

Asbestos shingles are attached to an exterior wall with nails. Shingle nails the same color as the shingle itself are sold with the shingles; usually the price of the nails is included in the selling price of the shingle. Three nail holes are predrilled in each shingle, 1 inch up from the bottom and evenly spaced.

ASPHALT SIDING

Asphalt sidings, while not necessarily aesthetically pleasing, are a very durable exterior finish covering. There are two basic types: roll and shingle. You may notice a similarity here between asphalt siding and shingles for roofs; in fact, they are installed in almost the same manner. Roll siding generally resembles brick or stone, having a pattern embossed on the surface. Roll siding is made of heavy felt saturated with asphalt, and with crushed slate embedded in the surface. Color choices are limited; the most popular is a reddish brown that resembles red brick (from a distance).

Asphalt siding is also available in shingle form, and is attached in much the same manner as conventional roofing shingle. In some parts of the country, it is not uncommon for contractors to use roofing shingles for sidewall application. On a house with a gambrel roof, for example, roofing shingles are applied to the roof and continued down the sides of the building. In this case the roof is actually part of the long sides of the house.

CEDAR SHINGLES

The last type of shingle siding is red cedar shingle or handsplit cedar shakes. By far the most attractive exterior shingle siding, it is also about the most expensive. Shingles or shakes are installed on a sidewall in very much the same manner as they are installed on a roof. The main difference is the exposure spacing for the shingles, which can usually be greater for sidewall application. Chapter 2, Cedar Shingles and Handsplit Shakes, covers the various types of shingles and shakes used for roofing. Generally speaking, cedar shingles are the same as for roof application. In addition, machine-grooved shakes are available which are manufactured from shingles and have striated faced and parallel edges. Actually, there is a wider selection of shingles and shakes when used for sidewall application. Grading requirements for sidewall installation of shingles and shakes are not as stringent as those required for a roof. In fact, all but a very few of the entire western red cedar shingle and handsplit shake family can be used on sidewalls. In each case the flexibility of shingles and shakes is clearly demonstrated. Unlimited by dimension, they may be applied on flat as well as curved surfaces. Design possibilities are nearly unlimited, not to mention a natural color variation which ranges from the lighter straw colors to the darker coffee (see Figure 10-2).

Differing surface textures (from the rugged shakes through the striated machine-grooved shake to the clean-lined, smooth shingle) offer a further choice in design approaches. A variety of application effects are also possible, such as staggering the butt lines or double coursing for deep shadow lines.

Estimating the quantity of any of the three types of shingles needed to cover sidewalls is similar. You must determine the total square footage of the sidewalls. If you stick with the standard exposure distances for each type of shingle, there should be no problem determining the required number of shingles necessary to do the job. If, however, you plan to increase the exposure, which can only be done with cedar shingles, then you will have to make allowances. In most cases this will mean that fewer cedar shingles will be required. It is always best to stay with the recommended exposure distance, however.

INSTALLING ASBESTOS SHINGLES

You should apply asbestos shingles only to a smooth, dry, and flat surface. Conventional exterior wall sheathing, such as ply-

Courtesy of Red Cedar Shingle and Handsplit Shake Bureau

FIG. 10-2. Cedar shingles look good on any sidewall, either in their natural color or painted.

wood, siding boards, or insulation board, are all suitable provided that they meet these requirements and have good nail holding ability. The nails you use to attach asbestos siding must be long enough to pass through the siding and well into the sheathing underneath. If the exterior sheathing has poor nail holding power, you should install nailing strips (1 × 2 inch or 1 × 3 inch furring strips) and attach the shingles to these rather than directly to the sidewall.

Because of the porosity of asbestos shingles, it is necessary to protect the sheathing from moisture. This is most commonly accomplished by first covering the exterior wall with asphalt saturated paper. Lengths of the paper run horizontally starting at the bottom and overlapping succeeding lengths. Fasten the paper with staples, simply to hold it in place. The bottom edge of the paper should lie about ¼ inch below the sheathing, and will be covered with the first course of shingles.

After the felt paper has been attached, fasten metal corner edging to all outside corners. "Bull-Nose" metal corner, as it is commonly called, has an interior groove into which the edges of the asbestos shingles slip. This metal corner is available in standard lengths and is one of the best ways to finish off corners on a wall. You can also attach metal drip edge or cap flashing over every window and door top.

Next, strike chalk lines 12 inches up from the bottom of the sheathing, which also should be the bottom of the felt paper and metal corner. This line will be your guide for the top edge of the first row of shingles. Starting at one end of the house, the first shingle is installed with one edge in the metal corner and the top aligned with the chalk line. Drive two nails through the two holes closest to the metal edging and before driving the third nail, slip an asphalt tab under the shingle so it is centered on the exposed end. The tab is simply a piece of saturated felt (usually 3 × 12 inches) and is used as added protection from water under all vertical joints.

The second asbestos shingle is butted against the first, aligned with the chalk line and nailed into place, again inserting a tab before the third nail is driven through the shingle. Continue attaching the shingle across the wall, butting each against the previous shingle, and maintaining alignment with the chalk line. Don't forget to insert a tab under each joint before nailing. When you finally get to within one shingle distance from the metal corner, you will probably have to cut that shingle for a proper fit.

Because of their brittleness, asbestos shingles are tricky to cut. The best way to cut a shingle is with the aid of a special tool known as an asbestos shingle cutter. The lumberyard or home improvement center that sold you the shingles will probably lend or rent one of these cutters to you. A second way to cut asbestos shingles is with a composition blade (used for cutting concrete block) in a handheld circular saw. The third way (and the poorest) to cut is with a saber saw using a special blade. Whenever you are cutting asbestos shingles, you should do the cutting outside and avoid breathing the dust, which is dangerous to your respiratory system.

I recommend that you borrow or rent a levery type shingle cutter. It will do the job and there is little worry about hurting yourself. To make the cut, place the marked shingle under the blade of the cutter and push down on the lever. The top jaw will press down on the lower jaw and make the cut.

Fit this last cut piece of shingle between the metal corner and the last shingle installed. Nail it into place and the first course is complete.

The second course of shingles will overlap the first by 1 inch. As luck would have it, the nail holes along the bottom of each shingle are 1 inch up from the edge. This makes aligning the second and succeeding courses easy; nails are inserted in these holes and the shingle is slid down until the nail shafts just touch the tops of the previous row; then it is nailed into place. Start the second row of shingles with a half shingle, then use full shingles until you reach the end of the wall. Remember to slip a tab half-way under the exposed edge of each shingle before driving the last nail. The second and succeeding courses of shingles are finished off the same as the first course.

Continue attaching rows of asbestos shingles until you are within one shingle width of the top of the wall. The top edge of this last row is covered with molding. The molding has a dual function: to secure the last row of shingles to the wall and to close the gap between the wall and soffit. The top molding should be nailed to the 2 × 4 inch nailer above the soffit and not through the shingle, as it will surely crack.

INSTALLING ASPHALT SIDING

Roll asphalt siding is very similar to roll asphalt roofing, and is installed in much the same manner. Roll asphalt sidings can be applied to any clean, flat, and dry exterior surface. *Flat* is the key when covering over old siding materials. If old walls have a covering of asphalt siding, for example, that has deteriorated over the years, this should be removed before you begin installing the new asphalt siding. The results of a new siding job are limited by the surface on which the new siding will be installed. In some cases it may be necessary to attach sheets of plywood over the sidewalls of the house to obtain a flat surface. This could amount to more time and money than you are willing to spend, as asphalt siding is supposed to be an economical type of exterior wall covering.

Before you begin to snap chalk lines around the house, you should unroll the siding into lengths of 12 to 18 feet. Next, lay these strips in a pile, on a smooth surface. This will help the asphalt to soften slightly and flatten out, making the material easier to work with. You should not work with this type of siding if the outside temperature is below 5°C. because at lower temperatures asphalt tends to become brittle. If you must work at these lower temperatures, you should store the siding in a warm place before unrolling to avoid cracking or splitting the mineral coating.

Strike chalk lines horizontally around the building at a distance above the lowest point, equal to ¼ inch less than the width of the siding material. If necessary, additional horizontal and vertical lines can be struck to ensure proper alignment of later courses. If the building is badly out of line—at the corners, for example—you may have to make other adjustments.

Attach the first strip of asphalt siding to the sidewall so that the top edge of the sheet is aligned with the chalk line. Nail the strip along the top edge with enough nails to hold it in place. The work will be much easier to accomplish if you have a helper to hold up one end of the strip while you nail towards him.

After you have driven enough nails to hold the strip in place, you can face nail it in place along the bottom. Nails should be driven in a straight horizontal line, approximately ½ inch up from the bottom edge, and spaced about 4 inches apart.

Use noncorrodible nails with checkered or smooth heads (0.025 inches in diameter) and long enough to penetrate at least ¾ inch into the wall surface or sheathing underneath. Nailheads should be colored to match the siding material being installed. This usually means black-headed nails for all mortar joints and other appropriate color nails for face nailing (that is, red for brick and gray for stone pattern).

The second strip (as well as succeeding courses) is attached to the sidewall so that the bottom edge overlaps the top of the first sheet by the amount of the selvage edge less the width of one mortar joint. This overlap should be about 4 inches. The second strip is secured in the same manner as the first; nails are driven along the top edge to hold the strip in place and then the strip is face nailed along the bottom, ½ inch up and with nails spaced approximately 4 inches apart. Succeeding courses are installed in the same manner (see Figure 10-3).

Treatment for end joints is similar to that used for rolled roofing. Adjoining edges of two strips are cut at right angles in such a way as to ensure continuity of the pattern. Some professionals will cut brick pattern asphalt siding so that no brick is cut in half, but instead will interlock with the adjoining strip.

A flashing strip is necessary for all end joints. The most common treatment is to use a 6-inch strip of no. 15 asphalt saturated felt paper as long as the height of the course. The flashing should extend from the selvage edge of the lower course down to the bottom of that lower strip. The strip of flashing is embedded in a suitable asphalt cement before being nailed into position. It is important that the flashing strip be centered so that adjoining edges of the strips in the joint will meet over the flashing.

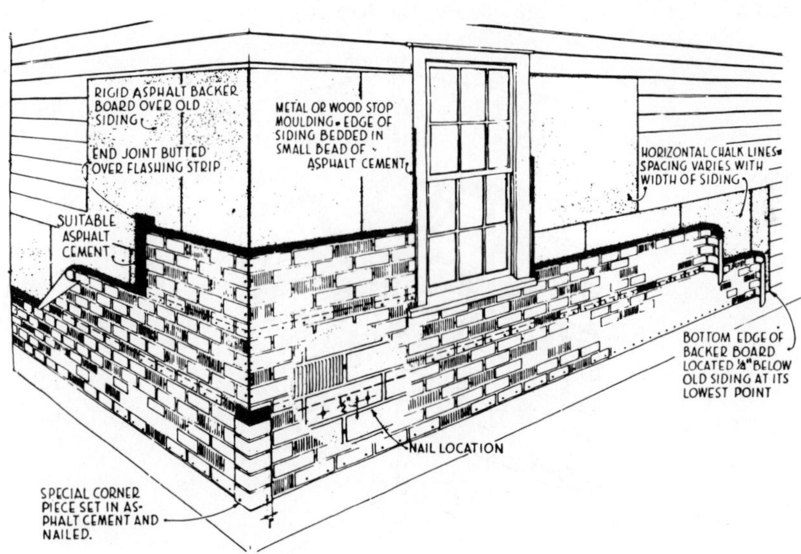

Courtesy of Asphalt Roofing Manufacturers Association

FIG. 10-3. Application of asphalt roll brick siding shows corner trim, end joint nailing, and general nailing details.

Outside corners are treated in several different manners, depending on your location. In high wind areas, for example, the edge of the strip that ends at a corner is attached over no. 15 asphalt cement. Then after both sides of the corners have been covered with asphalt siding a cap of rolled siding (made especially for outside corners) is installed over the joint. In areas where winds are rarely a problem, the asphalt cement is often omitted.

Inside corners are usually covered first with a 12-inch-wide strip of felt paper, and then coated with asphalt cement. When a strip ends at an inside corner it is embedded in the asphalt cement and nailed into place (see Figure 10-4).

Nails for both inside and outside corners are driven approximately ½ inch in from the edge and spaced 4 inches apart in a straight, vertical line.

The last strip of asphalt siding should end at the edge of the top of the wall. It is common practice to embed this last strip's top edge in a bead of asphalt cement. It is also common practice to protect this top edge from the weather, which is best accomplished by nailing wood molding or special metal stop (manufactured specially for the top edge) along the top edge.

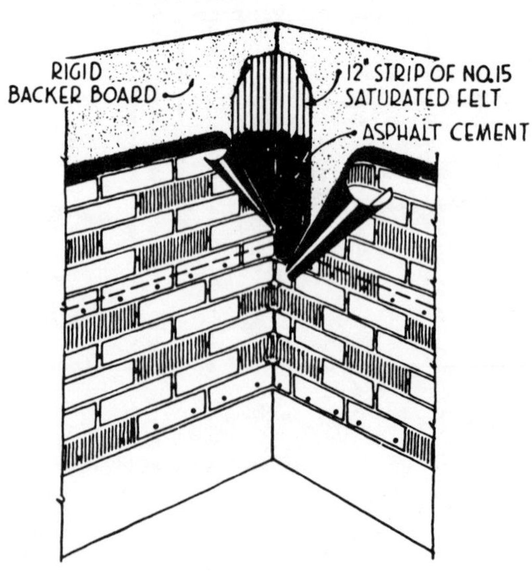

Courtesy of Asphalt Roofing Manufacturers Association

FIG. 10-4. Inside corner detail with asphalt roll brick siding.

To ensure that the asphalt siding remains flush against the sidewall, many professionals, in addition to nailing along the top and bottom edges of the siding, will drive nails into every vertical joint. Of course, the proper color nailheads should be used for this type of nailing. You should avoid driving the nails too tightly. Overdriven nails have a tendency to cause the siding to look as if it were quilted.

When the trim around window and door frames protrudes beyond the face of the wall surface, the siding is cut to fit up to and around the edge. The siding is then embedded in a narrow bead of asphalt cement before being nailed.

When the wood trim around the opening is flush with the siding, either a narrow wood molding or special metal stop is applied to the trim 1 inch from its edge. Then the siding is butted snugly against it. Before nailing the strip to the wall surface, it is embedded in a bead of asphalt cement.

INSTALLING CEDAR SHINGLES AND SHAKES

Surely one of the most attractive and durable types of exterior siding is red cedar shingles or handsplit shakes. These shingles are easy to install and require practically no maintenance. If left in their natural state, cedar shingles will mellow with age.

Cedar shingles are installed in much the same manner on a sidewall as on a roof, except that the exposure can be greater. Exposure is determined by the length of the shingle being installed. In single coursing, for example, the exposure must not be less than one-half the shingle length minus ½ inch. This exposure will ensure that there are at least two layers of shingles over the entire wall surface. Recommended exposures are 8½ inch for 18-inch shakes and 11½ inches for the 24-inch shake.

Most cedar shingles that are used for sidewalls are 18 inches long and from 2 to 12 inches wide. The Red Cedar Shingle and Handsplit Shake Bureau recommends that you use only the No. 1 grade shingle or shake for sidewalls.

Cedar shingles may be attached to any clean, dry, and smooth exterior wall. Again, as with other types of shingle siding, you may have to do a certain amount of work to prepare your sidewalls adequately. Cedar shingles are commonly attached to a sidewall in two ways: single and double coursing. The layout of both methods is basically the same, the major difference being that double coursing simply means that each course is two shingles thick.

The first step is to determine the number of courses you will be attaching to the sidewall. This will be based on the distance from the soffit to a point approximately 2 inches below the top of the foundation of the house. This height is divided into an equal number of parts depending, of course, on the recommended exposure for the shingles you are installing. You should make adjustments so that they will line up evenly with the bottom and top of principal windows as well as under the eaves.

The next step is to mark off the course locations. Some professionals simply mark every corner with a suitable mark to indicate the bottom of each course. Other builders use what is commonly known as a *story pole*. This is merely a straight piece of 1 × 4 or similar lumber, the same height as the wall. On this story pole are transferred the course bottom edge location. One unique feature about a story pole is that you can use it anywhere to check course location.

After the course locations have been determined, and adjusted for windows and door frames, you should cover the sidewall with building paper. Sheets are attached with staples horizontally around the building. Start at the bottom and overlap each succeeding course by about 3 to 4 inches. Next, using the story pole, indicate the bottom of the first course and strike a chalk line to help with alignment of the shingles.

The next step will be determined by how you plan to treat the corners of the building. Basically, there are two ways: you can attach corner boards (1 × 4 inch boards attached vertically) or you can have shingle corners. If the corner boards will be used to finish off the corners, you should install them before attaching the shingles. If shingle corners are to be used, you should know that there are two types; woven (as shown in Figure 10-5), where alternating courses extend, and mitered, where the edges of each corner shingle are cut on a bevel so it interlocks with the shingle of the course around the corner. Probably the easiest method is to use corner boards, much the same as was used in bevel siding (Chapter 8, "Wooden Siding") as shown in Figure 10-6.

Attach the first shingle to the wall so that one edge is against the corner board and the bottom edge lies along the chalk line.

Courtesy of Red Cedar Shingle and Handsplit Shake Bureau

FIG. 10-5. Corner treatment using red cedar shingles. Note how course edges are alternated. These are called "woven" outside corners.

Courtesy of Red Cedar Shingle and Handsplit Shake Bureau

FIG. 10-6. The easiest corner treatment is to use corner boards. The shingles are attached up to the edges of these boards.

Nail the shingle into place with two nails, spaced approximately 1 inch up from the bottom edge. If the shingle is more than 6 inches wide you can use three nails; if it is very wide you may have to use four nails to hold it in place. Install the remainder of the shingles to finish the same first course, ending at the corner board at the other end of the wall. Next, install the second course with the proper exposure.

When installing the second and succeeding courses, I have found that a chalk line (as an alignment aide) is not the best way to ensure straight lines. A much better way is to tack lightly a straight piece of 1 × 2 or 1 × 4 to the side wall so that its top edge indicates the bottom edge of the course being installed. Then, shingles are installed so that one edge butts against the previously installed shingle and the bottom edge of the shingle rests on the top of the straight edge. This method results in straight and true courses every time (see Figure 10-7).

Courtesy of Red Cedar Shingle and Handsplit Shake Bureau

FIG. 10-7. Use a bottom edge guide to help you get straight courses.

If you are installing cedar shingles so that the corners will have mitered or woven corners (the most common but not the easiest method) you should begin differently from the way explained above for corner boards. Here, the first shingle on both sides of the corner are either mitered or cut so they will overlap. They are nailed into place, and then the second course is attached, with the proper exposure. Succeeding course corner shingles are then installed until you reach the top. Then the courses, beginning with the first, are installed. In effect what we are doing here is finishing the corners first, and then installing the row shingles. This is the best way to ensure that the corners will be correct (see Figure 10-8).

Inside corner treatment is the same, regardless of the treatment for outside corners. For inside corners, fit a piece of lumber strip approximately 1½ inch square into the corner first. Then shingles are fit into the corner as each course ends. For the sake of appearance, you should stain the inside corner strip before installing.

Metal flashing should be attached over all window, door, or other openings before the cedar shingles are attached. This will ensure a watertight seal over the opening.

Courtesy of Red Cedar Shingle and Handsplit Shake Bureau

FIG. 10-8. Straight courses and woven corners are pleasing to look at.

As you attach the shingles to the sidewall, you should strive to accomplish three things:

1. All joints between shingle edges should be tight; trim where necessary to ensure this.
2. The bottoms of the shingles in each course should be on a straight line. Use a straightedge rather than a chalk line for the truest lines.
3. There should never be any vertical joints that run from one course to the next. Ideally, there should be at least 1 inch distance between all vertical joints.

If you have to cut cedar shingles, as you surely will have to, you will find that most vertical cutting can be easily accomplished with a sharp utility knife. Make horizontal cuts with a saber saw. You will also find that a small block plane will be the best way to square off the edges of shingles that are a little out. Fit shingles around window and door frames by first marking the shingle and then cutting with the saber saw.

After all the courses of shingles have been installed, you will have to finish off the top course. The two common ways are molding and shingles. Both are installed horizontally along the top edge of the last course and are, in effect, a finish between the last course and the soffit. Molding can be either ¼ round (¾ to 1 inch wide) or 1 × 2 or 1 × 4 inch lumber. (Personally, I think that a finish of shingles installed horizontally is the most attractive.)

As mentioned earlier, cedar shingles will not deteriorate if left as is; they will turn color, however. Usually cedar shingles will turn very dark when not in the direct rays of the sun (the north side of the house, for example) and silver-gray when on a side that is in direct sun (south side). These color changes may not always happen, especially in the more arid parts of the country, but they frequently do.

If you prefer to have all sides of the house the same shade of cedar color, it would be best to give the shingles a coat of some type of preservative. This will keep the cedar looking uniform all around the house. You will, however, have to recoat the shingles every three years or so.

11

BRICK, STONE, AND STUCCO

Masonry exterior sidewalls endure. Brick, stone, and the bonding agent cement offer advantages that can be found in no other building material. They are fireproof, rustproof, and unaffected by the sun, pests (insects, for example), or air pollutants. Masonry walls are permanent and exceptionally strong. Once properly constructed a masonry wall will require almost no maintenance and will last a lifetime. Thousands of homes all over the country are living proof of the ability of these materials to stand the test of time.

Yet, in spite of all of the advantages of masonry walls, most people shy away from this type of building material because of the assumption that it is very hard work, requiring years of apprenticeship. Although it is true that some aspects of masonry work are real work—a bag of cement weighs 94 pounds, for example—most other building work is equally hard; a bundle of roofing shingles weighs about 80 pounds, and has to be carried up onto a roof before installation. Since most of the work with brick, stone, and cement takes place on the ground, it is no more difficult than framing a house, for example. Also there are many different types of tools that are work savers; a wheelbarrow is one example. Common sense and planning are other work savers.

Experience is one thing that you probably will not have when you begin working with cement. This can only come after you have spent years working with these materials. But a conscientious approach, a well thought out work plan, patience, and careful work can help overcome a lack of experience. In fact, these requirements are necessary for any type of construction, whether masonry or wood. A thorough discussion of brick, stone, and cement work would easily fill the pages of this book and, therefore, is not possible in this chapter. What I hope to accomplish, however, is to give you some basic information for working with these materials. If the reader is planning to do more than make relatively simple repairs to existing stonework, it would be to your advantage to seek out more detailed information from other sources. In this short chapter I can only hope to lay some of the groundwork, but enough, I hope, to enable you to handle your own repairs and maintenance.

CEMENT

Portland cement is a mixture of raw materials that are finely ground, proportioned, and calcined to the fusion temperature (approximately 1500°C.) to give the desired chemical composition. The clinker resulting from calcination is then finely pulverized. When combined with water, these cements undergo a chemical reaction and harden to form a stone-like mass. This reaction is called *hydration* and these cements are termed *hydraulic cements*.

The raw materials used in the manufacture of portland cements include limestone, cement rock, oyster shells, coquina shell, marl, clay, shale, silica, sand, and iron ore. These materials are blended, pulverized, heated to extreme temperatures, and then pulverized again. The resulting product is called portland cement and it is the bonding agent for all types of masonry work.

There are several different types of portland cement manufactured to meet certain physical and chemical requirements. Normal portland cement is a general purpose type that is commonly available at lumberyards or other home improvement centers across the country. It is suitable for all types of construction where special requirements do not have to be met (for example, high heat resistance).

Portland cement will store indefinitely if it is kept dry. Contact with moisture, while still in the sack, will cause the cement to set up slower and with less strength. Therefore, cement should be stored indoors (in the garage, for example) and covered with some type of waterproof covering, such as plastic sheets. If before opening a bag of cement you feel lumps, try rolling the sack over a hard surface to break up these lumps. If the lumps cannot be broken up in this manner the cement should be returned to the seller for an exchange. Hard lumps indicate partial hydration, which will reduce the strength and durability of the cement.

When sand and water (in specified proportions) are added to portland cement, mortar or grout is formed. Mortar is used as a bonding agent for blocks, bricks, and stone. If, in addition to the sand and water, gravel or crushed stone are added, the mixture is commonly called concrete. If hydrated lime or asbestos fibers are added to the mortar mix it is transformed into the veneering material known as stucco.

Cement is also sold, under several brand names, premixed. That is, it contains portland cement, lime, sand, small stones, and even color. With these ready-mixed cements you simply add water and mix. Although the price of these premixed cements tends to be higher than plain portland cement, you will find it worthwhile for small jobs. Premixed cements are commonly available in 5, 10, 25, and 80 pound bags.

Mixing Cement

Mixing up a batch of cement, whether for patching a small crack or laying a brick wall, must be done according to some formula or recipe. There are two recipes for cement that have been worked out, and will be suitable for most types of masonry work. The first is commonly referred to as the 1:1:6 mix. The numbers here refer to the ratio of portland cement, lime, and sand in the mixture. The ratio remains the same whether you are mixing small or large batches. To illustrate: if you wanted to make a batch of portland cement that would fill a space of 1 cubic foot, you would use 1¼ gallons of portland cement, 1¼ gallons hydrated lime, and 7½ gallons of dry sand. Water, of course, must also be added and it generally takes about 4 to 5 gallons for a cubic foot of cement.

The easiest way to get consistent measurements is to use a pail (marked with gallon levels) for measuring and adding the ingredients.

Another cement mixture, using portland cement with lime already added at the factory, is commonly called the 1:3 mix. Here one part masonry cement to three parts sand will produce (when water is added) a mixture suitable for most masonry purposes.

It might be helpful, at this point, to describe how to mix a batch of cement. To begin with, all of the materials should be close at hand: bags of cement, sand (lime, if required), and clean water. If you are only making a small batch you can mix the materials on a piece of plywood or other suitable surface. If a larger batch is being mixed, you will find it easier to use a wheelbarrow, or possibly you should consider renting a cement mixer (see Figures 11-1 and 11-2).

Measure proportionate amounts of cement and sand, then put them in the mixing place (either the ground or mixer). Next, mix these ingredients until they are uniform and dry. Then make a depression in the center of the mixture and pour in about half of the water you think you will need (remember that about four to five gallons of water will be needed for each cubic foot of cement).

FIG. 11-1. Mix small batches of cement on a wooden platform or sheet of plywood.

FIG. 11-2. A cement mixer will prove a real time saver when mixing large quantities of cement.

Using a hoe, pull the dry ingredients into the puddle of water and continue mixing until the batch is of uniform consistency. You will probably have to add more water to the batch as you mix, and it becomes thick. If the mixture appears too thin and watery, add more of the sand and cement in proper proportions.

After you have thoroughly mixed the ingredients and you feel that the mixture is about right for the type of work you will be doing, test the mixture by pulling the hoe through the mixture and making a trough or furrow. If the sides of this furrow stand about where they were when you first drew the hoe across, and the mixture shakes freely off the hoe, then the mixture is about right. But if the sides of the furrow run down into the mass of cement, the mixture is too wet, and you will have to mix in more ingredients. If the mortar does not shake freely off the hoe, the mixture is too dry and you will have to add small amounts of water until you achieve the right consistency.

You should always wear a pair of leather gloves when working with cement. There are many irritants in cement and these will damage unprotected hands. In fact, you should wear gloves for all types of cement work except for such finishing jobs as shaping mortar joints, which require bare handed control.

When mixing the cement in a wheelbarrow, make sure that you scrape the sides often to ensure a uniform mix. If the consistency is not right, after you have mixed for awhile, add small amounts of either water or the sand/cement mixture until you achieve the right consistency.

STUCCO

Stucco walls are similar to plaster walls except, of course, cement is used instead of plaster. A mixture of cement that will be used for stucco commonly contains portland cement, fine grain sand (the standard 1:3 mix), and about 10 percent or $\frac{1}{10}$ part hydrated lime, measured by volume, to make the mix more workable. Some professionals like to add short asbestos fibers to the standard 1:3 mix instead of hydrated lime. Add water to the ingredients and mix until the batch is the consistency of putty. A good stucco mix contains only enough water to achieve the right consistency; too much water will increase the chances of cracks developing as the stucco dries.

Stucco is most commonly applied over wire mesh that has been fastened to the sidewall of the house. Sometimes, however, when the existing sidewall is masonry, for example, the stucco is applied directly over this as a finish covering. The second method (with the wire lath) does not produce the best results because the stucco may not adhere well over the entire surface.

Stucco is troweled over the screen using either the two-coat or three-coat method. With two-coat work, the stucco consists of a base coat and a lighter finish coat, with a finished thickness of at least $\frac{5}{8}$ of an inch. In three-coat work, the stucco is applied in stages commonly called "scratch, brown, and finish," with a total finish thickness of at least $\frac{7}{8}$ of an inch. With either method the basic idea is to build up layers of the stucco mix until the desired strength and texture is achieved. The wire screening helps to hold the stucco to the wall surface, and it is therefore important that part of the stucco be pressed through the mesh. When the stucco dries there will be globs of cement on both sides of the mesh forming a very strong wall covering. Care must be exercised when applying the first coat of stucco over the mesh because if too much pressure is used the stucco will be too thick on the backside of the mesh, causing more unevenness than necessary, and creating more work with the finish coat.

Texture can be applied with many different types of tools, each producing a different type of texture or design. A wooden float can be used with circular motions to create swirls or at angles to produce straight grained texture. A wooden float will leave the surface on the rough side. If a smoother texture is desired, use a metal trowel. The metal trowel will not result in a glass-like finish but it will be much smoother than if done with a wooden float. Many masons will finish off a wall by brushing the surface with a broom or wallpaper brush after the stucco has set up for several hours. Another texture can be achieved by pressing crumpled up newspaper into the almost set up stucco. The newspaper method will create a coarse texture that resembles some type of Spanish wall. Texture is interesting, and you are limited only by your imagination.

One very appealing aspect of stucco walls, in addition to the low maintenance, is that they can be repaired easily if they should ever become damaged. Any area up to about 2 square feet can be repaired quickly and effectively. Areas larger than this, however, will usually mean that the entire wall must be resurfaced.

To repair small areas—cracks, for example—you must first remove all loose or damaged pieces of the existing stucco. Use a putty knife, cold chisel, and a hammer for the larger work and a wire brush for the final cleaning. To be effective, new stucco must only be applied to a firm surface so in some cases you will have to remove the existing stucco down to the lath underneath. Work carefully and wear some type of eye protection.

When all of the loose pieces have been removed, undercut the edges of the area to be repaired, then wire brush the hole. Before the new coat of stucco is applied, the area should be thoroughly wet down and kept damp for at least twelve hours prior to filling with new cement. The purpose of this wetting is to create an area that will not draw the moisture from the new stucco too quickly, causing it to lose strength and crack.

Repairs are made in either of two ways depending on how deep the hole or crack is. If the repair will be from the metal lath underneath, apply the stucco in two coats, waiting two days between applications. The first coat is packed into the area with a trowel to ¼ to ½ inch from the surface. Then the area is kept damp for two days while it sets. After the two-day wait, the area is moistened again and the finish coat is applied and leveled with a trowel. If the patch is not very deep, it is repaired in one shot, in very much the same manner as the finish coat above.

After the finish coat has been applied, with either method, the patch must be kept damp for two or three days. Spray the area twice a day with a fine mist from a garden hose. If the area is in direct sunlight, or if heavy winds are common, cover the area with burlap, and keep this damp for two days. Stucco is strongest when it is cured slowly.

BRICKS

Brick walls are attractive, enduring, and almost maintenance free. They are also very strong. Bricks have been used for over 5000 years and are still the most popular building material for sidewalls, fireplaces, walks, and patios. A thorough discussion of building with just one of the 10,000 different size, shape, and textured bricks would easily fill these pages. Therefore, the information contained here must be limited to repairs for existing brick walls.

A brick wall, either structural or veneer, will last a lifetime (or longer) provided it was installed properly over a suitable footing, and maintained so there are no broken bricks, or missing or cracked mortar joints. Defects in a brick wall, most commonly in the grout or joints, will let excess water into the wall and cause further damage. Preventing the entrance of water is especially important in the northern sections of the country where trapped water will freeze and possibly cause some major damage to the sidewall.

If you own a house with brick walls you should periodically check all surfaces for areas that are in need of repair. Loose mortar and damaged bricks are not uncommon but are easy to repair. If, however, your search should uncover cracks that run vertically for more than a few courses then you should call in a reliable professional mason to have the problem area checked. Long vertical cracks can be an indication of insufficient footings that are moving and causing the wall to crack. Repairs in this case would be extensive. Individual circumstances will, of course, dictate the nature and extent of repairs.

Before small areas can be repaired, it will be necessary to remove all broken or loose mortar. If the brick or bricks around the area are also damaged these should be removed as well. Use a cold chisel and a hammer to remove crumbling and loose mortar from the joint. You should wear some type of eye protection as pieces of mortar or brick are likely to fly when struck with the chisel/hammer combination.

After the area has been cleaned of all loose mortar, brush the joint with a stiff brush to remove any loose particles. Next, dampen the area with a garden hose set on fine spray. While the area is soaking up the water, mix up a batch of cement using the standard 1:3 mix (1 part masonry cement, 3 parts fine sand, plus enough water to achieve a stiff mix).

When the mortar has been thoroughly mixed, put a manageable amount on a hawk and lift it to the area to be repaired. A hawk is simply a board (¾-inch thick plywood, 1 foot square) with a handle on the underside. If you are right-handed the hawk, with a load of mortar, is held next to the work with the left hand, while the right hand does the work. If you don't have a conventional hawk, use a suitable piece of lumber to hold the mortar while you work.

The joint being repaired is filled with the mortar using a pointing trowel, which is smaller than an ordinary trowel. The mortar is pushed into the joint, using the bottom of the pointing trowel. Pack the mortar tightly into the joint, and then finish off the face of the joint with either the point of the trowel or with a special finishing trowel or tool. You should strive to make the repaired joint look exactly like the other joints in the wall. For extra long joints—say, over three bricks—you may find the work a bit easier to accomplish if you use a joint filling tool. If you are repairing several joints in the same area that run both horizontal and vertical, pack all of these joints with the mortar first, then go back and finish off all vertical joints and then all horizontal joints (see Figures 11-3 and 11-4).

After all joints have been finished to your satisfaction, let the cement set up for a few hours, undisturbed. Then spray a fine mist over the repairs with a garden hose. The repair must be kept damp for at least three days. In hot weather this may mean that you will have to spray the area several times during the day to

Step 1

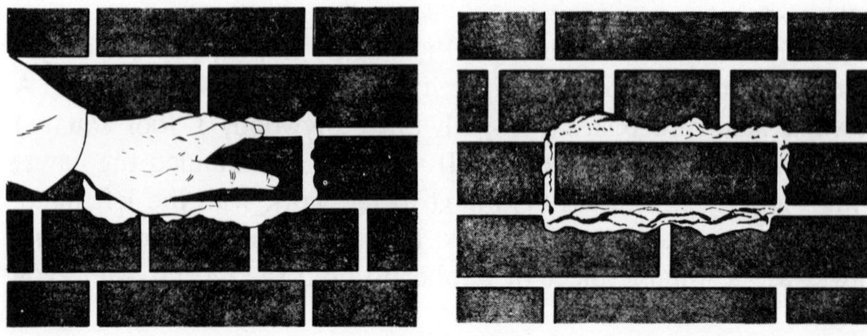

Step 2 Step 3

FIG. 11-3. Step 1: After the damaged brick has been removed and the area moistened, line the hole with cement. Step 2: Place a brick that has been soaked in water into the cement-lined hole, in line with other bricks in that course. Step 3: Pace additional cement around the edges of the new brick. The joints must then be finished off.

ensure that the repairs will not dry out too quickly. It may be necessary to cover the area with wet burlap if the area is in direct sunlight. When the repair has cured for at least three days, you can assume the cement has set properly. The next step is to clean the area to remove excess mortar from the joint or the face of the bricks. This is best done with a stiff wire brush. Work carefully, and don't press too hard with the brush, just enough to take the excess off the surface of the brick. After the area has been cleaned, the job is done and you can reasonably expect the repair to last a long time. However, you should check this particular area periodically.

FIG. 11-4. Joints between courses of brick or block are finished off with a special finishing tool.

STONE

In my opinion, nothing compares with stone for an exterior wall covering. In a stone wall you will find beauty and variety, not to mention that a stone wall will easily outlive the maker. Building a stone wall is a craft that requires not only a knowledge of basic masonry but a creative spirit as well. As with the other types of masonry work discussed in this chapter, a thorough coverage of the subject would fill these pages and many more. Readers who wish to learn how to build a stone wall will have to find additional information elsewhere. However, some of the basics of repair to existing walls made of stone will be discussed here.

About the only potential problems with a stone wall involve the joints between the stones. These should be looked after periodically because, as with a brick wall, holes and loose or missing mortar are invitations to future problems.

Pointing up a stone wall is similar to the same type of repairs on a brick wall. The damaged mortar must be removed and replaced with new material. This is done in just about the same manner as with repairs for a brick wall.

If stones should become loose—on a corner, for example—they should be removed, the area cleaned of all loose mortar, and then the old stone should be replaced in its original position but with new mortar. After the stone and new mortar have cured for a minimum of three days (kept damp all the time) the finish or pointing can be done. The pointing is done in the same manner as for brick walls except that the joints between the stones are often irregular rather than straight. The same tools—hawk and pointing trowel—are used for the finish work.

Another maintenance procedure that should be done periodically is checking and cleaning the joints between the stones. Generally speaking, most stains can be removed with a stiff brush and strong spray of water from the garden hose. However, if this method of cleaning fails to remove the stain, use a gentle laundry detergent and a stiff brush. Muriatic acid or other strong cleaners (commonly used for brick work cleaning) should never be used on stonework as they may do more harm than the stain.

Stucco, brick, and stone walls will last many lifetimes with only a minimum of care. If you own a house with masonry walls, look them over carefully at least once a year and make any necessary repairs as soon as possible. This little care will go a long way to ensure that your masonry walls endure the test of time.

12

VENTILATION AND INSULATION

Excessive moisture in some form is often the cause of condensation problems in the home. Ironically, the most aggravating and easily prevented problems are those caused by the movement of water vapor through walls and ceilings. These problems result in excessive maintenance costs, such as the need for frequent repainting and increased heating costs. Adequate ventilation used in conjunction with properly installed vapor barriers and insulation will help you to avoid most of these problems.

In the colder regions of the United States, notably where the January temperature averages 2°C. or lower, the first signs of spring may include dark stains on the house siding and peeling paint (see Figure 12-1). These unsightly blemishes often indicate a cold weather condensation problem. The formation of icicles or an ice dam at the cornice of a house after a heavy snowfall indicates another type of moisture problem that also requires correction.

CONDENSATION PROBLEMS

Condensation can be described as the change in moisture from a vapor to a liquid. In homes not properly protected, condensation caused by high humidities often results in excessive maintenance

FIG. 12-1. Peeling paint is often a sign of excess moisture escaping from the interior of the home.

costs. Water vapor within the house, when unrestricted, can move through the wall or ceiling during the heating season to some cold surface where it condenses, collecting generally in the form of ice or frost. During warm periods, the frost melts. When conditions are severe, the water from the melting ice in unvented attics may drip to the ceiling below and cause damage to the interior finish. Moisture can also soak into the roof sheathing or rafters and set up conditions that could lead to decay. In walls, water from melting frost may run out between the siding laps and cause staining or soak into the siding and cause paint to blister and peel.

Wood and wood-base materials used for sheathing and panel siding may swell from this added moisture and result in bowing, cupping, or buckling. Thermal insulation also becomes wet and provides less resistance to heat loss. Efflorescence may also occur on brick or stone of an exterior wall because of such condensation.

Changes in design, materials, and construction methods since the mid-thirties have resulted in houses that are easier to heat and more comfortable, but these same changes have accentuated the potential for condensation problems. New types of weather stripping, storm sash, and sheet material for sheathing in new houses provide tight air-resistant construction that restricts the escape of moisture generated in the house. Newer houses are also generally smaller and have lower ceilings resulting in less atmosphere to hold moisture.

Estimates have been made that a typical family of four converts about 3 gallons of water into water vapor per day. Unless excess water vapor is properly removed in some way (ventilation usually), it will either increase the humidity or condense on cold surfaces such as window glass. More serious, however, it can move in or through the construction, often condensing within the wall, roof, or floor cavities. Heating systems equipped with winter air-conditioning systems also increase the humidity in the home.

Most new houses have from 2 to 3½ inches of insulation in the walls and 6 or more inches in the ceilings. Unfortunately, the more efficient the insulation is in retarding heat transfer, the colder the outer surfaces become and unless moisture is restricted from entering the wall or ceiling, the greater the potential for moisture condensation. Moisture migrates toward cold surfaces and will condense or form as frost or ice on these surfaces.

Inexpensive methods of preventing condensation problems are available. They mainly involve the proper use of vapor barriers and good ventilating practices. Naturally, it is simpler, more inexpensive, and more effective to employ these during the construction of a house than to add them to an existing house.

Condensation will take place any time the temperature drops below the dewpoint (100 percent saturation of the air with water vapor at a given temperature). Commonly, under such conditions some surface accessible to the moisture in the air is cooler than the dewpoint and the moisture condenses on that surface.

During cold weather, visible condensation is usually first noticed on window glass but may also be discovered on cold surfaces of closet and unheated bedroom walls and ceilings. Condensation might also be visible in attic spaces on rafters or roof boards near the colder cornice area or it might form as frost. Such condensation or melting frost can result in excessive maintenance, such as the need for refinishing of window sash and trim, or even decay. Water from melting frost in the attic can also damage ceilings below.

Another area where visible condensation can occur is in crawl spaces under occupied rooms. This area usually differs from those on the interior of the house and in the attic because the source of the moisture is usually from the soil or from warm moisture-laden air which enters through foundation ventilators. Moisture vapor then condenses on the cooler surfaces in the crawl space. Such conditions often occur during warm periods in the late spring.

An increase in relative humidity of the inside atmosphere increases the potential for condensation on inside surfaces. For example, when inside temperature is 21°C., surface condensation will occur on a single glass window when outside temperatures fall to −23°C. and inside relative humidity is 10 percent. When inside relative humidity is 20 percent, condensation can occur on the single glass when outside temperatures are at about −14°C. When a storm window is added or insulated glass is used, surface condensation will not occur until the relative humidity has reached 38 percent when the outdoor temperature is −23°C. The above conditions only apply where storm windows are tight and there is good circulation of air on the inside surface of the window. When drapes or shades restrict air circulation, storm windows are not tight, or lower temperatures are maintained in such areas as bedrooms, condensation will occur at a higher outside temperature.

Condensation in concealed areas, such as wall spaces, often is first noticed by stains on the siding or by paint peeling. Water vapor moving through permeable walls and ceilings is normally responsible for such damage. Water vapor also escapes from houses by constant outleakage through cracks and crevices, around doors and windows, and by ventilation, but this moisture-vapor loss is usually insufficient to eliminate condensation problems.

Moisture, which is produced in a home or which enters a home, changes the relative humidity of the interior atmosphere. Ordinary household functions that generate a good share of the total amount of water vapor include dishwashing, cooking, bathing, and laundry work, as well as human respiration and evaporation from plants. Houses may also be equipped with central winter air conditioners or room humidifiers. Still another source of moisture may be from unvented or poorly vented clothes dryers.

Water vapor from the soil of crawl space houses does not normally affect the occupied areas. However, without good construction practices or proper precautions, it can be a factor in causing problems in exterior walls over the area as well as in the crawl space itself. Therefore, crawl spaces are another source of moisture that must be considered in providing protection.

Other sources of moisture, often unsuspected, can cause condensation problems. One such source can be a gas-fired furnace. It is desirable to maintain flue-gas temperatures within the recommended limits throughout the appliance, in the flue, the connecting vent, and other areas; otherwise excessive condensation problems can result. If all sources of excessive moisture have been exhausted in determining the reasons for a condensation problem, it is wise to have the heating unit examined by a competent heating engineer.

A distinct relationship exists in all homes between indoor relative humidity and outdoor temperature. The humidity is generally high indoors when outdoor temperatures are high and decreases as outdoor temperatures drop. In an exceptionally tight modern house where moisture buildup may be a problem, outside air should be introduced into the cold air return ducts to reduce relative humidity.

Many materials used as interior coverings for exposed walls and ceilings, such as plaster, dry wall, wood paneling, and plywood, permit water vapor to pass slowly through them during cold weather. Temperatures of the sheeting or siding on the outside of the wall are often low enough to cause condensation of water vapor within the cavities of a framed wall. When the relative humidity within the house at the surface of an unprotected wall is greater than that within the wall, water vapor will migrate through the plaster or other finish into the stud space; there it will condense if it comes in contact with surfaces colder than its dewpoint temperature. Vapor barriers are used to resist this movement of water vapor or moisture in various areas of the home.

The amount of condensation that can develop within a wall depends on: (1) the resistance of the intervening materials to vapor transfusion; (2) differences in vapor pressure; and (3) time. Plastered walls or ordinary dry walls have little resistance to vapor movement. However, when the surfaces are painted with an oil base paint, the resistance is increased. High indoor temperatures and relative humidities result in high indoor vapor pressures. Low outdoor vapor pressures always exist at low temperatures. Thus, a combination of high inside temperatures and humidities and low outside temperatures will normally result in vapor movement into the wall if no vapor barrier is present. Long periods of severe weather will result in condensation problems. Though fewer homes are affected by condensation in mild weather, many problems have been reported. Where information is available, it appears that the minimum relative humidities in the affected homes are 35 percent or higher. See Figure 12-2.

VAPOR BARRIERS

Vapor barrier requirements are sometimes satisfied by one of the materials used in a home's construction. In addition to integral vapor barriers, which are a part of many types of insulation, such materials as plastic-faced hardboard and similar interior coverings may have sufficient resistance when the permeability of the exterior construction is not too low. The permeability of the surface to such vapor movement is usually expressed in "perms," which are grains (438 grains per ounce) of water vapor passing through a square foot of material per hour per inch of mercury difference in vapor pressure. A material with a low perm value (1.0 or less) is a barrier, while one with a high perm value (greater than 1.0) is a "breather."

The perm value of the cold side materials should be several times greater than those used on the inside or warm side. A ratio of 1:5 or greater from inside to outside is sometimes used as a rule of thumb in selecting materials and finish. When this is not possible because of virtually impermeable outside construction (such as built-up roof or resistant exterior wall membranes), research has indicated the need to ventilate the space between the insulation and the outer covering. However, few specific data are available on ventilation requirements for walls.

Vapor barriers are used in three general areas of the house to minimize condensation and moisture problems: (1) walls, ceilings, and floors; (2) concrete slabs; and (3) crawl space covers.

Walls, Ceilings, and Floors

Vapor barriers used on the warm side of all exposed walls, ceilings, and floors greatly reduce movement of water vapor to

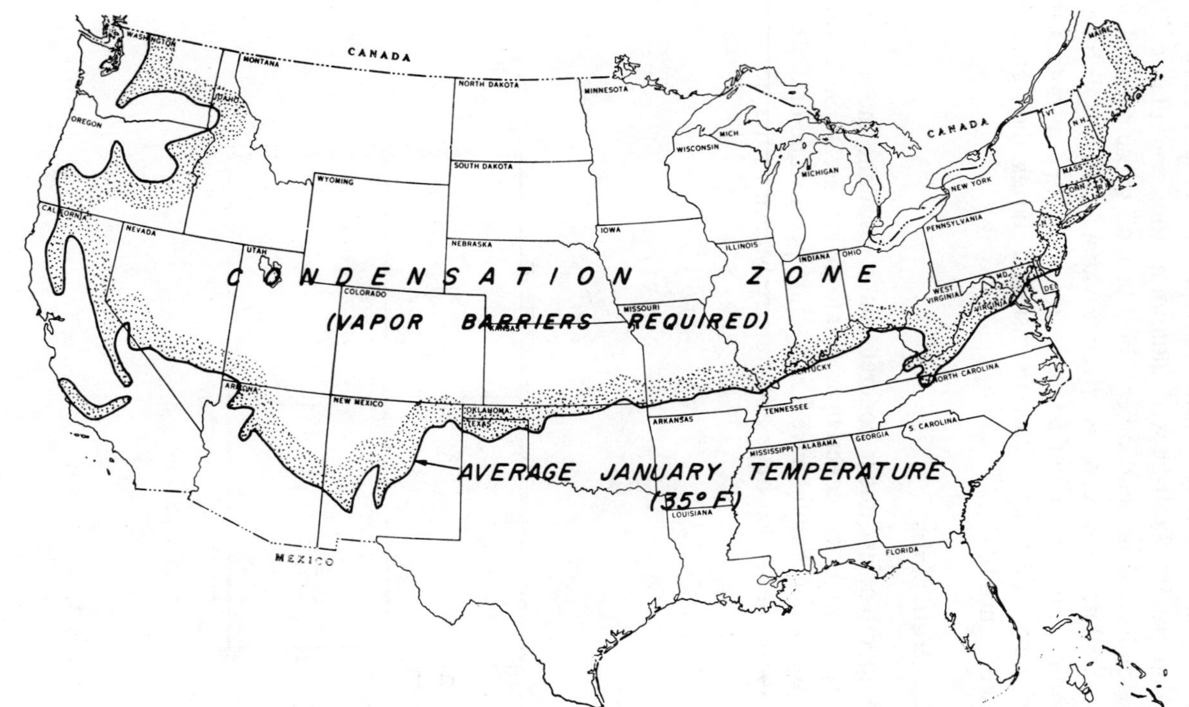

FIG. 12-2. Winter condensation problems occur where the average temperature for January is 35°F. or lower.

colder surfaces where harmful condensation can occur. For such uses it is good practice to select materials with perm values of 0.25 or less. Such vapor barriers can be a part of the insulation or a separate film. Commonly used materials are asphalt-coated or laminated papérs, kraft-backed aluminum foil, and plastic films such as polyethylene, and others. Foil-backed gypsum board and various coatings also serve as effective vapor barriers. Oil base or aluminum paints or similar coatings are often used in homes that did not have other vapor barriers installed during their construction (see Figure 12-3).

Concrete Slabs

Vapor barriers under concrete slabs resist the movement of moisture through the concrete and into living areas. Such vapor barriers should normally have a maximum perm value of 0.50. But the material must also have adequate resistance to the hazards of

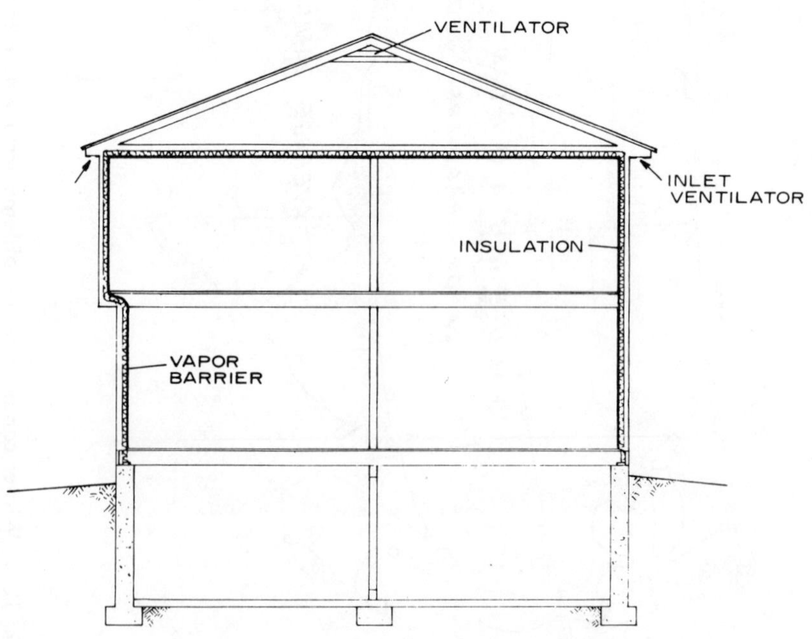

FIG. 12-3. Location of vapor barriers and insulation in full two-story house with basement.

pouring concrete. Thus, a satisfactory material must be heavy enough to withstand such damage and at the same time have an adequate perm value. Heavy asphalt laminated papers, papers with laminated films, roll roofing, heavy films such as polyethylene, and other materials are commonly used as vapor barriers under concrete slabs in new construction (see Figure 12-4).

Crawl Space Covers

Vapor barriers in crawl spaces prevent ground moisture from moving up and condensing on wood members. A perm value of 1.0 or less is considered satisfactory for such use. Asphalt-laminated paper, polyethylene, and similar materials are commonly used.

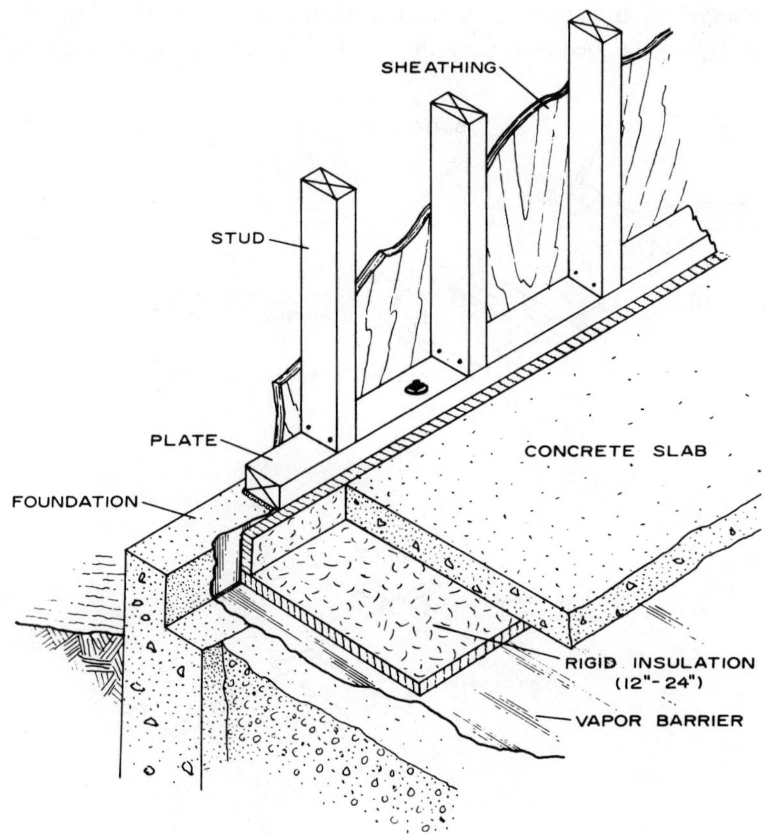

FIG. 12-4. Installation of vapor barrier under concrete slab.

Strength and resistance of crawl space coverings to mechanical damage can be lower than that for vapor barriers used under concrete slabs (see Figure 12-5).

New Construction

In new construction where low permeance vapor barriers are properly installed, most commercially available sheeting and siding materials and coatings can be used without creating condensation problems. However, in structures without vapor barriers, a low permeance material or coating on the outside can retard the escape of moisture that has been forced into the wall from the inside. An alternate finish for such situations is a penetrating stain, which does not form a coating on the wood surface and so does not retard the movement of moisture. Penetrating stains are very durable and easily refinished because they do not fail by blistering or peeling.

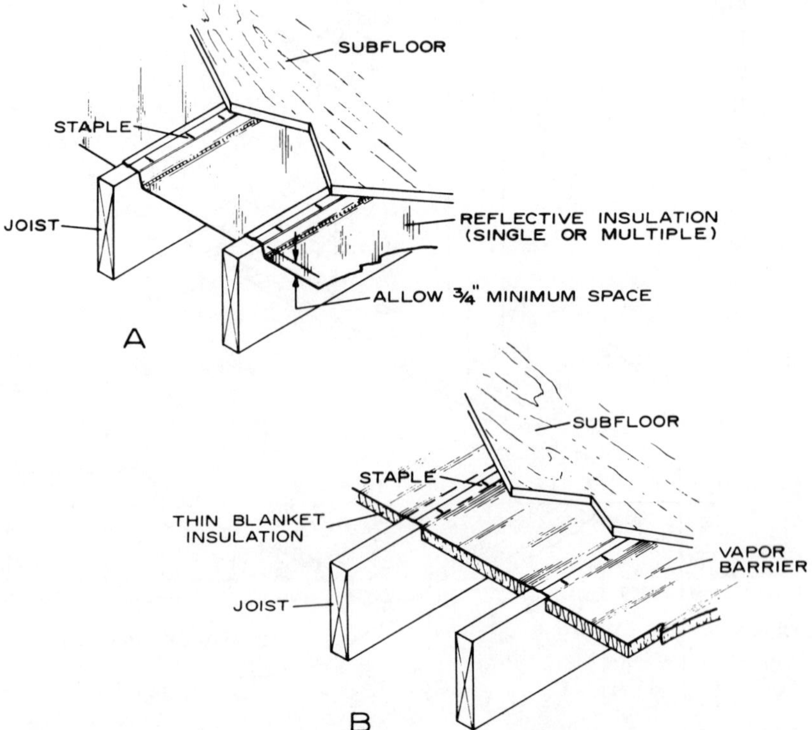

FIG. 12-5. Installation of vapor barriers and insulation over crawl space: (A) reflective insulation; and (B) thin blanket insulation.

When the older home has a paint peeling problem because of condensation, the siding should be painted with a white latex paint, which is very porous, and then spot-painted annually wherever peeling occurs. White paint is recommended because it does not fade and retains a good exterior appearance between yearly touch-ups.

Thermal insulation has a major influence on the need for vapor barriers. The inner face of the wall sheeting in an insulated wall, for example, is colder than the sheeting face in an uninsulated wall and consequently has a greater attraction to moisture. Thus, there is greater need for a vapor barrier in an insulated wall than in an uninsulated wall.

Ventilation used in proper amounts and locations is a recognized means of controlling condensation in buildings. Inlet and outlet ventilators in attic spaces, ventilation of rafter spaces in flat roofs, and crawl space ventilation aid in preventing accumulation of condensation in these areas. By introducing fresh air into living quarters during the winter, some humid air is forced out of the house while the incoming air has a low water vapor content. Well-installed vapor barriers may increase the need for ventilation in living quarters because little of the moisture generated can get out and may build up.

The use of both inlet and outlet ventilators in attic spaces aids in keeping the air moving and preventing accumulation of frost or condensation on roof boards in cold areas. "Dead" air pockets in the attic can normally be prevented by good distribution of inlet ventilators in the soffit areas. However, there is still a need for vapor barriers in the ceiling; ventilation alone, when insulation is used, does not prevent condensation problems. A good vapor barrier is especially needed under the insulation in a flat roof where ventilation can normally be provided only in the overhang.

Crawl space moisture, which results in high moisture content of the wood members, can be almost entirely eliminated by a vapor barrier over the soil. When such protection is used, the need for ventilation is usually reduced to only 10 percent of that required when a soil cover is not present.

During warm damp periods in early summer, moisture often condenses on basement walls or around the perimeter of the floor in concrete slab houses. Soil temperatures in the northern part of the United States remain quite low until summer, and surface temperatures of the floor or wall are often below dewpoint. When the concrete reaches normal temperature and the atmosphere changes, such problems are normally reduced or eliminated.

GOOD PRACTICE RECOMMENDATIONS

The control of condensation through the use of vapor barriers and ventilation should be practiced regardless of the insulation used. Normally, winter condensation problems occur in those parts of the country where the average January temperature is 2°C. or lower. Figure 12-2 illustrates this condensation zone. The northern half of the condensation zone has a lower average winter temperature and, of course, more severe conditions than does the southern portion. Areas outside this zone, such as the southeast and west coastal areas and the southern states, seldom have condensation problems. Vapor barriers should be installed at the time of construction in all new houses built within the condensation zone and proper ventilation procedures should be followed. These will ensure control over normal condensation problems.

A good rule of thumb to keep in mind when installing vapor barriers in a house is as follows: Place the vapor barrier as close as possible to the interior or warm surface of all exposed walls, ceilings, and floors. This normally means placing the vapor barrier between the subfloor and finish floor or just under the subfloor of a house with an unheated crawl space in addition to the vapor barrier placed over the soil. The insulation, of course, is normally placed between the studs or other framing members on the outside of the vapor barrier. The only exception is the insulation used in concrete slabs where a barrier is used under the insulation to protect it from ground moisture.

Crawl Spaces

Enclosed crawl spaces require some protection to prevent problems caused by excessive soil moisture. In an unheated crawl space this usually consists of a vapor barrier over the soil, together with foundation ventilators. In heated crawl spaces, a vapor barrier and perimeter insulation is used but foundation ventilators are eliminated.

To provide complete protection from condensation problems, the conventional unheated crawl space usually contains: foundation ventilators, a ground cover (vapor barrier), and thermal insulation between the floor joists. Foundation ventilators are normally located near the top of the masonry wall. In concrete block foundations, the ventilator is often made in a size that takes the place of one full block (see Figure 12-6).

The amount of ventilation required for a crawl space is based on the total area of the house in square feet and the presence of a vapor barrier soil cover. In placing the vapor barrier over the crawl space soil, adjoining edges should be lapped slightly and ends turned up on the foundation wall. To prevent movement of the barrier, it is good practice to weight down the laps and edges with bricks or stones.

Insulation batts, with an attached vapor barrier, are normally located between the floor joists. They can be fastened by placing the tabs over the edge of the joists before the subfloor is installed when the cover (vapor barrier) is strong enough to support the insulation batt. However, there is often a hazard of the insulation

FIG. 12-6. A typical basement ventilator, the size of a cement block, caulked to prevent entrance of excess moisture.

becoming wet before the subfloor is installed. Alternatives can be used with new or existing homes.

Friction-type batt insulation is made to fit tightly between the joists, and can be installed from the crawl space. Another type of insulation is reflective insulation, which usually consists of a Kraft paper with aluminum foil on each face. The reflective face must be placed at least ¾ inch away from the underside of the subfloor or other facing to be fully effective. Multiple or expanded reflective insulation might also be used. A thick blanket insulation can also be used between the joists. This is installed in much the same manner as the thicker insulations. When vapor barriers are a part of the flexible insulation and properly installed, no additional vapor barrier is ordinarily required.

A different approach to condensation problems is required when a heated crawl space is present. One method of heating, which is sometimes used for crawl space houses, utilizes the crawl space as a plenum chamber. Warm air is forced into the crawl space, which is somewhat shallower than those normally used without heat, and through wall and floor registers, around the outer walls, into the rooms above. When such a system is used, insulation is placed along the perimeter walls. Flexible insulation, with the vapor barrier facing the interior, is used between the joists, at the top of the foundation wall. A rigid insulation such as expanded polystyrene is placed along the inside of the wall, extending below the groundline to reduce heat loss. Insulation may be held in place with an approved mastic adhesive. To protect the insulation from moisture and to prevent moisture entry into the crawl space from the soil, a vapor barrier is used over the insulation below the groundline. Seams of the ground cover should be lapped and held in place with bricks or stones. Some builders even pour a thin (scratch coat) concrete slab over the vapor barrier. The crawl space of such construction is seldom ventilated.

In crawl space houses, as well as all other types of houses, the finish grade outside the foundation should be sloped to drain water away from the house.

INTERIOR WALLS

Flexible insulation in blanket or batt form is normally manufactured with a vapor barrier. These vapor barriers contain tabs along each edge and are stapled to the framing members. To minimize vapor loss and possible condensation problems, the best method of attaching is to staple the tabs over the edge of the studs. However, many contractors do not follow this procedure because it is more difficult and may cause some problems in nailing the finish wall covering. As a result, in many cases the tabs of the insulation are fastened to the inner faces of the wall studs. This usually results in some openings along the edge of the vapor barrier and, of course, a chance for water vapor to escape and cause problems. When insulation is placed in this manner, it is good to use a vapor barrier over the entire wall before the finish wall covering is installed.

Another factor in the use of flexible insulation having an integral vapor barrier is the protection required around window and door openings. When the vapor barrier on the insulation does not cover doubled studs and header areas, additional barrier material should be used for protection. Most well-informed contractors include such details in the application of their insulation (see Figure 12-7).

At junctions of interior partitions with exterior walls, care should be taken to cover this intersection with some type of vapor barrier. For best protection, insulating the space between the doubled exterior wall studs and the application of a vapor barrier should be done before the corner post is assembled. However, the vapor barrier should at least cover the stud intersections at each side of the partition wall.

Some of the new insulation forms, such as the friction type without covers, have resulted in the development of a new process of installing insulation and vapor barriers so as practically to eliminate condensation problems in the walls. An unfaced friction-type insulation batt is ordinarily supplied without a vapor barrier, is semirigid, and made to fit tightly between frame members spaced 16 to 24 inches on center. "Enveloping" is a process of installing a vapor barrier over the entire wall. This type of vapor barrier often consists of a 4-mil or thicker polyethylene or similar material used in 8-foot-wide rolls. After the insulation has been placed, rough wiring or duct work finished, and window frames installed, attach the vapor barrier over the entire wall with staples. Window and door headers, top and bottom plates, and other framing members are completely covered. After plaster base or dry-wall finish is installed, trim the vapor barrier around window openings.

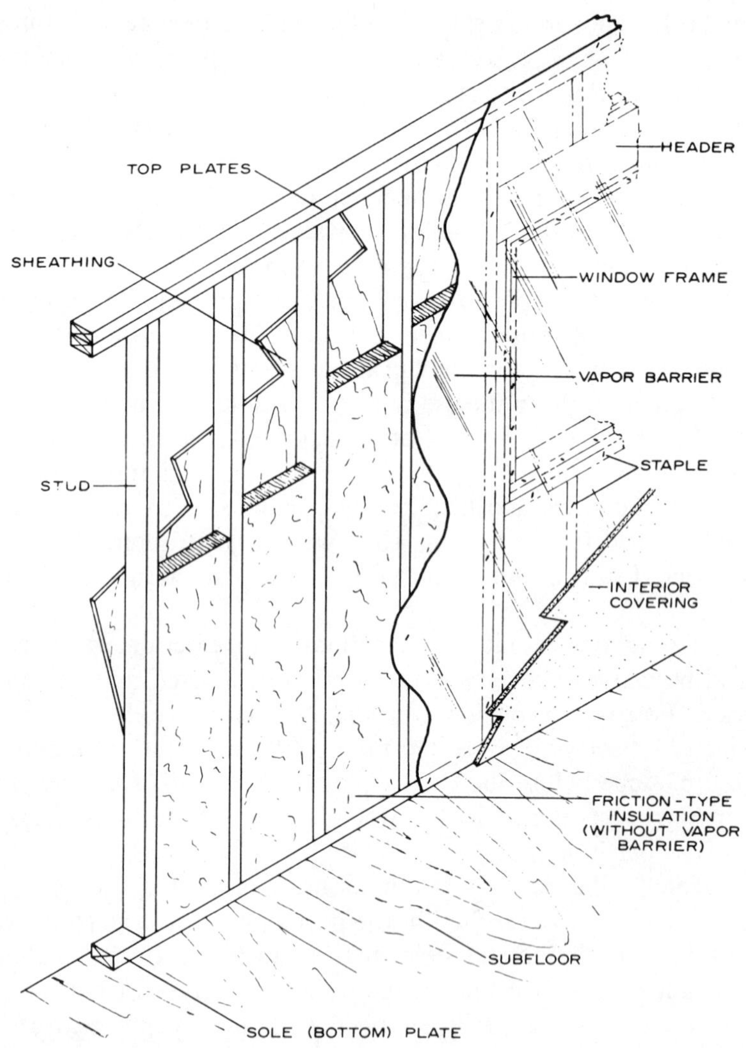

FIG. 12-7. Installing vapor barrier over friction-type insulation (enveloping).

Reflective insulations are often commonly used in new construction. Reflective insulations ordinarily consist of either a Kraft sheet faced on both sides with aluminum foil or the multiple-reflective "accordion" type. Both are made to use between the studs or joists. To be effective, it is important when using such insulation that there is at least ¾ inch space between the reflective surface and the wall, floor, or ceiling surface. When a reflective insulation is used, it is good practice to use a vapor barrier over the studs or joists. Place the barrier over the frame members just under the dry wall or plaster base. Gypsum board commonly used as a dry-wall finish can be obtained with an aluminum foil on the inside face which serves as a vapor barrier. When such material is used, the need for a separate vapor barrier is eliminated.

CEILINGS AND ATTICS

Insulation in ceilings normally consists of the batt or fill-type. However, to provide for good condensation control, a vapor barrier should always be provided. When an insulation batt is supplied with a vapor barrier on one face, no additional protection is normally required. Place the batts with the barrier side down, so that they fit tightly between ceiling joists. Batts with the vapor barrier attached can also be stapled to the bottom edge of the joists before the ceiling finish is applied. At the junction of the outside walls and rafters, a space should always be left below the roof boards to provide a ventilating airway.

Ventilation of attic spaces and roof areas is important in minimizing water vapor buildup. However, while good ventilation is important, there is still a need for vapor barriers in ceiling areas. This is especially true of the flat or low-slope roof where only a 1 to 3 inch space above the insulation might be available for ventilation.

In houses with attic spaces, the use of both inlet and outlet ventilation is recommended. Placing inlet ventilators in soffit or friezeboard areas of the cornice, and outlet ventilators as near the ridge line as possible, will assure air movement through a "stack" effect. The difference in height between inlet and outlet ventilators normally assures air movement even on windless days or nights (see Figure 12-8).

The minimum amount of attic or roof space ventilation required is determined by the total ceiling area. The use of both inlet and outlet ventilators is recommended whenever possible. Divide the total ceiling area by the number of ventilators used to find the recommended square foot area of each. For example, a gable roof with inlet and outlet ventilators has a minimum required total

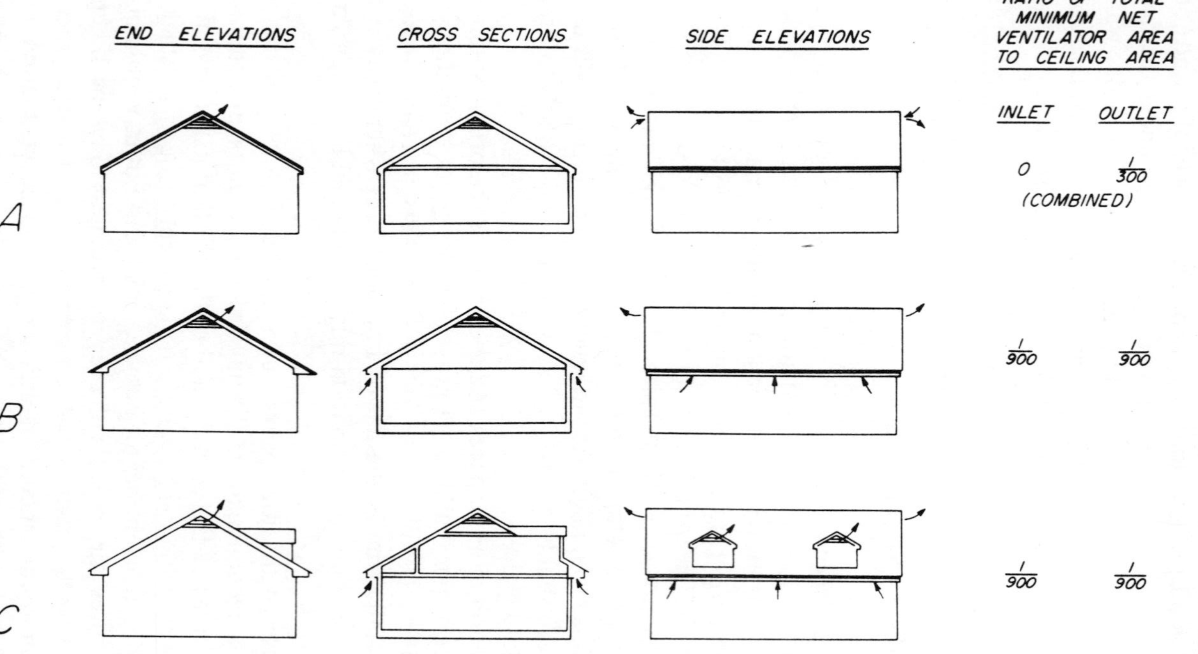

FIG. 12-8. Ventilating areas of gable roofs: (A) louvers in end walls; (B) louvers in end walls with additional openings at eaves; (C) louvers at end walls with additional openings at eaves and dormers. Cross-section of (C) shows free opening for air movement between roof boards and ceiling insulation of attic room.

inlet and outlet ratio of 1/900 of the ceiling area. If the ceiling area of the house is 1,350 square feet, each net inlet and outlet ventilating area should be 1,350 divided by 900 or 1½ square feet.

If ventilators are protected with no. 16 mesh screen and plain metal louvers, the minimum gross area must be 2 × 1½ or 3 square feet. When one outlet ventilator is used at each gable end, each should have a gross area of 1½ square feet (3 divided by 2). When distributing the soffit inlet ventilators to three on each side, for a small house (total of 6), each ventilator should have a gross area of 0.5 square feet. For long houses, use six or more ventilators on each side.

Inlet ventilators in the soffit may consist of several designs (see Figure 12-9). It is good practice to distribute them as much as possible to prevent "dead" air pockets in the attic where moisture might collect. A continuous screened slot satisfies this requirement. Continuous slots or individual ventilators between roof members should be used for flat-roof houses where roof members serve as both rafters and ceiling joists. Locate the openings away from the wall line to minimize the possible entry of wind-driven snow. A soffit consisting of perforated hardboard can also be used to advantage but the holes should be no larger than ⅛ inch in diameter. Small metal frames with screened openings are also available and can be used in soffit areas. For open cornice design, the use of a friezeboard with screen ventilating slots should be satisfactory. Perforated hardboard might also be used for this purpose. The recommended minimum inlet ventilation ratios should be followed in determining total net ventilating areas for both inlet and outlet ventilators.

To be most effective, outlet ventilators should be located as close as possible to the highest portion of the ridge. They may be placed in the upper wall section of a gable-roofed house in various forms (see Figure 12-10). In wide gable-end overhangs, with ladder framing, a number of screened openings can be located in the soffit area of the lookouts. Ventilating openings to the attic space should not be restricted by blocking. Outlet ventilators on gable or hip roofs might also consist of some type of roof ventilator. Hip roofs can utilize a ventilating gable (modified hip). Protection from blowing snow must be considered, which often restricts the use of a continuous ridge vent. Locate the single roof ventilators along the

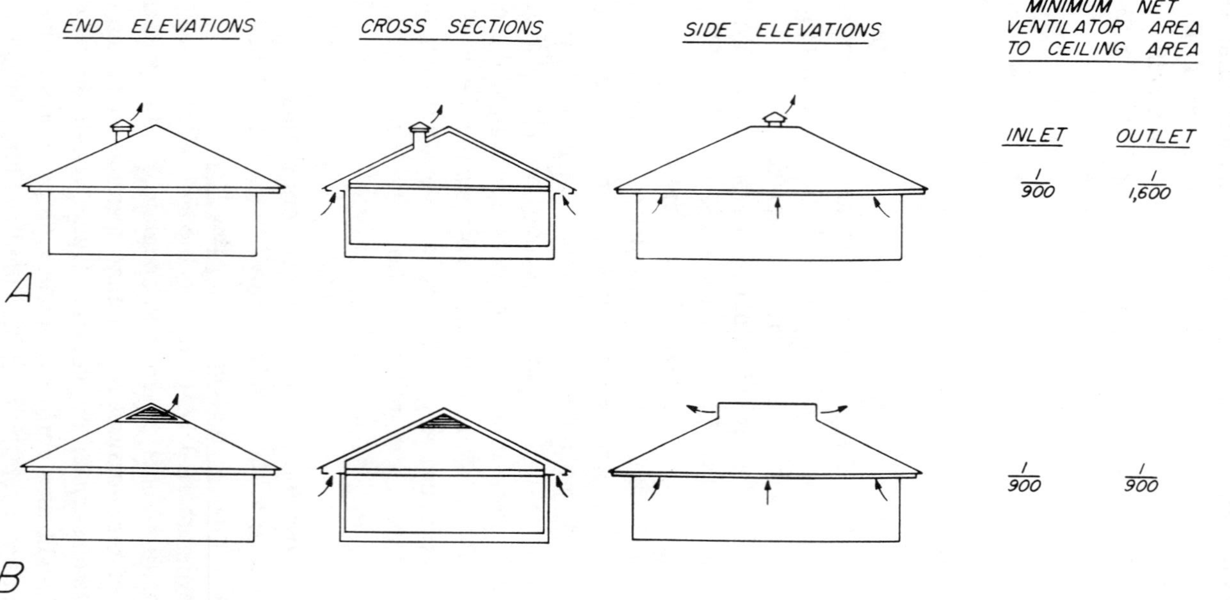

FIG. 12-9. Ventilating areas of hip roofs: (A) inlet openings beneath eaves and outlet vent near peak; (B) inlet openings beneath eaves and ridge outlets.

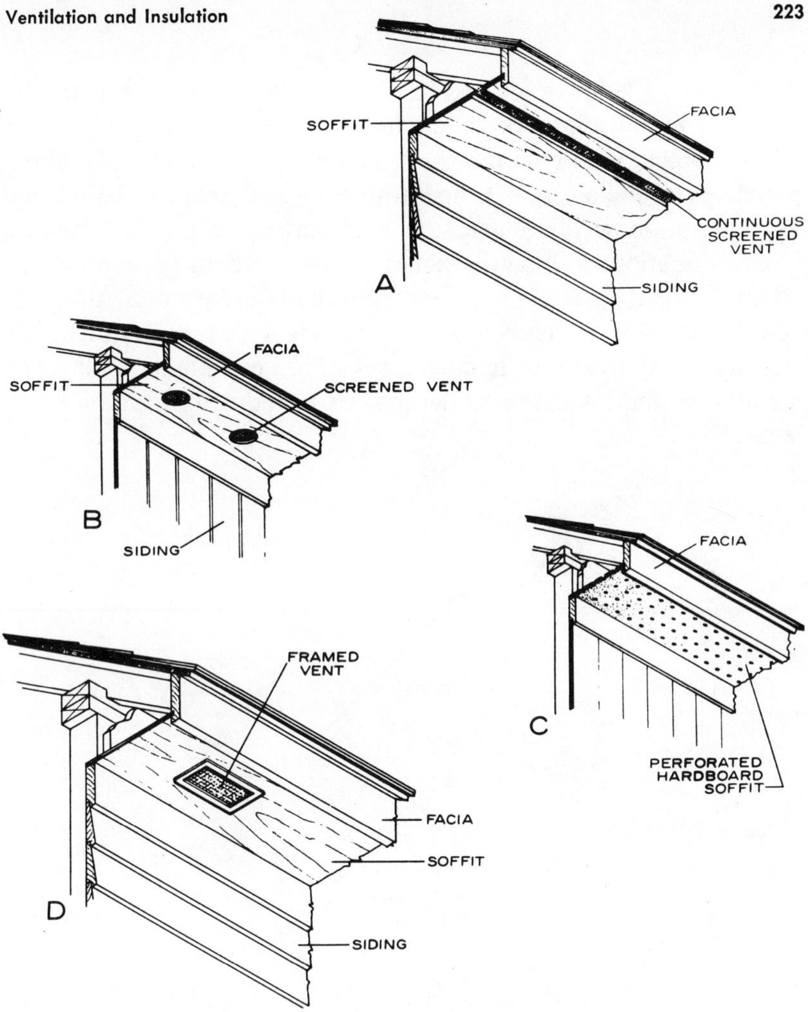

FIG. 12-10. Inlet ventilators in soffits: (A) continuous vent; (B) round vents; (C) perforated; (D) single ventilator.

ridge toward the rear of the house so they are not visible from the front. Outlet ventilators might also be located in a chimney as a false flue which has a screened opening to the attic area.

Water leakage into walls and interiors of houses in the snow belt areas of the country is sometimes caused by ice dams and is often mistaken for condensation. Such problems occur after heavy snowfalls when there is sufficient heat loss from the living quarters to melt the snow along the roof surface. The water moves down the roof surface to the colder overhang of the roof where it freezes.

This causes a ledge of ice and backs up water, which can enter the wall or drip down into the ceiling finish (see Figure 12-11).

Ice dam problems can be minimized, if not entirely eliminated. By reducing attic temperatures by adequate insulation and ventilation, snow melting at the roof surface is greatly reduced. Good insulation, 6 or more inches in the northern sections of the country, greatly reduces heat loss from the house proper. Adequate ventilation, in turn, tends to keep attics dry with temperatures only slightly above outdoor temperatures. This combination of good ventilation and insulation is the answer to reducing ice dam problems.

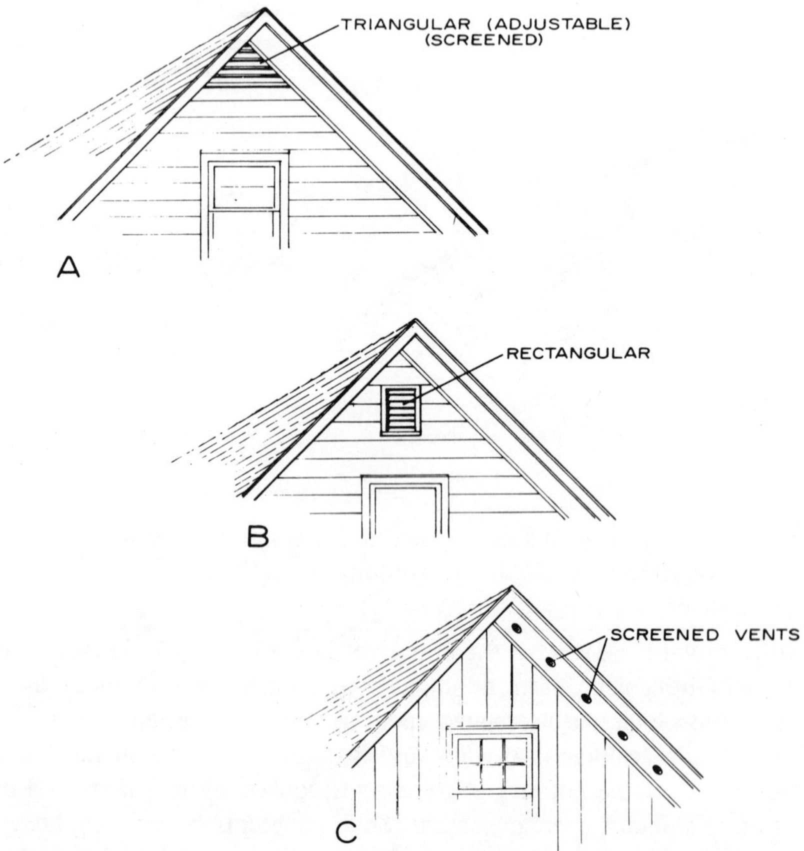

FIG. 12-11. Gable outlet ventilators: (A) triangular gable end ventilator; (B) rectangular gable end ventilator; (C) soffit ventilators.

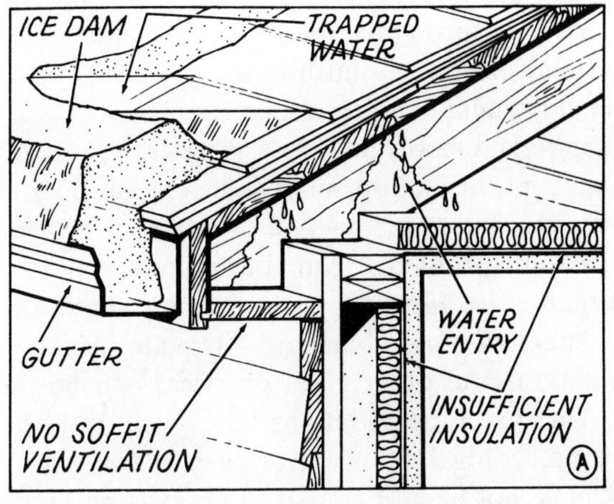

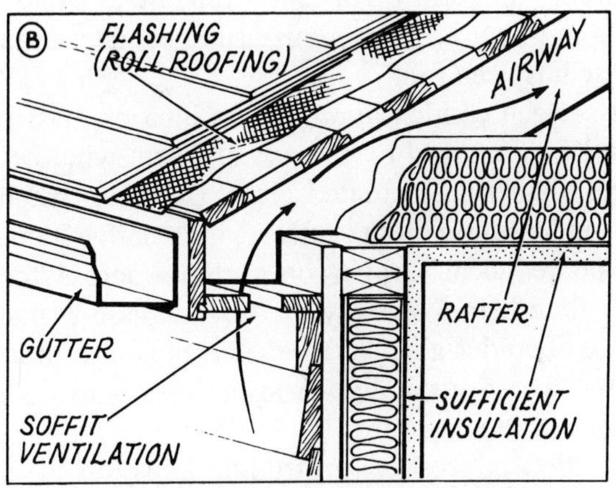

FIG. 12-12. Ice dams: (A) insufficient insulation and ventilation can cause ice dams and water damage; (B) good ventilation, insulation, and roof flashing minimize problems.

Another protective measure is provided by the use of a flashing material. A 36-inch width of 45-pound roll roofing along the eave line will provide such added protection.

Walls and doors to unheated areas such as attic spaces should be treated to resist water vapor movement as well as to minimize heat loss. This includes the use of insulation and vapor barriers on all wall areas adjacent to the cold attic. Vapor barriers should face the warm side of the room. In addition, some means should be used to prevent heat and vapor loss around the perimeter of the door. One method is through some type of weather strip. The door itself should be given several finish coats of paint or varnish which will resist the movement of water vapor.

If further resistance to heat loss is desired, a covering of ½ inch or thicker rigid insulation, such as insulation board or foamed plastic, can be attached to the back of the door.

Condensation problems can be eliminated by specifying proper construction details during the planning stages of the house. Correct placement of vapor barriers, adequate insulation, the use of attic ventilation, and other good practices can be incorporated at this time. These recommendations have been outlined and illustrated in the preceding sections. However, when one or more of these details have not been included in an existing house and condensations occur, they are often more difficult to solve. Nevertheless, methods can be used to minimize such condensation problems after the house has been built.

Visible surface condensation on the interior glass surfaces of windows can be minimized by the use of storm windows or by replacing single glass with insulated glass. However, when this does not prevent condensation on the surface, the relative humidity in the room must be reduced. Drapes or curtains across the windows hinder rather than help. Not only do they increase surface condensation because of colder glass surfaces, but they also prevent the air movement that would normally warm the glass surface and aid in dispersing some of the moisture.

Condensation or frost on protruding nails, on the surfaces of roof boards, or other members in attic areas normally indicates the escape of excessive amounts of water vapor from the heated rooms below. If a vapor barrier is not already present, place one between the joists under the insulation. Make sure the vapor barrier fits tightly around ceiling lights and exhaust fans, caulking where necessary. In addition, increase both inlet and outlet ventilators to conform to the minimum recommendations covered earlier. Decreasing the amount of water vapor produced in the living areas is also helpful.

Surface condensation in unheated crawl spaces is usually caused by excessive moisture from the soil or from outside the house. To eliminate this problem, place a vapor barrier over the soil.

Reducing high relative humidities within the house to permissible levels is often necessary to minimize condensation problems. Discontinuing the use of room-size humidifiers or reducing the output of automatic humidifiers until conditions are improved is helpful. The use of exhaust fans and dehumidifiers can also be of value in eliminating high relative humidities within the house. When possible, decrease the activities that produce excessive moisture, such as bathing, laundry, and cooking. This is especially important in homes with electric heat.

Concealed condensation is, in essence, a surface or similar condensation that takes place within a component such as a wall cavity when a condensing surface is below the dewpoint. In cold weather, condensation often forms as frost. Such conditions can cause staining of siding, peeling of paint, and possibly decay in severe and sustained conditions. These problems are usually not detected until spring after the heating season has ended. The remedies and solutions to the problems should be taken care of before repainting or re-siding is attempted. Several solutions might be:

1. Reduce or control the relative humidity within the house.
2. Add a vapor-resistant paint coating such as aluminum paint to the exterior walls and ceilings.
3. Improve the vapor resistance of the ceiling by adding a vapor barrier between ceiling joists.
4. Improve attic ventilation.

GLOSSARY

Airway—A space between roof insulation and roof boards for the movement of air.

Alligatoring—Coarse checking pattern characterized by a slipping of the new paint coating over the old coating so that the old coating can be seen through the fissures.

Asphalt—Most native asphalt is a residue from evaporated petroleum. It is insoluble in water but soluble in gasoline, and melts when heated. Used widely in building for waterproofing roof coverings of many types.

Attic ventilators—In houses, screened openings provided to ventilate an attic space. They are located in the soffit area as inlet ventilators and in the gable end or along the ridge as outlet ventilators. They can also consist of power-driven fans used as an exhaust system. (See also Louver.)

Barge board—A decorative board covering the projecting rafter (fly rafter) of the gable end. At the cornice, this member is a facia board.

Batten—Narrow strips of wood used to cover joints or as decorative vertical members over plywood or wide boards.

Batter board—One of a pair of horizontal boards nailed to posts set at the corners of an excavation. It is used to indicate the desired level, and also as a fastening for stretched strings to indicate outlines of foundation walls.

Beam—A structural member transversely supporting a load.

Bearing partition—A partition that supports any vertical load in addition to its own weight.

Bearing wall—A wall that supports any vertical load in addition to its own weight.

Bed molding—A molding in an angle, as between the overhanging cornice, or eaves, of a building and the sidewalls.

Blind nailing—Nailing in such a way that the nailheads are not visible on the face of the work; usually at the tongue of matched boards.

Blind stop—A rectangular molding, usually ¾ by 1⅜ inches or more in width, used in the assembly of a window frame. Serves as a stop for storm and screen or combination windows and to resist air infiltration.

Blue stain—A bluish or grayish discoloration of the sapwood caused by the growth of certain moldlike fungi on the surface and in the interior of a piece. Made possible by the same conditions that favor the growth of other fungi.

Bodied linseed oil—Linseed oil that has been thickened in viscosity by suitable processing with heat or chemicals. Bodied oils are obtainable in a great range of viscosity, from a little greater than that of raw oil to just short of a jellied condition.

Boiled linseed oil—Linseed oil in which enough lead, manganese, or cobalt salts have been incorporated to make the oil harden more rapidly when spread in thin coatings.

Bolster—A short horizontal timber or steel beam on top of a column to support and decrease the span of beams or girders.

Boston ridge—A method of applying asphalt or wood shingles at the ridge or at the hips of a roof as a finish.

Brace—An inclined piece of framing lumber applied to wall or floor to stiffen the structure. Often used on walls as temporary bracing until framing has been completed.

Brick veneer—A facing of brick laid against and fastened to sheathing of a frame wall or tile wall construction.

Bridging—Small wood or metal members that are inserted in a diagonal position between the floor joists at midspan to act both as tension and compression members for the purpose of bracing the joists and spreading the action of loads.

Built-up roof—A roofing composed of three to five layers of asphalt felt laminated with coal tar, pitch, or asphalt. The top is finished with crushed slag or gravel. Generally used on flat or low-pitched roofs.

Butt joint—The junction at which the ends of two timbers or other members meet in a square-cut joint.

Cant strip—A triangular-shaped piece of lumber used at the junction of a flat deck and a wall to prevent cracking of the roofing which is applied over it.

Cap—The upper member of a column, pilaster, door cornice, molding, and the like.

Casement frames and sash—Frames of wood or metal, enclosing part or all of the sash, which may be opened by means of hinges affixed to the vertical edges.

Casing—Molding of various widths and thicknesses used to trim door and window openings at the jambs.

Checking—Fissures that appear with age in many exterior paint coatings, at first superficial, but which in time may penetrate entirely through the coating.

Checkrails—Meeting rails sufficiently thicker than a window to fill the opening between the top and bottom sash made by the parting stop in the frame of double-hung windows. Most commonly beveled.

Collar beam—Nominal 1- or 2-inch thick members connecting opposite roof rafters. They serve to stiffen the roof structure.

Column—In architecture: a perpendicular supporting member, circular or rectangular in section, usually consisting of a base, shaft, and capital. In engineering: a vertical structural compression member which supports loads acting in the direction of its longitudinal axis.

Combination doors/windows—Combination doors or windows used over regular openings. They provide winter insulation and summer protection and often have self-storing or removable glass and screen inserts. This eliminates the need for handling a different unit each season.

Concrete plain—Concrete either without reinforcement, or reinforced only for shrinkage or temperature changes.

Condensation—In a building, beads or drops of water (and frequently frost in extremely cold weather) that accumulate on the inside of the exterior covering of a building when warm, moisture-laden air from the interior reaches a point at which the temperature no longer permits the air to sustain the moisture it holds. Use of louvers or attic ventilators will reduce moisture condensation in attics. A vapor barrier under the gypsum lath or dry wall on exposed walls will reduce condensation in them.

Construction, frame—A type of construction in which the structural parts are wood or depend on wood frame for support. In codes, if masonry veneer is applied to the exterior walls, the classification of this type of construction is usually unchanged.

Corbel out—To build out one or more courses of brick or stone from the face of a wall, to form a support for timbers.

Corner bead—A strip of formed sheet metal, sometimes combined with a strip of metal lath, placed on corners before plastering to reinforce them. Also, a strip of wood finish three-quarters-round or angular placed over a plastered corner for protection.

Corner boards—Used as trim for the external corners of a house or other frame structure against which the ends of the siding are finished.

Corner braces—Diagonal braces at the corners of frame structure to stiffen and strengthen the wall.

Cornice—Overhang of a pitched roof at the eave line, usually consisting of a facia board, a soffit for a closed cornice, and appropriate moldings.

Cornice return—That portion of the cornice that returns on the gable end of a house.

Counterflashing—A flashing usually used on chimneys at the roofline to cover shingle flashing and to prevent moisture entry.

Crawl space—A shallow space below the living quarters of a basementless house, normally enclosed by the foundation wall.

Cricket—A small drainage-diverting roof structure of single or double slope placed at the junction of larger surfaces that meet at an angle, such as above a chimney.

Cross-bridging—Diagonal bracing between adjacent floor joists, placed near the center of the joist span to prevent joists from twisting.

Cut-in brace—Nominal 2-inch thick members, usually 2 x 4's, cut in between each stud diagonally.

Decay—Disintegration of wood or other substance through the action of fungi.

Deck paint—An enamel with a high degree of resistance to mechanical wear, designed for use on such surfaces as porch floors.

Density—The mass of substance in a unit volume. When expressed in the metric system, it is numerically equal to the specific gravity of the same substance.

Dewpoint—Temperature at which a vapor begins to deposit as a liquid. Applies especially to water in the atmosphere.

Direct nailing—To nail perpendicular to the initial surface or to the junction of the pieces joined. Also called *face nailing*.

Dormer—An opening in a sloping roof, the framing of which projects out to form a vertical wall suitable for windows or other openings.

Downspout—A pipe, usually of metal, for carrying rainwater from roof gutters.

Dressed and matched (tongued-and-grooved)—Boards or planks machined in such a manner that there is a groove on one edge and a corresponding tongue on the other.

Drier paint—Usually oil-soluble soaps of metals such as lead, manganese, or cobalt, which, in small proportions, hasten the oxidation and hardening (drying) of the drying oils in paints.

Drip—(1) A member of a cornice or other horizontal exterior-finish course that has a projection beyond the other parts for throwing water off. (2) A groove in the underside of a sill or drip cap to cause water to drop off on the outer edge instead of drawing back and running down the face of the building.

Drip cap—A molding placed on the exterior top side of a door or window frame to cause water to drip beyond the outside of the frame.

Ducts—In a house, usually round or rectangular metal pipes for distributing warm air from the heating plant to rooms, or air from a conditioning device or as cold air returns. Ducts are also made of asbestos and composition materials.

Eaves—The margin or lower part of a roof projecting over the wall.

Expansion joint—A bituminous fiber strip used to separate blocks or units of concrete to prevent cracking due to expansion as a result of temperature changes. Also used on concrete slabs.

Facia or fascia—A flat board, band, or face, used sometimes by itself but usually in combination with moldings, often located at the outer face of the cornice.

Filler (wood)—A heavily pigmented preparation used for filling and leveling off the pores in open-pored woods.

Fire-resistive—In the absence of a specific ruling by the authority having jurisdiction, applies to materials for construction not combustible in the temperatures of ordinary fires and which will withstand such fires without serious impairment of usefulness for at least one hour.

Fire-retardant chemical—A chemical or preparation of chemicals used to reduce flammability or to retard spread of flame.

Fire stop—A solid, tight closure of a concealed space, placed to prevent the spread of fire and smoke through such a space. In a frame wall, this will usually consist of 2 × 4 inch cross blocking between studs.

Fishplate—A wood or plywood piece used to fasten the ends of two members together at a butt joint with nails or bolts. Sometimes used at the junction of opposite rafters near the ridge line.

Flashing—Sheet metal or other material used in roof and wall construction to protect a building from water seepage.

Flue—The space or passage in a chimney through which smoke, gas, or fumes ascend. Each passage is called a flue, which together with any others and the surrounding masonry make up the chimney.

Fly rafters—End rafters of the gable overhang supported by roof sheathing and lookouts.

Footing—A masonry section, usually concrete, in a rectangular form wider than the bottom of the foundation wall or pier it supports.

Foundation—The supporting portion of a structure below the first floor construction, or below grade; including the footings.

Frieze—In house construction, a horizontal member connecting the top of the siding with the soffit of the cornice.

Frostline—The depth of frost penetration in soil. This depth varies in different parts of the country. Footings should be placed below this depth to prevent movement.

Fungi, wood—Microscopic plants that live in damp wood and cause mold, stain, and decay.

Fungicide—A chemical that is poisonous to fungi.

Furring—Strips of wood or metal applied to a wall or other surface to even it and normally to serve as a fastening base for finish material.

Gable—In house construction, the portion of the roof above the eave line of a double-sloped roof.

Gable end—An end wall having a gable.

Girder—A large or principal beam of wood or steel used to support concentrated loads at isolated points along its length.

Gloss enamel—A finishing material made of varnish and sufficient pigments to provide opacity and color, but little or no pigment of low opacity. Such enamel forms a hard coating with maximum smoothness of surface and a high degree of gloss.

Grain—The direction, size, arrangement, appearance, or quality of the fibers in wood.

Grain, edge (vertical)—Edge-grain lumber has been sawed parallel to the pith of the log and approximately at right angles to the growth rings; that is, the rings form an angle of 45 degrees or more with the surface of the piece.

Grain, flat—Flat-grain lumber has been sawed parallel to the pith of the log and approximately tangent to the growth rings; that is, the rings form an angle of less than 45 degrees with the surface of the piece.

Grain, quartersawn—Another term for edge grain.

Grout—Mortar made of such consistency (by adding water) that it will flow into the joints and cavities of the masonry work and fill them solid.

Gusset—A flat wood, plywood, or similar type member used to provide a connection at an intersection of wood members. Most commonly used at joints of wood trusses. They are fastened by nails, screws, bolts, or adhesives.

Gutter—A shallow channel or conduit of metal or wood set below and along the eaves of a house to catch and carry off rainwater from the roof.

Gypsum plaster—Gypsum formulated to be used with the addition of sand and water for base-coat plaster.

Header—(1) A beam placed perpendicular to joists and to which joists are nailed in framing for chimney, stairway, or other opening. (2) A wood lintel.

Heartwood—The wood extending from the pith to the sapwood, the cells of which no longer participate in the life processes of the tree.

Hip—The external angle formed by the meeting of two sloping sides of a roof.

Hip roof—A roof that rises by inclined planes from all four sides of a building.

Humidifier—A device designed to increase the humidity within a room or a house by means of the discharge of water vapor. Humidifiers may be either individual room-size units or larger units attached to the heating plant to condition the entire house.

I-beam—A steel beam with a cross section resembling the letter *I*. It is used for long spans as basement beams or over wide openings, such as a double garage door, when wall and roof loads are imposed on the opening.

Insulation board, rigid—A structural building board made of coarse wood or cane fiber in ½- and 25/32-inch thicknesses. It can be obtained in various size sheets, in various densities, and with several treatments.

Insulation, thermal—Any material high in resistance to heat transmission that, when placed in the walls, ceiling, or floors of a structure, will reduce the rate of heat loss.

Jack rafter—A rafter that spans the distance from the wallplate to a hip, or from a valley to a ridge.

Jamb—The side and head lining of a doorway, window, or other opening.

Joint—The space between the adjacent surfaces of two members or components joined and held together by nails, glue, cement, mortar, or other means.

Joist—One of a series of parallel beams, usually 2 inches in thickness, used to support floor and ceiling loads, and supported in turn by larger beams, girders, or bearing walls.

Kiln dried lumber—Lumber that has been kiln dried often to a moisture content of 6 to 12 percent. Common varieties of softwood lumber, such as framing lumber, are dried to a somewhat higher moisture content.

Knot—In lumber, the portion of a branch or limb of a tree that appears on the edge or face of the piece.

Lath—A building material of wood, metal, gypsum, or insulating board that is fastened to the frame of a building to act as a plaster base.

Lattice—A framework of crossed wood or metal strips.

Leader—See Downspout.

Ledger strip—A strip of lumber nailed along the bottom of the side of a girder on which joists rest.

Let-in brace—Nominal 1-inch thick boards applied into notched studs diagonally.

Light—Space in a window sash for a single pane of glass. Also, a pane of glass.

Lintel—A horizontal structural member that supports the load over an opening such as a door or window.

Lookout—A short wood bracket or cantilever to support an overhang portion of a roof, or the like, usually concealed from view.

Louver—An opening with a series of horizontal slats so arranged as to permit ventilation but to exclude rain, sunlight, or vision. See also Attic ventilators.

Lumber—Lumber is the product of the sawmill and planing mill not further manufactured other than by sawing, resawing, and passing lengthwise through a standard planing machine crosscutting to length, and matching.

Lumber, boards—Yard lumber less than 2 inches thick and 2 or more inches wide.

Lumber, dimension—Yard lumber from 2 inches to, but not including, 5 inches thick and 2 or more inches wide. Includes joists, rafters, studs, plank, and small timbers.

Lumber, dressed size—The dimension of lumber after shrinking from green dimension and after machining to size or pattern.

Lumber, matched—Lumber that is dressed and shaped on one edge in a grooved pattern and on the other in a tongued pattern.

Lumber, shiplap—Lumber that is edge-dressed to make a close rabbeted or lapped joint.

Lumber, timbers—Yard lumber 5 or more inches in least dimension. Includes beams, stringers, posts, caps, sills, girders, and purlins.

Lumber, yard—Lumber of those grades, sizes, and patterns which are generally intended for ordinary construction, such as framework and rough coverage of houses.

Masonry—Stone, brick, concrete, hollow-tile, concrete-block, gypsum-block, or other similar building units or materials of a combination of the same, bonded together with mortar to form a wall, pier, buttress, or similar mass.

Mastic—A pasty material used as a cement (as for setting tile) or a protective coating (as for thermal insulation or waterproofing).

Metal lath—Sheets of metal that are split and drawn out to form openings. Used as a plaster base for walls and ceilings and as reinforcing over other forms of plaster base.

Millwork—Generally all building materials made of finished wood or manufactured in millwork plants and planing mills are included under the term "millwork." It includes such items as inside and outside doors, windows and frames, blinds, porchwork, mantels, panelwork, stairways, moldings, and interior trim. It normally does not include flooring, ceiling, or siding.

Miter joint—The joint of two pieces at an angle that bisects the joining angle.

Moisture content of wood—Weight of the water contained in the wood, usually expressed as a percentage of the weight of the ovendry wood.

Molding—A wood strip having a curved or projecting surface used for decorative purposes.

Mortise—A slot cut into a board, plank, or timber, usually edgewise, to receive tenon of another board, plank, or timber to form a joint.

Mullion—A vertical bar or divider in the frame between windows, doors, or other openings.

Muntin—A small member that divides the glass or openings of sash or doors.

Natural finish—A transparent finish that does not seriously alter the original color or grain of the natural wood. Natural finishes are usually provided by sealers, oils, varnishes, water-repellent preservatives, and other similar materials.

Nonbearing wall—A wall supporting a load other than its own weight.

Nosing—The projecting edge of a molding or drip. Usually applied to the projecting molding on the edge of a stairtread.

Notch—A crosswise rabbet at the end of a board.

O.C., OC, and On Center—The measurement of spacing for studs, rafters, joists, and the like, in a building from the center of one member to the center of the next.

Outrigger—An extension of a rafter beyond the wall line. Usually a smaller member nailed to a larger rafter to form a cornice or roof overhang.

Paint—A combination of pigments with suitable thinners or oils to provide decorative and protective coatings.

Paper, building—A general term for papers, felts, and similar sheet materials used in buildings without reference to their properties or uses.

Paper, sheathing—A building material, generally paper or felt, used in wall and roof construction as a protection against the passage of air and sometimes moisture.

Parting stop or strip—A small wood piece used in the side and head jambs of double-hung windows to separate upper and lower sash.

Partition—A wall that subdivides spaces within any story of a building.

Penny—As applied to nails, it originally indicated the price per hundred. The term now serves as a measure of nail length and is abbreviated by the letter *d*.

Perm—A measure of water vapor movement through a material (grains per square foot per hour per inch of mercury difference in vapor pressure).

Pier—A column of masonry, usually rectangular in horizontal cross section, used to support other structural members.

Pigment—A powdered solid in suitable degree of subdivision for use in paint or enamel.

Pitch—The incline slope of a roof or the ratio of the total rise to the total width of a house: for example, an 8-foot rise and 24-foot width is one-third pitch roof. Roof slope is expressed in the inches of rise per foot of run.

Pitch pocket—An opening extending parallel to the annual rings of growth that usually contains, or has contained, either solid or liquid pitch.

Pith—The small, soft core at the original center of a tree around which wood formation takes place.

Plate—*Sill plate:* a horizontal member anchored to a masonry wall. *Sole plate:* bottom horizontal member of a frame wall. *Top plate:* top horizontal member of a frame wall supporting ceiling joists, rafters, or other members.

Plough—To cut a lengthwise groove in a board or plank.

Plumb—Exactly perpendicular; vertical.

Ply—A term that denotes the number of thicknesses or layers of roofing felt, veneer in plywood, or layers in built-up materials, in any finished piece of such material.

Plywood—A piece of wood made of three or more layers of veneer joined with glue, and usually laid with the grain of adjoining plies at right angles. Almost always an odd number of plies are used to provide balanced construction.

Pores—Wood cells of comparatively large diameter that have open ends and are set one above the other to form continuous tubes. The openings of the vessels on the surface of a piece of wood are referred to as pores.

Preservative—Any substance that, for a reasonable length of time, will prevent the action of wood-destroying fungi, borers of various kinds, and similar destructive agents when the wood has been properly coated or impregnated.

Primer—The first coat of paint in a paint job that consists of two or more coats; also the paint used for such a first coat.

Putty—A type of cement usually made of whiting and boiled linseed oil, beaten or kneaded to the consistency of dough, and used in sealing glass in sash, filling small holes and crevices in wood, and for similar purposes.

Quarter round—A small molding that has the cross section of a quarter circle.

Radiant heating—A method of heating, usually consisting of a forced hot water system with pipes placed in the floor, wall, or ceiling; or with electrically heated panels.

Rafter—One of a series of structural members of a roof designed to support roof loads. The rafters of a flat roof are sometimes called *roof joists.*

Rafter, hip—A rafter that forms the intersection of an external roof angle.

Rafter, valley—A rafter that forms the intersection of an internal roof angle. The valley rafter is normally made of double 2-inch thick members.

Rake—Trim members that run parallel to the roof slope and form the finish between the wall and a gable roof extension.

Raw linseed oil—The crude product processed from flaxseed and usually without much subsequent treatment.

Reflective insulation—Sheet material with one or both surfaces of comparatively low heat emissivity, such as aluminum foil. When used in building construction the surfaces face air spaces, reducing the radiation across the air space.

Reinforcing—Steel rods or metal fabric placed in concrete slabs, beams, or columns to increase their strength.

Relative humidity—The amount of water vapor in the atmosphere, expressed as a percentage of the maximum quantity that could be present at a given temperature. The actual amount of water vapor that can be held in space increases with the temperature.

Resorcinol glue—A glue that is high in both wet and dry strength and resistant to high temperatures. It is used for gluing lumber or assembly joints that must withstand severe service conditions.

Ribbon (girt)—Normally a 1 × 4 inch board let into the studs horizontally to support ceiling or second floor joists.

Ridge—The horizontal line at the junction of the top edges of two sloping roof surfaces.

Ridge board—The board placed on edge at the ridge of the roof into which the upper ends of the rafters are fastened.

Roll roofing—Roofing material, composed of fiber and saturated with asphalt, that is supplied in 36-inch wide rolls with 108 square feet of material.

Roof sheathing—The boards or sheet material fastened to the roof rafters on which the shingle or other roof covering is laid.

Rubber-emulsion paint—Paint, the vehicle of which consists of rubber or synthetic rubber dispersed in fine droplets in water.

Saddle—Two sloping surfaces meeting in a horizontal ridge, used between the back side of a chimney, or other vertical surface, and a sloping roof.

Sand float finish—Lime mixed with sand, resulting in a textured finish.

Sapwood—The outer zone of wood, next to the bark. In the living tree it contains some living cells (the heartwood contains none), as well as dead and dying cells. In most species, it is lighter colored than the heartwood. In all species, it is lacking in decay resistance.

Sash—A single light frame containing one or more lights of glass.

Sash balance—A device, usually operated by a spring or tensioned weatherstripping, designed to counterbalance double-hung window sash.

Saturated felt—A felt that has been impregnated with tar or asphalt.

Scratch coat—The first coat of plaster, or cement, which is scratched to form a bond for the second coat.

Scribing—Fitting woodwork to an irregular surface. In moldings, cutting the end of one piece to fit the molded face of the other at an interior angle to replace a miter joint.

Sealer—A finishing material, either clear or pigmented, that is usually applied directly over uncoated wood for the purpose of sealing the surface.

Seasoning—Removing moisture from green wood in order to improve its serviceability.

Semigloss paint or enamel—A paint or enamel made with a slight insufficiency of nonvolatile vehicle so that its coating, when dry, has some luster but is not very glossy.

Shake—A thick handsplit shingle, resawn to form two shakes; usually edge-grained.

Sheathing—The structural covering, usually wood boards or plywood, used over studs or rafters of a structure. Structural building board is normally used only as wall sheathing.

Sheet metal work—All components of a house employing sheet metal, such as flashing, gutters, and downspouts.

Shellac—A transparent coating made by dissolving LAC, a resinous secretion of the lac bug (a scale insect that thrives in tropical countries, especially India), in alcohol.

Shingles—Roof covering of asphalt, asbestos, wood, tile, slate, or other material cut to stock lengths, widths, and thicknesses.

Shingles, siding—Various kinds of shingles, such as wood shingles or shakes and nonwood shingles, that are used over sheathing for exterior sidewall covering of a structure.

Shiplap—See Lumber, shiplap.

Shutter—Usually lightweight louvered or flush wood or nonwood frames in the form of doors located on each side of a window. Some are made to close over the window for protection; others are fastened to the wall as a decorative device.

Siding—The finish covering of the outside wall of a frame building, whether made of horizontal weatherboards, vertical boards with battens, shingles, or other material.

Siding, bevel (lap siding)—Wedge-shaped boards used as horizontal siding in a lapped pattern. This siding varies in butt thickness from ½ to ¾-inch and in widths up to 12 inches. Normally used over some type of sheathing.

Siding, Dolly Varden—Beveled wood siding that is rabbeted on the bottom edge.

Siding, drop—Usually ¾-inch thick and 6 and 8 inches wide with tongued-and-grooved or shiplap edges. Often used as siding without sheathing in secondary buildings.

Sill—The lowest member of the frame of a structure, resting on the foundation and supporting the floor joists or the uprights of the wall. The member forming the lower side of an opening, as a door or window sill.

Sleeper—Usually a wood member embedded in concrete, as in a floor, which serves to support and fasten subfloor or flooring.

Soffit—Usually the underside of an overhanging cornice.

Soil cover (ground cover)—A light covering of plastic film, roll roofing, or similar material used over the soil in crawl spaces of buildings to minimize moisture permeation of the area.

Soil stack—A general term for the vertical main of a system of soil, waste, or vent piping.

Sole or sole plate—See Plate.

Solid bridging—A solid member placed between adjacent floor joists near the center of the span to prevent joists from twisting.

Span—The distance between structural supports such as walls, columns, piers, beams, girders, and trusses.

Splash block—A small masonry block laid with the top close to the ground surface to receive roof drainage from downspouts and to carry it away from the building.

Square—A unit of measure—100 square feet—usually applied to roofing material. Sidewall coverings are sometimes packed to cover 100 square feet and are sold on that basis.

Stain, shingle—A form of oil paint, very thin in consistency, intended for coloring wood with rough surfaces, such as shingles, without forming a coating of significant thickness or gloss.

Storm sash or storm window—An extra window usually placed on the outside of an existing one as additional protection against cold weather.

Story—That part of a building between any floor and the floor or roof above.

String, stringer—A timber or other support for cross members in floors or ceilings. In stairs, the support on which the stair treads rest; also stringboard.

Stucco—Most commonly refers to an outside plaster made with portland cement as its base.

Stud—One of a series of slender wood or metal vertical structural members placed as supporting elements in walls and partitions.

Subfloor—Boards or plywood laid on joists over which a finish floor is to be laid.

Tail beam—A relatively short beam or joist supported in a wall on one end and by a header at the other.

Tenon—The projecting part cut on the end of a board, plank, or timber, for insertion into a corresponding hole (mortise) in another piece of lumber to form a joint.

Termites—Insects that superficially resemble ants in size, general appearance, and habit of living in colonies; hence, they are frequently called white ants. Subterranean termites establish themselves in buildings not by being carried with lumber, but by entering from ground nests after the building has been constructed.

Termite shield—A shield, usually of noncorrodible metal, placed in or on a foundation wall or other mass of masonry or around pipes to prevent passage of termites.

Toenailing—To drive a nail at a slant with the initial surface in order to permit it to penetrate into a second member.

Tongued-and-grooved—See Dressed and matched.

Trim—The finish materials in a building, such as moldings, applied around openings (window trim, door trim) or at the floor and ceiling of rooms (baseboard, cornice, and other moldings).

Truss—A frame or jointed structure designed to act as a beam of long span, while each member is usually subjected to longitudinal stress only, either tension or compression.

Turpentine—A volatile oil used as a thinner in paints and as a solvent in varnishes. Chemically, it is a mixture of terpenes.

Undercoat—A coating applied prior to the finishing or top coats of a paint job. It may be the first of two or the second of three coats. In some usages of the word it may become synonymous with priming coat.

Under layment—A material placed under finish coverings, such as flooring or shingles, to provide a smooth, even surface for applying the finish.

Valley—The internal angle formed by the junction of two sloping sides of a roof.

Vapor barrier—Material used to retard the movement of water vapor into walls and prevent condensation in them. Usually considered as having a perm value of less than 1.0. Applied separately over the warm side of exposed walls or as part of batt or blanket insulation.

Varnish—A thickened preparation of drying oil or drying oil and resin suitable for spreading on surfaces to form continuous, transparent coatings, or for mixing with pigments to make enamels.

Vehicle—The liquid portion of a finishing material; it consists of the binder (nonvolatile) and volatile thinners.

Vent—A pipe or duct that allows flow of air as an inlet or outlet.

Vermiculite—A mineral closely related to mica, with the faculty of expanding on heating to form lightweight material with insulation quality. Used as bulk insulation and also as aggregate in insulating and acoustical plaster and in insulating concrete floors.

Volatile thinner—A liquid that evaporates readily and is used to thin or reduce the consistency of finishes without altering the relative volumes of pigments and nonvolatile vehicles.

Water-repellent preservative—A liquid designed to penetrate into wood and impart water repellency and a moderate preservative protection. It is used for millwork, such as sashes and frames, and is usually applied by dipping.

Weatherstrip—Narrow or jamb-width sections of thin metal or other material to prevent infiltration of air and moisture around windows and doors. Compression weather stripping prevents air infiltration, provides tension, and acts as a counterbalance.

INDEX